LINGUISTIC DYNAMISM IN SOUTH ASIA

LINGUISTIC DYNAMISM IN SOUTH ASIA

M.J. Warsi (Ed.)

GYAN

GYAN PUBLISHING HOUSE
NEW DELHI-110002

Linguistic Dynamism in South Asia

Rs. 650

ISBN: 978-81-212-1010-2

Published in 2008 in India by
Gyan Publishing House,
4741/23, Main Ansari Road Darya Ganj
New Delhi-110002
Phones : 23282060, 23261060
Fax : (011) 23285914
E-mail: gyanbooks@vsnl.com
Website : http : // www.gyanbooks.com

Laser Typesetting by : Quick Media, Delhi
Printed at : Singhal Print Media, Delhi

TO

Professor Murray B. Emenean

who is no more in this World
but
whose memory and scholarship will always be a source of strength for all of us.........

TO

Professor Harvey E. Emerson

[illegible] who is no more in this world

but

[illegible]

[illegible]

Contents

Foreword

Linguistic areas, i.e. areas in which 'languages belonging to more than one family show traits in common which do not belong to the other members of one of the families have been recognized for a very long time. India (the Indian subcontinent) is a linguistic area, of the Balkan, Caucasian, Southeast Asian type, in which there are 'languages belonging to more than one family but showing traits in common which are found not to belong to the other members of (at least) one of the families'.

Investigation in Indian linguistic area has so far not dealt with vocabulary items, non-grammatical in usage, except for some that are peculiar to the Indian cultural scene, such as caste designation. Basic vocabulary items are on the whole not so easily dealt with, since there have been few studies of the semantic structures of these as they occur in the languages of India, in contrast with their semantic structures elsewhere and particularly in the Indo-European language family, which would provide the background for the Indo-Aryan items of northern India.

I hope that this book by **M.J. Warsi** will meet the requirements for which it has been edited and the scholars, researchers and students of linguistics will find it of great value.

March 16, 2004

Murray B. Emeneau
Professor Emeritus (Linguistics)
University of California at Berkeley

Acknowledgements

I am indebted to the pioneering scholars in all the countries for their findings and contributions to this outcome. I am particularly grateful to those who have personally and liberally shared their insights with me.

My dedication is a modest way of expressing my gratitude to Professor Uday Narayan Singh Director CIIL, Mysore, Professor Fatemeh Keshavarz, Chairperson, Department of Asian and Neareastern Languages and Literatures and Professor Beata Grant, Director, Religious Studies Program at Washington University in St. Louis. I am also thankful to Professor A.R. Fatihi, AMU, Aligarh and Professor O.N. Koul for their encouragement.

I am happy, in addition, to be able to acknowledge a profound personal debt to Professor George L Hart and Kaushalya Hart of University of California at Berkeley for introducing me to Profeesor Murray B Emeneau.

My greatest debt is to (Late) Professor Murray B. Emeneau for writing few lines as the preface of this book, inspite of his poor health condition at that time (in the year 2004)

The entire manuscript has benefited immeasurably from the careful reading of my brother Dr. M. K. Warsi. Other friends Nirmal Kumar Azad, Dr. Doel Mukerjee and Najeebul Hasan Khan deserve special thanks for their suggestions and encouragement.

The careful editorial work by the staff of Gyan Publishing House also improved the manuscript. I am personally thankful to Mr. Amit Garg for taking extra care while printing the book.

M J Warsi

Washington University in St. Louis

January 2008

Introduction

The last decade has seen an unprecedented growth in the study of language contact, shift and variations associated partly with the linguistic effects of globalization and increased migration all over the world. Language change and shift are culturally normal, and all combinations of known languages can be heard in rural contexts, with language choice in daily communication being based foremost on traditional language protocol. It is argued that variation is common in this geographical area, conceding that shift can also occur, but that the idea of a linguistic area is certainly fundamental to the notion of diffusion.

More than three hundred languages are spoken in South Asia than in any other region of the world. Many of these languages are however only dialects of a parent language. Language attitude examines the way external factors have influenced and are influencing language change, focusing on how changing social contexts are reflected in language use. Language change explores the attitudes, values and assumptions that shape the way we use language. In this study it has been seen that how language change operates within different genres.

B K Rana in his paper observes that Nepal followed the policy of one language one culture. So, in a democratic system peoples asserted their language rights. The Maoists radicals also exploited language issues of Nepal. It also became an important agenda for them. In the event of king's direct rule, it is now widely feared that Rights Movement in Nepal will halt for sometime. The concerned language communities will also experience a setback. But, those communities will continue endeavoring to preserve their languages and somehow slow down the process of language death in the country.

Chao-chih Liao of National University of Kaohsiung rightly accessed the situation and argues that the language assets theory is proposed to urge foreign brides in Taiwan to talk confidently with their children in their native language (L1), rather than Mandarin or Taiwanese. There should be (complementary) Cambodian, Myamarian, Vietnamese, Thai, and Indonesian schools established for these children; communities might help teach in these schools. Taiwanese in USA have complementary Mandarin/Taiwanese classes, since mothers are highly educated and have peer connections. The foreign brides in Taiwan can so too. They should be also encouraged to run for the position of legislators, to be influential at a higher level.

According to **Harbir Arora** and **Karumuri V. Subbarao**, Hindi-Urdu does not have a dative marker in such constructions. To them, such a wide range of functions performed by dative *ku* in Dakkhini where it either replaces the genitive or extends its domain to perform variety of functions in different constructions demonstrates how an existing category is exploited to maximam possible extent. The additional occurrence of dative in comparative constructions, in capabilitative constructions in Dakkhini and dative with time adverbials in Dakkhini is a case of **extention of functions** without its category being changed. To conclude, they have demonstrated that the syntactic reanalysis of an existing category results among other things in (i) categorychange (î) change in function (îi) extention of functions as well as (iv) change in the position of a constituent. The syntactic change that took place in the above mentioned syntactic constructions in Dakkhini provides insights into the nature of syntactic change.

Salman Al-Azami's paper attempts to look into the differences in linguistic usage between first and second generation Sylheti and non-Sylheti Bangladeshis in

Manchester. The research investigates the changes in the Bengali language from its standard form at different levels of linguistics and tries to find the similarities and dissimilarities between the changes made by the first and second generation speakers in the community. The research also covers areas such as the differences in terms of bilingualism between Sylhetis and non-Sylhetis and the linguistic manipulations done by these speakers from standard Bengali. Semi-structured interviews and a participant observation were undertaken to find the results that showed that the second generation Sylhetis are able to communicate in Sylheti due to practice at home. The study finds that the Bengali language has undergone some changes at sound, word and sentence levels, though the changes are mere manipulations rather than anything else. These manipulations take place because the respondents find themselves between two linguistic cultures. The study observes that the first generation non-Sylhetis frequently use code-mixing and code-switching while using Bengali. Most of the first generation Bangladeshis was found to be multilingual as they know Hindi/Urdu as their third language. The study also found that frequent visits to Bangladesh, active participation in community activities, living in close proximity, bringing spouses from Bangladesh, using Bengali/Sylheti at home etc. play significant roles in maintaining Bengali/Sylheti among the first generation. The present study should play a positive role in paving the way for much more research on the language maintenance and shift among the Bangladeshis in the UK.

At Liverpool Hope University College **Manel Heart's** examination of bilingual studies specifically the area of English-Sinhala code-switching in relation to its diverse patterns become more interesting. Although much has been written on Sri Lankan English as a variety of New English, little attention has been devoted up to now to ascertain how this variety in association with Sinhala, the majority language of Sri Lanka, has continued to influence the speech of Sinhala-English bilinguals in the 21st century, during which the number of these bilinguals has increased substantially. In this paper, Manel examine the patterns of code-switching used by 18 Sinhala-English bilinguals and discuss the significance of these patterns to Sri Lankan English speech. On the basis of this data Manel argue that these patterns go a long way in explaining how the different languages are appropriated and extended in ways which are creative and sophisticated. Manel suggested that in-depth analysis of this kind is necessary for showing that code-switching is one of the many linguistic choices available to bilinguals in Sri Lanka and for understanding how 'mixed' language is used for negotiating a distinct identity in this context.

A very interesting study on language development by a well known linguist **Udaya Narayana Singh** of India focuses on minority and smaller language communities. First, he discusses the issue of the use of language technology as an instrument of change in such communities in South Asia, and its implication on language and education planning in such developing countries. Secondly, the paper recalls the classification of 'Language Standardization' into 'Primary' and 'Secondary' standardizations as proposed in Singh (1994), and attempts to show how – in order to effectively employ the secondary standardization strategies in smaller language groups, use of language technology allows rapid development, often combining standardization and modernization of these languages together. Thirdly, he argues that Language Planning theory requires a typology of multilingual contexts in a cline, where membership to a given type has consequences for development of language technology, too. Since different languages in a multilingual and pluri-cultural matrix have different roles and functions, and consequently, different degree of importance, adoption of language technology initiatives could have a leveling effect on development of such smaller or restricted languages on par with majority languages.

B N Patnaik in his study draws attention to food talk in Oriya which has remained unnoticed so far by scholars working on this language. It deals, in some detail, with only those constructions that are greeting expressions. He maintains that food talk is by no means restricted to Oriya, and instances of it can be found as well in Bengali, Hindi, Telugu and Kannada, among other South Asian languages, and speculates how some food talk expressions may have come to be used as expressions of greeting.

Avadesh K Mishra very thoroughly studied and seen that Kurukh has changed in such a way that it has become more homogenized with the surrounding languages. From a typological heterogeneity situation it has moved to a typological homogeneity situation. Kurukh has borrowed features from Indo-Aryan as well as Munda languages, and having done so it has incorporated features of both the language families and thus has become more consistent with the typology of this region rather than with the typology of the family. The changes are language contact induced changes. If these languages were not in contact, these changes would not have arisen. The language has developed differently: instead of loss, it has gained structures by way of both adoption and adaption. The language has changed in a drastic way in order to move towards typological homogeneity of the region.

In his paper on *the plural markers of kui–kuvi revisited,* **Panchanan Mohanty** observes that (1) Kui and Kuvi have only two plural markers, viz. /-*rV*/ for the masculine and /-*ka*/ for the non-masculine stems. (2) /-*s*-/ and /-*n*-/ should be treated as the feminine and the neuter markers respectively in these languages. (3) These markers developed most probably under the influence of the surrounding NIA languages which employ separate plural markers for the neuter nouns and also due to a pressure to retain the archaic consonant-ending Proto-Dravidian stem-structure in these languages which are quite conservative by nature.

Rajesh Kumar in his paper has discussed Hindi infinitival constructions as an example of mixed categories. Throughout the paper, he has shown that the Hindi infinitival phrases have internal syntax of a VP, the partial internal syntax of an NP and the external distribution of an NP. Then he concluded that one should recognize both VP and NP structure with regard to infinitival phrases. Infinitive phrases are too endocentric to analyze as the exocentric structure. Hence proposing plausible phrase structures of Hindi infinitival phrases while pointing out the problems of each proposal, he came to the phrase structure that consists of DP outer layer plus internal VP. The proposed phrase structure provides the principled account of the empirical generalizations found in Hindi infinitival phrases, at the same time they maintain theoretical assumptions of the phrase structure.

Shailender Kumar Singh's paper argues that trans-generational reproduction of aesthetic character has historical-ethnographic structure. Important thing to be noticed here is that India as a transgenerational ethnographic entity never seem to be in the process of fading. Multiplicity of identity, at any category level, is visible. Characteristics such as stratified roles, cross-cultural overlapping, regional variations, cross-linguistic geographic boundaries, ethno-behaviorism, stratified social structures and hierarchical polities are either anaphoric or patchable. Pluralistic ethos is, therefore, neither on compromise nor on suppressed visibility. Hierarchical ties are indicatively justifiable. Singularity is seldom allowed to act as a definable parameter either in identity creation or in identity projection. The principle of projection is hardly always governed by a single local governing; rather all categorical constituents are multiplied in such a way that each conducts itself in a very smooth and negotiated manner.

He further believes that postcolonial ecology has created the possibility of extending and expanding the new interconnectedness in which a sharp division between the

East and the West is no longer based upon the dichotomy of have and haven't but mostly upon how the gap between two has wrongly been read. No doubt, the tests of extensiveness and intensity of the new order are yet to be done objectively as well as subjectively. However, this can be viewed as a filter and a guide model to the different levels of existing differences.

Offering a unique perspective on language contact, shift and variations, this volume contains a broader spectrum in understanding the complex linguistics phenomena of South Asia. Accordingly, the phenomenon of language contact has been approached from a variety of perspectives by the invited linguists and scholars of many different orientations.

List of Contributors

1. **Udaya Narayana Singh**
   Central Institute of Indian Languages, Mysore, India
   Email: udaya@ciil.stpmy.soft.net
2. **Chao-chih Liao**
   National University of Kaohsiung
   Email: ccliao@nuk.edu.tw
3. **B.K. Rana**
   Independent Researcher, Nepal
   Email: bk_rana@yahoo.com
4. **Panchanan Mohanty**
   University of Hyderabad, India
   Email: panchananmohanty@rediffmail.com
5. **Harbir Arora and Karumuri V. Subbarao**
   University of Delhi
   Email:harbir.arora@gmail.com
6. **A Salman Al-Azami**
   Manchester, UK
   Email: salmanalam50@yahoo.com
7. **Manel Herat**
   Liverpool Hope University College
   Email: heratm@hope.ac.uk
8. **B.N. Patnaik**
   Central Institute of Indian Languages, Mysore
   Email: patnaik@iitk.ac.in
9. **Awadesh K. Mishra**
   North Eastern Hill University, Shillong
   E-mail: awadhesham@yahoo.com
10. **Rajesh Kumar**
    University of Texas at Austin, USA
    Email: rkumar@mail.utexas.edu
11. **Shailendra Kumar Singh**
    Mahatma Gandhi international Hindi university
    Email: tosksingh@rediffmail.com

1

Language Technology and Changes Brought by Language Planning: Minority Language Communities in India

Udaya Narayana Singh

Introduction

Anyone raising the issue of integrating language technology with minority language development a few years ago would have faced severe criticism. When a large number of speakers of such languages live below the poverty line, the critics would argue, how could one even dream of bringing their languages on technology platform? Although the worst cases of economic deprivation lie in Africa (for example, Zambia with 86% below thc poverty line as per 1993 statistic top the list), South Asian countries are also equally vulnerable if we look at the figures[1] of Nepal (42%), Bangladesh (35.6%), and Pakistan (35%). It is not that only they are doing badly in terms of this indicator, even India (25%) and Sri Lanka (22%) are lagging way behind the developed nations. We cannot compare them with smaller countries like Taiwan (with only 1% below the poverty line) or sparsely populated countries in Europe (for example). But compare the South Asian countries with better managed nation-states like USA with a large population (which shows 12.7% below the poverty line).

But even if we leave apart this counter-argument on economic ground, technology was itself at a nascent stage in the developing countries, depending on age-old communication techniques such as radio and television as well as tape recorders. And these countries had a kind of GDP rate that would not allow them to invest further on education through mass media. With $1.1 billion GDP-PPP in Bhutan, $1.2 billion in Maldives, and $30.6 billion in Nepal, South Asia is perhaps the home of some of the poorest countries in the world, notwithstanding little better figures of Bangladesh ($209.9 billion) and Pakistan ($266.2 billion). However, compared to these countries, India (with her GDP-PPP of $2,395.4 billion, which is still way behind China's $5,019.4 billion) could have invested in infrastructures needed to make mass media an instrument of not only public entertainment, but also a mode of education. Given the fact that a large number of minority as well as major languages are actually instances of divided language communities – divided between India and Nepal (even major languages like Nepali and Maithili – important for both countries), India and Sri Lanka (Tamil), India and Bangladesh (both Bangla and Chakma), or India and Pakistan (at least, Urdu, Panjabi, and Sindhi communities), it is possible that what India could do for language education using mass media would greatly benefit the other South Asian nations, too. This comment applies equally to other areas of technology such as IT and Computational Technology.

This paper broadly covers three areas of language development with special focus on minority and smaller language communities in this context. First, it discusses the issue of use of language technology as an instrument of change in such communities in South Asia, and its implication on language and education planning in such developing countries. Secondly, it attempts to show how – in order to effectively employ various strategies of cannon formation among smaller language groups, use of language technology allows rapid development, often combining standardization and modernization of these languages together. Thirdly, it also shows that Language Planning theory requires a typology of multilingual contexts in a cline, where membership to a given type has consequences for language development as well as nation building.

I. Language Technology as an Instrument of Change

I will devote this section to first discussing how South Asia is placed in language-related technology development, and then present my arguments as to why I think language technology could bring in enormous changes for smaller language groups.

In the entire South Asian region, there are numerous agents of change at work at present. What has impeded this rapid force of change is conflict of interest, or perception of clash of interest among these developing countries. Such perceptions are bound to change in near future as they go along the race to development. In the entire post-world war II period, or after almost all these nations gained independence, they have engaged in a vain search for villains and scapegoats[2]. The result has been a kind of disintegration. But the forces that encourage dissensions and misunderstanding among the South Asian nations tend to forget what Girard says in this context: "The killing of the scapegoat provides a means for the formation of a new social unanimity and cohesion, as acquisitive mimesis is transformed into conflictual mimesis, which is resolved by the destruction of someone arbitrarily designated as the cause of the conflict". One should not be surprised if all these countries one day understands the game-plan of the "others", and decide to work with some minimum program that were mutually beneficial. This common ground could well be in alleviating poverty, provision of shelter, eradication of literacy, and use of technology as an instrument of change in the education sector. My conjecture is that this would result in a better human development index score in all South Asian nations.

Turning to the present situation in Asia, it is not surprising that in terms of Human Development Index[3], Bangladesh occupies the lowest spot with a score of 0.478

as against Japan's score of 0.933 and Norway's world-best figure of 0.942. Other South Asian countries are not much better than Bangladesh in terms of physical quality of life of their inhabitants – with Maldives and Sri Lanka doing slightly better with 0.743 and 0.741 scores, respectively, and India way behind at 0.577, with Pakistan (0.499), Bhutan (0.494) and Nepal (0.490) quite comparable with Bangladesh figures. So, one can very well ask this question if this picture is going to change in near future. The answer I think is positive.

Let us consider the changes that have already taken place in India. Although India happens to house the world's largest number of cinema-viewers with 2,860 million (as per 1998 figure), penetration of television into our homes has not been more than 60.1 per 1,000, even if the absolute number of such homes with television is 63 million. Suffice it to say that other South Asian nations are nowhere near India's figure. In early 60's. India had only a few TV sets but in 1972, there were 84,000 TVs. By the end of '80s, the number crossed 1.5 Million and 1985 saw 7 Million TV sets. In 1998, it had crossed 58 Million mark. It had to do with CNN's direct broadcasting of Iraq war in 1991, after which trans-national television became a reality – first with dish antenna, and then with satellite transmission of numerous channels. It is, therefore, very much possible to utilize this opportunity to create both corpus and content in the domain of educational television with a professional touch.

The development in India[4] was possible because television was introduced quite early in India (in 1959 with only one transmitter). In the next two decades, India had 18 transmitters. Soon after the INSAT Satellite was launched by India (in 1982), the number of transmitters went up to first 172 (in 1985), and then 672 (by 1995). By 1997, India had 868 transmitters. From the very beginning, thought was given to make television as a supplementary medium of education in India. By the mid-'90s, the country also developed a strong industrial base for manufacturing

COUNTRIES	Telephone	Radio[1]	Television[1] (For 1000)	Newspaper[1]	Cinema Viewers	P.C. [1] (2000 fig)	Mobile[1]
India	43.78	1.16e+08 [1.10e-06]	63 m [60.01]	5,221 (1998) 4.97 per 1m	2,860m (1998) [2,724.58 per 1000]	4.6 m Rank 16 [4.38 per 1000]	2.93 m (2000)
Bangladesh	8.26	6.15e+06 [4.44e-05]	0.77 m [5.56]	NA	NA	0.2 m [1.44]	283,000 (2000)
Bhutan	-	37,000 [17.29]	11,000 [5.14]	NA	NA	5,000 [2.33]	NA
Maldives	168.26	35,000 [106.16]	10,000 [30.33]	NA	NA	5,500	1,290 (1997)
Nepal	13.87	840,000 [31.73]	130.000 [4.91]	NA	NA	0.07 m [2.64]	NA
Pakistan	28.92	6.15e+06 [1.35e+07] [8.95e-06]	3.1 m [20.57]	352 (1999) [2.33 per 1 m]	NA	0.59 m [3.91]	158,000 (1998)
Sri Lanka	79.91	3.85e+06 [0.00]	1.53 m [77.49]	NA	NA	0.135 m [6.83]	228,604 (1999)
Topmost fig	1700.95	980,000 Costa Rica 251.53 for 1000	1385.68 [400 m]	5,221 [106.68]	2860 m [5452.31]	161 m [727.26]	69.209 m [883.66]
Top Country	Luxem-bourg	2309.45 per 1000 Christmas Island	Christmas Island *China*	India *Ethiopia*	India Iceland	USA San Marino	USA (2003) Iceland
Bottommost	2.12	Equatorial Guinea	500 [144.67]	4.83 per 1m [1]	75,970 [14.54 per 1000]	150 [0.19 per 1000]	0
Bottom Country	Niger	Albania [1e+06]	Nauru Suriname	Bermuda	San Marino Malaysia	Vanuatu Congo	Niue (1991)

and selling television sets. The "cable operators" altered the scenario further. Each international event - whether it is Asian Games in 1982, or World Cup Cricket later - gave a boost to the TV-industry. By mid-'90s, 58 million out of 150 million odd households had TV sets. Still, while majority of Indians lived in villages (about 70 per cent), and a majority of television sets (about 70 per cent) were in the urban areas. According to the state-controlled national channel - Doordarshan, the percentage of rural viewers has been on the increase in the recent times – making it nearly 51 per cent of the total viewers. In spite of this impressive increase in the composition of rural viewers in the country, overall penetration of television in rural households has been very small. A 1994 study (titled INSAT Effects Study[5]) indicated that only about 12 per cent of the rural households had a television set. The Indian Space Research Organisation (ISRO) too conducted a SITE-experiment[6] (Satellite Instructional Television Experiment) which showed that in community viewing situations, the ratio of men and women viewers is 70:30. Over the years, there has of course been a tremendous upsurge in TV-viewership, which is clear from TRP ratings of popular TV programs.

So far, we have only considered the electronic media. Meanwhile, in the field of personal computers, India has made it to a world-rank of 16th with 4.6 million systems. However, penetration of computers is only 4.38 per 1,000 persons. The telephony figures (43.78 per 1,000) as well as huge upturn in cellular connectivity in India (from 18.6 million in March, 1998 to 50.9 million in December, 2002[7] have also improved the picture of networking. The current world average penetration for the developing world is 6 lines per 100 people and the average for the world as a whole is 10 lines per 100 people. In India it is roughly 6 lines per 100 people, as of January 2004[8] . Further, in about 600,000 villages in India, the Viallage Panchayat telephones (VPT) used to be only 343,000 in September 1999, but in the next three years, the figures have become 510,000. As one can see, the Indian telecommunication network is undergoing a revolutionary change, in terms of coverage, quality and range of services. As of September 1999, the network equipment capacity has grown to 22.63 million lines in about 25,394 exchanges and has registered an annual growth rate of 16.5 percent over the last six years, which is among the fastest in the world. The Indian telecom sector over the next five years is expected to have an annual growth of over 20 percent according to J P Morgan, a global equity research and investment company[9]. All this was possible because since 1985, however, significant trunk capacity has been added in the form of fiber-optic cable and a domestic satellite system with 254 earth stations making it possible for cellular telephone service to be offered in metropolitan cities. The demand for the next 10 years is estimated to be 81.83 million lines at an annual rate of 12-13 percent through internal accruals alone. The projected demand gap is expected to range between 20 and 25 million lines in 2007. As for cell-phones. only 8 licenses were issued for Cellular Mobile Telephone service in 4 metro cities in November 1994, which jumped up to another 34 licenses to 14 companies for 18 telecom circles by the end of 1995. By June 2003, the total number of cellular phones in India was 15.2 million.[10] Compare this with all-US figure of 124 million cell phones.

The print media also showed great progress. With 5,221 daily newspapers published in India, it is close to the world best figure. One again, this was possible because India made an early beginning. William Bolts, an ex-employee of the East India Company attempted to start the first newspaper in India in 1776. But Bolts had to beat a retreat under the disapproving gaze of the Court of Directors of the Company. The Bengal Gazette by James Augustus Hicky was started in 1780. The colonial establishment started the Calcutta Gazette. It was followed by another private initiative the Bengal Journal. In Madras (now called Chennai), too, The Madras Courier was started in 1785 by Richard Johnson. It got its second newspaper when, in 1791 Hugh Boyd, came out of the Courier quit and founded the Hurkaru. The passing of the Indian Telegraph Act in 1885, and later (after 1951) its extension to the whole of India, coupled with establishment of the two news channels, PTI (Press Trust of India) on August 27, 1947 and UNI (United News of India) in 1961 had contributed to this tremendous growth of newspapers in India. And with the reach of the Terrestrial television to 53% all-India and 80% in cities, and Cable and satellite television occupying 20% all-India, and 46% of urban areas, there has been an upturn.

Still, the reach of our print media has not been more than 4.97 per 1,000 persons until some time ago. According to one statistics, print media reach to 25% all over India and to 46% urban households now[11] . Still, with entry of news media through radio and television into a large number of households over the last one decade, availability of a large number of channels everywhere, and the reach of India's satellites and beaming technologies could contribute a lot to minority languages education in this country. India's literacy programs depended to a large extent on traditional classroom type of teaching. The projects like 'Operation Blackboard' in India are best examples of our dependence on traditional methods for teaching and learning among the smaller language groups. And even when 'Country-wide classroom' programs were started by state-owned television, its reach, style, content and utility left much to be done. This picture has also to undergo a sea-change and a careful as well as coordinated planning.

Coming to the crux of the problem, the difficulty with any such planning in India would mean greater penetration of broadband, which is only 0.02% now. The broadband is an always-on network capable of providing interactive voice, data and video services on public networks. Once this kind of facility is available in South Asia, the face of language education could be changed. Technically, true broadband would be capable of providing minimum asymmetric bandwidth of 1.5kbps. However the Telecom Regulatory Authority of India (TRAI) is still wondering whether to jump-start at 128kbps or straight away hit the benchmark of 256 kbps (where the US benchmark speed is 200 kbps). At present, internet is the only service available on broadband in India, as other services are not driven so much by the market force. Obviously, this figure of 0.02% is the lowest compared among the countries with IT domination. The Confederation of Indian Industries (CII), in its report called 'Vision 2010' identifies the following reasons for this low broadband penetration:

(*a*) Low PC penetration.

(*b*) Broadband being an expensive option still.

(*c*) The required infrastructure is at the nascent stage

(*d*) Security and service related problems with wider use of broadband.

To complicate the matter further, while the Broadband-to-Internet ratio in developed countries is 75%, in India it is 5%. Any furtherance of broadband technology is linked with the GDP growth of our countries in this region.. When GDP increases, and one has more spending power, more and more people are likely to go for the Broadband. Now, even the content creators shy away from investing anything more in the business. But one can see it coming to India in near future. At present, there is more need for TV content on broadband, and it is in this content, language technology content and tools developers can play a major role. CII report predicts that India would be among the top five broadband countries by 2010.

As a consequence, electronic media in many countries have begun being used on a large scale in education for indigenous languages. Language revitalization is gaining momentum in many countries now, the best examples of which are increased interest in conceptualization of new technological projects for indigenous languages (such as the

'Shell-book project' in Papua New Guinea) as well as important publications in this area (such as The Green Book of Language Revitalization in Practice, edited by Leanne Hinton and Kenneth Hale (2001; San Diego, CA: Academic Press) which devotes 80 out of 400 pages for a section on technology. One still needs to be cautioned about the limitation of all technologies, no matter how powerful they may be.

It is in this context that we need to understand that computers cannot become 'surrogate' mothers passing down the rich linguistic knowledge from one generation to another. Only the living speakers of a minority language can do that. As long as they have the desired urge and the right instinct that would ensure their languages to survive, language preservation efforts would bear positive results. On the other hand, precisely on this ground that even adult speakers of a minority language have begun to give up their languages world-wide, one found scholars like Courtney B. Cazden writing: "In one oft-cited metaphor, the collective language resources of any community will be a leaky bucket in need of endless refilling unless or until the community's youngest members are learning that language in the home. Realistically, many young parents are themselves not fluent speakers, and so some non-authentic ("non-natural") forms of support, electronic or not, are needed."

This leads us also to the moral debate on the use of non-authentic or doctored material in language education – so very essential in modern text-book writing techniques. Although it is true that authentic language structure and texts would be such "original texts, films, and recordings of language usage ...that accurately reflect how a language community employs its heritage tongue" (Villa, 2002), those engaged in pedagogical activities would know that following such rigid standards would defeat the very purpose of teaching texts from smaller languages, as there would be certain necessary deviations and manipulations that would positively grade the reading texts. McHenry (2002:) shows that "materials embodying and supporting both authentic and non-authentic language use can have significant educational value. It all depends on the program's governing purpose and values".

II. Introduction: Models of Language Development

While trying to propose a model of language development in the countries lagging behind in the development race, we need to ask some basic questions to ourselves: When do languages develop? What changes must come about for them to be called 'developed languages'? The standard response in literature in Language Planning has been that all undeveloped languages have creative capability but they are not put to use in certain advanced contexts. Putting them in writing or using them in school and higher education or in mass media would provide such contexts.

This leads us to another question: What changes must occur in the body of such languages for them to being used in such and other advanced contexts? The standard response given by almost all is 'standardization'. There have been some additions while they talked about standardization though. For instance, characteristics such as consistency or legitimacy or utility in intellectual domains etc have followed. We are told that vernaculars require "a uniform and consistent norm of writing...widely accepted by its speakers" (Haugen 1994: 4340), or that they must also be "legitimized" as State languages (Williams 1992:24). Similarly, they must provide planners with "motivation for literacy" as well as "computerization" (Le Page 1992: 120-38). Such languages also need to be "intellectualized" (Garvin 1955). A combination of all these or some of these will provide occasion for others to admit these languages in the 'privileged club', as it were.

In 1994, in Meta (39.2)[12] [3] I had proposed a dichotomy of Primary vs. Secondary Standardization applicable to developing countries. Let me start from there: All developing countries have to resolve the problem of finding an appropriate model of development. The point was that early language standardization was took place naturally, without models to follow; languages of today have a number of models of primary development before them. These latter languages are described as having adopted a 'Secondary Standardization' strategy. Obviously, when languages develop naturally, they take longer time to develop because of lack of planned interventions. Depending on the degree of intervention by the planners, the secondarily standardized languages show a kind of cline or gradation. More often than not, in cases of the latter type, it is very difficult to differentiate between the periods of standardization and modernization. Both these processes go hand in hand in respect of these languages because of the time constraints within which these latecomers bloom. It is more than a convention that when a language undergoes primary standardization, the processes of modernization follow it soon after, in course of time.

We all know that those days are gone when languages could develop on their own. One difference between the advent of modernism in course of the last two centuries and the postmodern situation prevailing today is that all languages in today's world advance and develop because of various internal and external pressures, and because of the ensuing tensions. As against this, there was a time when a language could develop as a consequence of either natural historical forces or chance emergence of a towering literary personality. Such primarily standardized languages, however, had no model before them to follow. In comparison, languages of today have a number of models of primary development before them, and they have an option to follow any one of these models (with suitable modifications, wherever necessary) or chart a completely new course by scrupulously avoiding the known courses of action.

For today's languages to develop, therefore, there have to be policies that have already worked elsewhere which have to be re-implemented. Alternatively, there must be models which can be translated, if the elites that influence decision process of the state want it to be so. The options here are between being innovative or being translative. It would not take one long to realize that between these two options, translativity is a better, surer and faster way to develop. Innovation (howsoever ideal it may be theoretically), like any act of creativity, runs the risk of being a failure and counter-productive. If nothing, it is surely more time consuming than any translative strategy. It is not surprising that many of the underdeveloped and developing languages today start from a point where they attempt at translating metaphors, myths, proverbs, terms, sciences, cultures, and language structures. Many, of course, end up translating attitudes and fashions first, which relegates the twin task of textual transference and language development to the background. Where this does not happen, and when a number of texts are actually transferred, the source and target languages show a tendency of 'coming together' or converging. I would not hesitate to imagine that both linguistic convergence and massive amount of Code-switching and Mixing emerge from translative actions which members of converging speech communities use as 'gap-filling devices' – as techniques that erase distances. In the process, they also try recreating certain language functions, triggered by bilingualism. In many other cases, it may also give rise to a kind of linguistic dominance or improvement of status of one language over the others in the same speech area. That is the reason why many languages of the Third World — be it Hindi in India or Hausa in Nigeria — very quickly learn the art of dominating over other indigenous languages, at least in formal speech functions. As it can be seen, there is a scope for different configurations of languages in space to emerge in a multilingual possibilities.

III. Types of Multilingual Societies

I would like to argue here that the typology of multilingual contexts, each with different national identities and having different experiences in language development, can be viewed as a cline. At one extreme, are Type A societies where language is almost anthropomorphized by its speakers. In some Type A communities, language is revered and is regarded almost as an object of worship. In these societies, children learn the language when they are young and it remains with them as long as they live. Their language becomes a matter of passion for which the community is ready to make bigger sacrifices. Bangladesh is an example of this Type A society.

At the other extreme lie Type-Z communities that view language as a tool or skill. Such communities may use different 'tools' (languages) for different purposes, for example, using a particular language for business or to establish linkages or associating one language with leisure activities or as a library language or a religious language or using it as the medium of mass communication. These societies are often (but not necessarily always) unable to be passionate enough about their language to use it as an instrument of nation-building. Singapore with its four national language communities offers a picture that comes closer to this kind of postulation. Here we find a number of interesting strategies being used, including cultivation of new country-internal norms such as Singlish.

Analyzing other multilingual communities around the world and plotting them on the cline would show that this typology does not conceptualize language situations as all-or-none or mutually exclusive as was often assumed in earlier typologies. I suggest that the features of many of these types overlap with neighboring types and together present a cascade that poses an interesting challenge for language planning agencies. For this reason, I would like to argue that language planning models have to be eclectic and pluralistic to accommodate these differences.[13]

In order to understand the extent of multilingualism in South Asia, one must refer to the other paper in this volume on the 'Status of Smaller Languages in India' (Udaya Narayana Singh & Anju Saxena), which will clearly outline the challenge. Although South Asian nations offer remarkable similarities in many respects that have to do with plurality of languages and cultures, they vary in a number of other indicators. Just as I have discussed the indicators related to language technology and mass media here, one needs to look at the variation in density of population (and consequently, in "Physical Quality of Life"(PQLI index) in overall GNP, Per Capita Income, population density and the standard of living, etc. As one could notice there, the common person in South Asia faces more or less the same predicaments in everyday life.

In Singh (2003), I had addressed this important question of language loss in multilingual situations, and then compared the South Asian scenario with the developed countries facing the grave threat of minority language attrition. There are different estimates about the extent of possible language loss in the world in the next 50 years. But there is no doubt that with the disappearance of these languages, their lexical rainbow, registral styles, textual ranges, knowledge bases and traditions will also disappear. At the same time, as David Bradley (2003) shows in the context of Yi and Lisu, there are ethno-linguistic minorities who have successfully braved the great challenges to maintain and promote their languages by linking the languages with education. Long ago, in the oft-quoted paper on 'Two types of linguistic relativity', Dell Hymes (197), too, had shown similar cases. This kind of language loss is a major concern in the developing world already as there have been erosion of multilingual base in countries such as Australia, Canada, New Zealand and USA already. For example, we can plot the decline in the percentage of speakers of indigenous languages among the Indigenous populations of Canada in the following manner:

1951	1961	1971	1981	1991	1996
87.4	75.5	57.1	29.3	32.7	26

The US Scenario is equally grim. Bright (1994)[14] and Mithun (1999:1)[15] put the number of indigenous languages originally spoken at around 300. As reported in McConvel, & Thieberger (2001), Chafe (1962)[16] had counted 211 languages as still living in the USA and Canada in 1960[17]. Of these, only 89 (42%) had speakers of all ages. Thirty years later Zepeda and Hill (1991:136)[18] estimate that 51 (approx. 24%) of those 211 languages have disappeared. Campbell (1994)[19] and Campbell & Mithun (1979)[20] predict that 80% of the North American languages spoken at the turn of this century 'will die in this generation'. The prediction is for 20-30 Indigenous languages will survive in North America by 2040. Australia also has disturbing statistics. Out of about 300 languages spoken in 1800, there has been a decrease of 90% in the number of such speakers of all age groups who can speak their heritage language fluently. The number of indigenous people speaking their own languages declined from 100% in 1800 to 13% in 1996. If these trends continue unchecked, there will no longer be any Indigenous languages spoken in Australia by 2050.

Compare the above with a recent survey conducted by Padmanabha, Mahapatra, Verma and McConnel (1989)[21] surveyed - out of the total of 114 languages with 10k plus speakers listed in the 1981 Census, about 96 languages, and they found about fifty of them to have written modes of expression. The general observation here as well as in works of other sociolinguists who wrote on India (cf. Pandit 1976)[22] has been that South Asia has been able to retain its multi-ethnic and pluri-lingual character from many centuries.

There are of course reasons behind this trend of language retention. In India each major language in India acts as a link with other languages. Every language area consists of at least 3 inter-languages. All of the widely accepted and understood languages have many variants. For example, Hindi alone has forty-eight variants. One reason for such linguistic diversity is the complex social realities of South Asia: Indian languages reflect the intricate levels of social hierarchy and caste. Secondly, another reason for this diversity is that Indians have this typical characteristic of being not just bilingual but multi-lingual. Multilingualism in India has nothing to do with education; it is found among illiterates, as well. In different contexts/ domains, people use different languages. The 1931 census added a question on bilingualism, and 1991 census even had a question dealing with trilingualism. Census figures show that the percentage of India's bilingual population in 1991 (19.44%) was significantly higher than in 1961 (9.7%), 1971, (13.04%) and 1981 (13.44%). In 1991, 7.26% of the population claimed to be trilingual.

If we go back to the extent of multilingualism in India, we find that after Independence, the 1961 and 1971 census figures[23] show 193 classified languages out of a total of 1,652 mother tongue labels and "raw" labels numbering 3,000. This jumped to around 7,000 in the 1981 census. The 1991 census then touched an all-time high figure (10,000). It was then that 'rationalization' of these labels became a big challenge in India. In fact, the problem in India lies is in defining 'mother tongue". According to the census definition, mother tongue is "the language spoken in childhood by the person's mother to the person. If the mother died in infancy, the language mainly spoken in the person's home in childhood." The emphasis in the 1881 and 1891 census was on mother tongue as the language 'ordinarily spoken in the household', and in 1901, to languages 'ordinarily used'. It was extended in 1911 and 1921 to 'ordinarily used in his own home'. In 1931, 1941 and 1951, it was stipulated as the language first spoken 'from the cradle'. The confusion and its source are very clear from the above approach of the Census of India. With Census using sophisticated GIS software, and a lot of technology tools, these problems will hopefully go from the current census operations onwards. The other problem with minority languages has to do with their identity. Language loss does not seem to be an issue in India but the predicament of the language planner in India is that language labels change every decade. For example, Angika, Bajjika, or Galong are labels that went out of use recently but we have no dearth of new labels; e.g. Rajbanshi, Kokborok or Gorkhali. There are instances of language revival, as in case of Nepali. There are also campaigns for giving a rightful place of a minority language such as Konkani and Santali. There are even cases of survival of languages spoken by transplanted communities such as Saurashtri Tamil. Many generations of settlers in Andaman and Nicobar also retained their languages. If we dig deep into the decennial census tables of other South Asian countries, similar trends can be found in different degrees.

In several studies, Emeneau[24], Masica[25], Subbarao[26], Abbi[27] and in my own work, I have pointed out at different times (Singh 1976; Singh et al, 1986)[28] that South Asia witnesses two opposite patterns of convergence and divergence in languages. Some languages split and new speech forms and labels emerged, as in Indo-Aryan – Sanskrit & Prakrit to Apabhramshas to Modern Indian languages. Some languages (like Tamil) changed without accompanying changes in their names or labels. Further, merger of structures or linguistic convergence was a common process by which dissimilar and divergent languages become more like one another. When this happens on social plane, unified varieties emerge, like Sadari or Nagamese. Socio-linguistically, too, South Asia shows tremendous similarities. Speech variation is the order, and cultural habits, rituals, and belief-systems show an equal extent of plurality. In a Times of India's web-portal, Sandy Sundaram (April 16, 2003)[29] in her 'Speaking Free', recollected the peculiar predicament of many multilingual Indians:

> Father was posted in the 'true' Telugu districts; it was but natural that we siblings spoke purest Telugu. Grandma, being a true Tamilian, made sure we also spoke Tamil, and tutors gave us the basics of English. Mother, being a very wise lady, engaged a Hindi tutor. To complicate matters, father went to Calicut and

Mangalore, making us reasonably proficient in Kannada and Malayalam. This multi-lingual upbringing can be a boon and a curse.

Does so much multilingualism mean that South Asia is a perennial problem zone? I raise this question because Language Planning literature is filled with suggestions that situations like these offer 'wicked problems', and they are neither 'tamed' nor 'tamable' (See Singh 1992 for a discussion on these concepts)[30]. I see here a defeat of approaches to planning, and a great role for multilingual education, and especially language education using technological tools.

Reorganisation of Indian states based on 'linguistic' principle from 1956 created a complicated national fabric where each major language is a minority language in another state. Tamil in Karnataka or in Kerala can be a case in point. Further, fierce competition for survival or for challenge to outsmart the other had also created what I had then called a 'Sunflower syndrome' (Singh 1990)[31] – a mutual dislike among all competing languages and mother-tongues and the matter has only worsened because of lack of dialogue and a severe insurgency problems. Once again, web-based and mass media based language teaching facility can build the bridges between any two such pair of languages in conflict.

From the Indian experience, one could see that language has worked as a factor in making of 'Nations' as well as 'Regions'. We are already aware from what happened in South Asia during the last one hundred year. Nations have been 'made' in so many ways in this region.This shows that language can be an important factor in the region formation; for example, lingualisation in Indonesia's use of Bahasa and the revitalization/resurgence of linguistic identity in Bangladesh. It is not that there are no conflicts in South Asia. Conflict resolution has been the biggest challenge in multilingual nations. From the internal dynamics of modern-day nation states, we can easily identify a series of dichotomies at work. Often two opposite forces operate through which human aggregates of a region attempt self-definition. While the factor of ethnicity prompts them to press for self-identity, the pressure of civic society teaches one to keep this feeling subdued. Further, when a country opens up to foreign trade, immigration, etc. it has no other option than to adhere to global narratives of liberal universalism. Thus, Globalism vs. Localism would always become an important point of debate here. To that extent, too, South Asian minority languages cannot afford to stay away from the global trend of language technology R & D work. Cleavage between compromise and control could create great differences. Control theory believes that those without the defining ethnic qualities lack respect. In that case, what about those without much bargaining power because of sheer lack of numerical strength or economic clout? At the core of this control theory then is the plan that a majority ethnicity will try translating differences by adopting a system to control both values and resources of the minorities. Alternatively, it will manipulate the technology tools in its favour and offer only a shadow technology to the minority communities.

V. Concluding Remarks

To sum up, we need to re-evaluate our approach to understanding the nature of conflicts and tensions that have to do with the development of language, race and ethnicity in multi-cultural spaces. We also have to reassess how we could possibly relate them to the advancements in language technology development. In case of problems with language development, which is further compounded by prejudice. The role the victims play and are willing to play in language revitalization and preservation activities must be clearly stated.

Although for some, cross-lingual comparisons may seem useless, re-thinking of group relations is very important even now. Schermerhorn (1970; 1978)[32] for example, advocates a cross-cultural study of the dynamics of majority and minority relations. However, in the context of national development that impacts language planning, our central concern should be to find out under what conditions our linguistic groups disintegrate or are isolated and finally adopt strategies to change those conditions.

Since different languages in a multilingual and pluricultural matrix have different roles and functions, and consequently, different degree of importance, adoption of language technology initiatives could have a leveling effect on development of such smaller or restricted languages on par with majority languages.

It is suggested that the above three issues raised in this paper pose interesting challenge for language technologists as well as language planning agencies engaged in the welfare of linguistic minorities. The paper shows that the planning models have to be eclectic and pluralistic to accommodate these differences.

References

Abbi, Anvita, 1992. Reduplication in South Asian languages. Delhi: Allied Publishers.

Abbi, Anvita, 1994. Semantic universals in Indian languages. Shimla: Indian Institute of Advanced Study.

Bellinger, Charles A. (2001). The Genealogy of Violence: Reflections on Creation, Freedom, and Evil. London: Oxford University Press.

Bradley, David (1998) Minority language policy and endangered languages in China and Southeast Asia. In K. Matsumura (ed.) Studies in Endangered Languages, 49-83. Tokyo: Hituzi Syobo.

Bradley, David. (2003) Plenary Talk, Nov 8, 2003 at the UNESCO Conference on Language Development, language Revitalization and Multilingual Education in Asia, Mahidol Univ, Bangkok; Nov. 6-8.

Bright, William. (1994) Native American Indian languages. Native North American Almanac, ed. by Duane Champagne, 427—47. Detroit: Gale Research. Repr. in Native America: Portrait of the peoples, ed. by D. Champagne, 397—439. Detroit: Visible Ink, 1994.

Campbell, Lyle. 1994. Language death. In R.E. Asher, ed, The encyclopedia of language and linguistics, Vol. 4, 1960-1968. Oxford: Pergamon Press.

Campbell, Lyle and Marianne Mithun, eds. 1979. The Languages of Native America: Historical and Comparative Assessment. The University of Texas Press, Austin.

Cazden, Courtney B. (2002) 'Afterwords'. Language Learning & Technology, 6.2:116-117.

Census of India, 1961, 1971, 1981, 1991. New Delhi: Office of the Registrar General of India.

Chafe, Wallace. (1962) Estimates regarding the present speakers of North American Indian languages. International Journal of American Linguistics 28: 162-171.

Dell Hymes (1966). 'Two types of linguistic relativity'. In Bright, W. (Ed.), Sociolinguistics. The Hague: Mouton. 131-56

Emeneau, Murray B. 1956. "India as a Linguistic Area." Language 32:1.3-16

Grierson, George Abraham. (1886-87). Linguistic Survey of India (LSI). Calcutta. (Published in parts, 1896-1927).

Haugen, Einar; J.D. McClure; and D. Thomson, eds. 1981. Minority languages today. Edinburgh: Edinburgh University Press.

Hinton, L., & Hale, K. (2001). The green book of language revitalization in practice. San Diego, CA: Academic Press.

Huntington, Samuel P. 1976. 'The change to change: modernization, development and politics'. Comparative Politics, 3: 283-322.

Joshi, Subhash. (1998) 'Reach, Access and Utilization of Television'. [Ref: www.orbicom.uqam.ca/in_focus/ columns/en/archives/ 1998_aout.html]

LePage, Robert B. and Andree Tabouret-Keller. 1985. Acts of Identity: Creole-based Approaches to Language and Ethnicity. New York: Cambridge University Press.

Masica, Colin P., 1976. Defining a linguistic area (South Asia). Chicago: The University of Chicago Press.

Masica, Colin P., 2001. The definition and significance of linguistic areas: methods, pitfalls, and possibilities (with special reference to the validity of South Asia as a linguistic area). The Yearbook of South Asian Languages and Linguistics 2001, 205 – 67.

McConvell, P. and N Thieberger (2001) Australia State of the Environment Technical Paper Series (Natural and Cultural Heritage), Series 2. Government of Australia: Department of the Environment and Heritage, 2001.

Mithun, Marianne. (1999) The Languages of Native North America. Cambridge: Cambridge University Press.

Padmanabha, P., B.P. Mahapatra, V.S.Verma, G.D.McConnell. (1989) The Written Languages of The World : A Survey of the Degree and Modes of Use (2. INDIA, Book 1, Constitutional Languages, Book 2, Non-Constitutional Languages). Jointly published by the International Centre For Research on Bilingualism and Office of the Registrar General, India, Laval University Press, Quebec.

Pandit, Prabodh B. 1976. Languages in Plural Society. Delhi: Manohar.

Schermerhorn, R.A. 1970. Comparative Ethnic Relations: A Framework for Theory and Research. New York: Random House.

Singh, Udaya Narayana. 1976. Negation in Bengali and the order of constituents. IL, 37.4 : 295-303.

Singh, Udaya Narayana. 1986. Polar verbs in selected South Asian languages and their combinability. (Jointly with K.V. Subbarao and S.K. Bandyopadhyay). In Bh. Krishnamurti, Colin P. Masica and Anjani Kumar Sinha, eds. South Asian Languages : Structure, Convergence and Diglossia. Delhi : Motilal Banarsidass. 244-269.

Singh, Udaya Narayana. 1987. 'On some issues in Indian multilingualism. In: Perspectives in Language Planning, eds. By Udaya Narayana Singh & R.N. Srivastava, 153-65. Calcutta: Mithila Darshan.

Singh, Udaya Narayana. 1990. On Language development : the Indian perspective. In Bahner, Joachim Schildt & Dieter Viehweger, eds. Proceedings of the 14th International Congress of Linguists. Berlin: Akademie Verlag. 1460-71.

Singh, Udaya Narayana. 1992. On language planning and development: A pluralistic paradigm. Shimla: Indian Institute of Advanced Study (IIAS) and Delhi: Munshiram Manoharlal.

Singh, Udaya Narayana. 1994. 'Translation as a way of growing', Meta, 39.2: 94-99.

Singh, Udaya Narayana. 2003. Language development and nation building in multilingual contexts, Plenary Talk, Nov 8, 2003 at the UNESCO Conference on Language Development, Language Revitalization and Multilingual Education in Asia, Mahidol Univ, Bangkok; Nov. 6-8.

Subbarao, K.V. 1984. A Study of Linguistic Typology, Language Contact and Areal Universals in the Subcontinent, University of Delhi.

Sundaram, Sandy. (2003) 'Speaking Free' in Times of India's web-portal; April 16, 2003.

United Nations (2002) Human Development Reports. Alse see: http://hdr.undp.org/statistics/data/

Villa, Daniel J. (2002) 'Integrating technology into minority language preservation and teaching efforts: an inside job'. Language Learning & Technology, 6.2: 92 -101.

Zepeda, O. and J.H. Hill (1991) The Condition of Native American Languages in the United States. In R.H. Robins and E.M. Uhlenbeck, Robins (editors). Endangered Languages. Oxford: Berg Publishers.

References

1. http://www.nationmaster.com/graph-T/eco_pop_bel_pov_lin based on *CIA World Factbook*, December 2003.
2. While describing the theories of Girard and Kierkegaard, Charles K. Bellinger (2001) argues that in post-modern sociology, 'Scapegoating' is a unique way of achieving or creating disintegration, and the "others" often like to follow this option. We seem to be convinced about the stories and scenario where there is this familiar villain who must get bashed at the end, flagging the victory of the 'desired' one.
3. Human Development Reports, United Nations 2003; Also see: http://hdr.undp.org/statistics/data/
4. Media Penetration in South Asia as of 2003:
5. Subhash Joshi (1998).
6. [Ref: http://www.isro.org/old_sat.htm]

7. Source: Indian Department of Telecommunication
8. Ref: www.diehardindian.com/infra/telecom.htm
9. As of now, India possesses 1,468,000 route kilometers of Trunk Automatic Exchange (TAX); 86,601 route kilometers of microwave systems and 108,032 route kilometers of optical fibre systems in the long-distance transmision network, as on 31 September, 1999.
10. Source: Cellular Operators Association of India
11. Source: http://en.wikipedia.org/wiki/Mass_media_in_India
12. Ref: Singh (1994).
13. To the extent this is needed, it draws from the pluralistic paradigm as presented in Singh (1992).
14. Bright, William. (1994).
15. Mithun, Marianne. (1999).
16. Chafe, Wallace. (1962).
17. As reported in McConvell, P. and N Thieberger (2001)
18. Zepeda and Hill (1991:136) Zepeda, O. and J.H. Hill (1991).
19. Campbell, Lyle. (1994).
20. Campbell, Lyle and Marianne Mithun, eds. (1979).
21. Padmanabha, P., B.P.Mahapatra, V.S.Verma, G.D. McConnell. (1989).
22. Pandit, Prabodh B. (1976).
23. Census of India, 1961, 1971, 1981, 1991.
24. Emeneau, Murray B. (1956).
25. Masica, Colin P. (1976).
26. Subbarao, K.V. (1984).
27. Abbi, Anvita (1992).
28. Singh, Udaya Narayana (1976) and also in Singh, Udaya Narayana, K.V. Subbarao and S.K. Bandyopadhyay (1986).
29. Sundaram, Sandy. (2003).
30. Singh, Udaya Narayana (1992).
31. Singh, Udaya Narayana (1990).
32. Schermerhorn, R.A. (1970).

2

Foreign Female Spouses and Language Changes in Taiwan

Cha-chih Liao

Introduction

A common feature with Huang (2000), Liao (2000), and Tse (2000) is that none cited a possible language repertoire in Taiwan to include Cambodian, Myanmarian, Tagalog, Vietnamese, Thai, etc. After 2017, Taiwan is predicted to be much more multilingual than ever, owing to an increase in foreign female spouses, who are welcomed first by low socioeconomic groups and gradually by mid-to-high socioeconomic classes.

My study is based on webpage data, discussions and interviews. I searched webpages for keywords 'Taiwan,' 'foreign brides,' and 'language' in April and October 2004 to get private, advertising, news and academic pages. Many classroom discussions were done. Three elementary school teachers together with four students born and/or raised by foreign mothers were interviewed, a total of 154 undergraduates asked to write their impressions, intuitions and observations about foreign wives. At last two sessions of interviews were done by 24 and 92 undergraduates in April and November 2004, respectively, one such spouse each for earning extra credits and concern about language phenomena in Taiwan. Most webpages emphasize negative aspects of foreign brides and their children, whereas interviewing elementary school children shows the positive. According to teachers, all these children get along well with peers, never absent from class and showing no cultural or language barriers with peers at all. Children do not know any other children in their surroundings who can communicate with them in their mother's language. Their mothers speak with them primarily in Mandarin and Taiwanese. When I told them to learn their mother's language also to be better equipped for a possible future job as translator or interpreter, they were evidently happy. No foreign mothers whose children were interviewed spoke to their children in their own native language. Hsue (2003) rightly implies that some foreign mothers think their native language is inappropriate in Taiwan and do not want to communicate with children in their own native language. Throughout the history of English language (Baugh and Cable 2002), we find that a powerful/wealthy people's language is also powerful. The history of English language repeats in Taiwan, perhaps in every corner of the world as a universal phenomenon.

Students' interviews with 116 (24 + 92) foreign brides indicate that all lead happy married lives. Those without a happy marriage might not be so accessible. Most foreign brides show low L1 loyalty: their children forget the mother's language easily owing to disuse in the community of practice (term used by Eckert and McConnell-Ginet [2003]).

When I predicted languages spoken in Taiwan by the year 2017, one law professor at National University of Kaohsiung who earend his PhD in Germany said, "In Germany, all you hear around is Turkish." I checked German population figures via the Internet and found, "German 91.5%, Turkish 2.4%, other 6.1% (largely Serbo-Croatian, Italian, Russian, Greek, Polish, Spanish, etc.)." With Turks occupying only 2.4% of that country's population (http://education.yahoo.com/reference/factbook/gm/popula.html as of April 2004), the Taiwanese professor felt as if Germany were a Turkish-speaking land. Speaking Turkish in Germany is quite a 'marked' phenomenon, readily noticed and discordant to hearing. On the afternoon of Mid-autumn festival (September 28, 2004), I went swimming and was surprised to find myself within a pool of all Asian foreigners; I understood nothing of what they said. Most Taiwanese neglect this phenomenon, however, because they are in the dominant group and cannot 'hear' them. The socioeconomic status of speakers of a language partly set the fate for the audibility of the language.

In recent years we find many Vietnamese, Thai and Indonesian restaurants and food vendors, run by women from these countries, married to Taiwanese husbands. Eating in one of those restaurants, we hear them talking with friends in L1 with mixing codes of Taiwanese and/or Mandarin.

Throughout history, Taiwan has been inhabited by different peoples (Huang 2000). This island may be one of the cradles of Austronesian–a composite of more than 1800 languages–whose speakers number 300 million, distributing from some islands off South America, to Madagascar in Africa, between Taiwan and New Zealand (http://www.bnxt.com.tw/mag/2003_11_15/2003_11_15_1459.html). In 2017, Taiwan should have many speakers of Vietnamese, Indonesian, Thai, Cambodian, Myanmar, Tagalog and pidgins derived from the above languages, plus Mandarin, Taiwanese and/or English. Yet as far as Mandarin and Taiwanese speakers are in the mainstream culture, most people will pretend not to know it. These phenomena are like English- speaking people in Taiwan: many do not bother to learn Taiwanese or Mandarin. Language status forges its speakers' mindset: people in a High Language group have a sense of superiority and generally do not bother to learn inferior groups' languages.

Taiwan's Ministry of Interior Affairs calculated 12.5% of children born in 2002 were included a foreign or Mainland

Chinese spouse. In 2008, Taiwanese first graders are predicted to be 12.5% from such families. Around Year 2017, when these children finish high school and enter the job market, many new languages spoken by adults will be found in Taiwan. College/university teachers will also begin to teach the new group of Taiwanese, whose L1 might be a Southeast Asian tongue, not Taiwanese or Mandarin. For them to have a little knowledge about intercultural differences between Taiwan and Southeast Asian countries from now on, might help. As shown in http://library.taiwanschoolnet.org/cyberfair2004/fly7536/narrative.htm, in 2003 at Hsin-yi Elementary School in Panchiao City, Taipei County, a number of first- and second-graders had foreign mothers. In other words, by Year 2017, their children will be 20 years old or over, working or attending universities; teachers are advised to prepare.

In 1998, 10,413 marriage registrations included a foreign spouse (Hsue, 2003), 7.1% of a total of the 145,976 marriage registrations. After 2000, the annual rate becomes higher than 11%. Those foreigners decide to marry to Taiwanese men because their home economy needs improvement. These wives gave birth to 5.1% of all newborn babies in 1998. By the end of June 2003, there were 270,000 foreign and Mainland Chinese female spouses in Taiwan. Foreign male spouses comprise 10%, female ones 90% of the marriage registrations. Male spouses distribute mostly in metropolitan, female ones in non-metropolitan areas.

Yang (2003) pointed out that foreign and Mainland Chinese brides encountering the problems: mental adjustment, cultural differences, illiteracy, language, social interaction, lacking systems to support them, religion conflicts, and the education of their children. However, interviews with 92 foreign brides done in November 2004 show only one did not receive education in her own nation (Table 1)

Table 1 Foreign Brides' education in their native countries

None	1	1.1%
Elementary	13	14.3%
Junior high	23	25.3%
Senior high	35	38.5%
College & U	19	20.9%

In Taiwan, foreign female spouses, no matter how long they have been married and lived in Taiwan, bear the derogatory title of 'foreign bride.' Liao (2004) used the term international daughter-in-law in Taiwan to refer to this group. There is inequality implied in the term of daughter-in-law, which still invokes in me negative feelings. The title of this paper is decided intentionally to be neutral: foreign female spouse.

1. Foreign Brides in Hierarchical Statuses

Language inadequacy proposal is shown in Yang (2003) mentioned above and Hsue (2003) mentioned below. The pride and prejudice of Liao (2004) about the dominant language of Taiwanese is well manifested. At Tongkang, Pingtong County, many fishermen marry Vietnamese. With father always at sea, Mother speaks no Taiwanese or Mandarin. The children only learn Vietnamese; when they enter elementary school, they are despised by peers (http://big5.huaxia.com.tw/sdbd/sh/00097967.html). Yang (2003) told the story of a fishmen's family at Chichin, Kaohsiung County: all male members got married to foreign women from Thailand, Indonesia, the Philippines, Vietnam, or Mainland China, and led a happy extended family life. The reason they sought brides outside Taiwan is that Taiwanese parents do not like their daughters to be married into a fishermen's family–too much agony, bitterness and/or suffering in heavy manual tasks. However, these brides are mostly overseas Chinese, so that they do not have problems in verbal communication. All of them speak a little Hokkien (called Taiwanese in Taiwan).

Foreign spouses may be categorized into several kinds: (1) Mainland Chinese women married into a Taiwanese family, more restricted by Taiwanese law than women from Southeast Asia; however, they speak Mandarin and have no language barrier. They are also Chinese; some Taiwanese, especially those 40 or older, feel them prestigious because of their language, since that the Nationalist Government promoted Mandarin using Beijing dialect as the standard, at least 1949-88. However, Shih-hsin Reading Club decided that Mainland Chinese and Southeastern Asian spouses are both called 'foreign brides;' the former hail from the People's Republic of China; and Taiwan is the Republic of China. (2) Overseas Chinese spouses. Their parents or grandparents are overseas Chinese and they marry to men in Taiwan. They enjoy a higher social status than the third kind. (3) Foreign brides, native speakers of Indonesian, Vietnamese, Thai, Cambodian, Malay etc. The term "bride" refers to any newlywed woman, yet foreign bride also refers to one married into a Taiwanese family for more than ten years. As for male foreign spouses, they seem not negatively labeled, for they generally come from developed countries like the USA, UK, or Western Europe. They are even admired and respected.

In Taiwan, the trend of marrying a foreign lady seemed to begin in the 1970s. During those days, many Thai and Philippine ladies were lured to Taiwan to marry rural men. Many ran away while back in the Philippines or Thailand to renew or extend visas. In the 1980s, Taiwanese men began marrying Indonesians. In 1994-97 Thais occupied the major part of foreign spouses (Li 2001). Since 1996, Vietnamese have become Taiwanese favorites. As of September 16, 2003, they comprised 62% of all foreign spouses, Indonesian 15.3%, and Thai 6% (http://big5.xinhuanet.com/gate/big5/www.fj.xinhuanet.com/hxlw/2003-12/16/content_134850...). Below the reader can find my own investigation done in October 2004, showing the Vietnamese occupy 67.2% of wives from Southeastern Asia (Mainland Chinese wives excluded). At the outset, only inferior groups in Taiwan (such as handicapped, elderly, and/or low-socioeconomic class), not highly educated, wed Southeast Asians. Since 1999, many highly educated, salaried people (medical doctors, professors, technicians, engineers, etc.) have had spouses from these lands (http://big5.xinhuanet.com/gate/big5/ www.fj.xinhuanet.com/hxlw/2003-12/16/content_134850). Yet gradually more complicated linguistic phenomena were not noticed by Huang (2000), Liao (2000) or Tse (2000).

Taiwan is an immigrat society: Cambodians, Maymarians, Indonesians, Thais, or Vietnamese serving as housemaids, manual workers, and/or spouses of Taiwanese. Many Vietnamese wish to come to Taiwan, where a month's salary equals annual income in Vietnam. They are willing to marry to men of the interior sort with the real purpose of helping improve their parents' lives in Vietnam. As of 2000, more foreign wives naturalized as Taiwanese citizens are of Vietnamese extraction; Indonesia, Cambodia, the Philippines, and Myanmar follow in descending order of numbers. The finding seems to be similar to that in Table 2, done in 2004.

2. Language Problem

Hsue (2003) seemed to have a sense of superiority as a Taiwanese, as if Taiwanese or Mandarin were superior to Vietnamese, Indonesian or Thai when claiming the foreign mothers from low-socioeconomic families, have deficit language ability and their abilities to educate the next generation are worrisome. It is also the concept of many Taiwanese about Southeastern Asian people's languages.

In this study, we will see if foreign mothers also think their language is inferior and do not want to teach their children in their own tongue. We hope to build foreign brides' confidence in communicating with their children in their mother tongue. Eighteen years hence, Taiwan will have Mandarin and Taiwanese as High Languages while Cambodian, Myanmarian, Vietnamese, Thai, and Indonesian languages as Low. New dialects may be produced too by mixing such languages with Taiwanese and/or Mandarin. At least there will be pidgin or creole Taiwanese and Mandarin. Foreign brides speak Taiwanese as pidgin, while their children might find different Taiwanese spoken by Taiwanese people.

Matchmakers for foreign brides usually have the bride-to-be's photo and basic data of what language(s) the lady can speak. Usually, if Vietnamese/Indonesian/Thai women want to be Taiwanese housewives, they go to a language school to learn Taiwanese or Mandarin before applying to be matched. Taiwanese men have to deposit some money and wait for chances to meet girlfriends in the lady's country. If she says yes, then the lady comes to Taiwan for the wedding. When any newlywed housewife runs away, the matchmaker matches another lady with only minimal extra charge. Interviews done in November 2004 show that 69.6% of foreign brides learned or spoke Mandarin before emigrating to Taiwan, 29.3% Taiwanese and 15.2% Hakka.

A foreign bride who insists on talking in her native language can be viewed lacking respect for the husband's family. Besides, no one understands her; she can only talk to herself and/or her children. It is simply impossible for them to be loyal to their own language. When they are reluctant to speak with their children in their own language, children do not acquire it. One reason they cannot speak thus with their children is dependence on the husband's family: in-laws might be unhappy to see she speaks with children in her native language. They are isolated and not educated with open attitude toward languages. Other reasons for their low loyalty may be that (1) they are afraid that their children may speak Indonesian, Vietnamese, etc. outside the home domain and reveal the identity of being born by a foreign mother, from an underdeveloped country, reflecting their lack of self-confidence; (2) they are afraid that the children might not speak good Taiwanese or

Mandarin and could not catch up with Taiwanese peers at school; (3) they have been habitually speaking Mandarin or Taiwanese since their marriage; and (4) they once tried, but children seemed to forget the language very soon, and they lost patience.

At the webpage of http://www10.brinkster.com/ccs51/03-2-6.htm (as of April 10, 2004) discussion groups exchange information about Vietnamese marrying Taiwanese living in Taiwan: what they like and dislike, what happy families they create, etc. In the messages we find code-switching to Vietnamese: wongsha ('husband'), and masha ('wife'). The webpage master proposed that Taiwanese husband and family members should teach the foreign bride Taiwanese or Mandarin to decrease communication problems. My idea: a husband and his family members can simultaneously learn their in-laws' language.

The Taipei County Government issued a handbook of Taiwanese and Vietnamese for wives to learn Taiwanese, husbands to learn Vietnamese. The County Government is planning issuing Taiwanese-Indonesian handbooks to facilitate the learning of Indonesian by husbands, and Taiwanese by wives (http://fineprint.yam/com/?url=http://news.yam.com/ettoday/et_life/news/200403/2004031811..)

Many Taiwanese worry about the education of the next generation of these foreign female spouses. In January 2004, one kindergarten teacher told me, "We have several children born of Vietnamese brides, whose Mandarin speaking ability is very poor. Their mother is reluctant to teach them Vietnamese, and unable to teach them fluent Taiwanese or Mandarin. They will become low achievers in kindergarten, elementary school, and later. Education of this group of children will be a big problem." Master of http://www10.brinkster.com/ccs51/03-2-6.htm describes the phenomenon: "Utterances of these children are not like Mandarin or Vietnamese. No one understands them. Some kids 18 months old cannot say 'Papa' or 'Mama' clearly." He further responds to the statement above: "In Europe, every child can speak at least three languages, because they hear so many languages spoken around them. Parents can let these children contact with different people to prevent some strange accents." Among 6670 websites when I searched the terms of 'Taiwan' and 'foreign brides', I did not see more than two people encouraging foreign mothers to speak their native language to children. I propose a policy of one parent speaking one language; later the children will be experts in three languages: Taiwanese, Mandarin, and the mother's native language.

Vietnamese brides hope to be able to read Vietnamese newspapers. They also hope to attend classes of Mandarin or Taiwanese (Li, 2001). They resent the label of 'foreign brides' when they have two children and have been married for years. They believe they are brides only on their wedding day, not forever. Foreign wives and mothers are not good terms either, because they are also derogatory. Taiwanese should not think Taiwanese and Mandarin as more cultivated languages than Vietnamese, Indonesian, etc. They need to cultivate the spirit of multiculturalism to embrace these wives and mothers. Officially, such people are called wai-ji-pei-ou ('foreign spouses'). In Min-yi-lun-tan ('Popular Opinions'), a Mainland Chinese bride, Liu Wei-xin, said 'foreign spouse' or 'foreign bride' is equivalent to 'prostitute' or 'poverty.' The ever- changing governmental policies toward these spouses imply derogation (United Daily News 2004: March 7; http://www.cyberbees.org/blog/ archives/ 002904.html). I hereby propose language assets theory to encourage foreign wives to use L1 to let children acquire the mother tongue. Still, those who tried complained children forget them soon and are reluctant to talk with them in L1. Some are more willing to grow up with children in L2 (second language)—that is mainstream Taiwanese and Mandarin.

3. Taiwanese to Learn Southeastern Asian Languages?

I asked a class of 40 students, only one woman indicated a desire to learn Southeast Asian languages if such classes are offered free of charge. None of 43 students in another class would like to, being worried about their future career above everything else. Perhaps 20 years later these foreign brides will shout to ask their children to learn Mother's tongue. People think of keeping their tradition when they reach middle age, because they have been able to make their own living and have extra time to think of a higher level achievement in the motivation or life hierarchy.

A person's native speech is regarded as an integral part of his family background, a sign of his local identity (Blom and Gumperz 1989: 411). It is sad that most foreign brides (38.4% as shown below) choose to give up their native speech, teaching children in limited Taiwanese and Mandarin because they are afraid that learning of their own native speech might interfere with children's learning of Taiwanese and Mandarin.

By identifying himself as a dialect speaker both at home and abroad, a member symbolizes pride in his community and in its distinct contribution to society at large (Blom and Gumperz 1989: 411). Here in Taiwan, a foreign bride cannot identify herself as her own native language speaker both at home and in the community, and are thus invisible. It seems the children will not think of learning their mother tongue to preserve the culture until they are past 30 years old, able to survive in their occupation.

4. Foreign Brides are Modifying the Job Market

Beginning with November 2003, Taipei Municipal Hospital for Women and Children has had clinical time for outpatients of foreign female spouses, with overseas Chinese voluntary workers from Vietnam, Indonesia, Cambodia, and Myanmar as translators between doctors and patients (http:/ /www.cyberbees.org/blog/archives/002904.html).

Lin Hui-chen, a Vietnamese bride living in Hsinchu, works as an interpreter by Tai-yuan Textile Factory because she speaks excellent Mandarin, English and Vietnamese. She is also one of the best helpers of the police in dealing with cases involving foreign people. Her language ability makes her a best friend of Vietnamese in Taiwan, bridging the gap between Taiwanese police officers/factory managers and Vietnamese laborers. She helps Vietnamese women fill in application forms, etc. to naturalize into Taiwanese. She set a good example for foreign brides in Taiwan (Chang 2003; http://www.greenpeace.com.tw/board/soap/posts/312.html). In many hospitals, aside from voluntary translators, multilingual written messages of common diseases and symptoms are used too (Chi Huan-ting, personal communication). With an increase in foreign female spouses and their children, more translators are in demand.

5. What Taiwanese government and communities have done

In September 2003 the Ministry of Interior Affairs issued a 90-page book, Brochure for Social Welfares of Foreign and Mainland Chinese Spouses in Taiwan, written in Chinese, indicating foreign spouses can consult the brochure if they have problems in language, adjusting themselves to Taiwanese culture, etc. While the book is written in Chinese, few foreign wives in Taiwan can read it. Besides, the book is for wives from Mainland China versus those from Cambodia, Indonesia, Myanmar, the Philippines, Thailand, Vietnam and other nations. The government seems always tackling urgent affairs and seldom pleases people.

Since 1996, Chiafu ('Family Support') began to offer economic supports to foreign brides. Among 366 families supported, as of August 2003, most of them are in non-metropolitan areas. Yang (2003) demonstrates the concept of language inadequacy in the social workers serving to support families with one foreign parent. The children are deficit in both economy and language ability. Each April, since around 1999, Taiwanese communities hold Water Pouring Festival for Thai workers and wives in Taiwan, a good example for Taiwanese to value and respect Southeast Asian customs. Hopefully, these activities can extend to embrace customs from Vietnam, Cambodia, Myanmar, Indonesia, etc.

If foreign spouses have problems in Taiwan, telephone services are available for them in English, Vietnamese, Indonesian, Cambodian and Thai for two hours each day in the Ministry of Interior Affairs (United Daily News, September 19, 2003; http://udn.com/PE2004/comment/20031001438723564/20031002479960312.shtml). One has to be aware of the specific time for service in her own language. Once missing the time, she has to wait until the next day.

Hsin-yi Elementary in Panchiao City, Taipei County, offers complementary evening school for foreign spouses (http://library.taiwanschoolnet.org/cyberfair2004/fly7536/narrative.htm). To combat the language problem, Meinong Town, Kaohsiung County, began to offer Mandarin Literacy classes for foreign spouses in 1995, the first such class in Taiwan (Hsia 1995). Financially sponsored by MOE (Ministry of Education), Yi-hsing Elementary School, in Pingchen County City, Tao-yuan, offers foreign brides courses of 'Classes for Adjustment and Growth for Foreign Brides' for four years, teaching Mandarin phonetic symbols, sentence making, literacy, and newspaper reading, communication with spouse, parents and children, as well as among in-laws, and understanding traffic signs (United Daily News, October 6, 2004:B2).

From August 19 to October 9, 2003, the Taichung County government, finding over 5000 foreign brides in its administration region, offered a free 'Adjustment Class for Foreign Brides' including language and written language recognition lessons (http:// big5.huaxia.com/tw/sdbd/sh/00097967.html). In October 2004, this government of the major hometown to foreign female spouses in Taiwan took its first trip to Vietnam, to understand better issues of foreign wives (United Daily News October 9, 2004: b4). In November 2003-January 2004, one Vietnamese Catholic nun, studying in Religion Graduate School of Fu-Ren Catholic University, in Taipei County, decided to offer a free Vietnamese class, sponsored by International Action and Cooperation Team, to ten Taiwanese, who wanted to serve Vietnamese spouses in Taiwan.

Lihsin Foundation offered the telephone of 02-2304-9595 and Ministry of Interior Affairs set the special line of 113 for women (including foreign brides) and minors to call if they have any problem. Both lines have telephone receivers in foreign tongues. On April 18, 2004, I learned that the English service time is 8:00-10:00 Monday to Friday; Vietnamese, 10:00-12:00; Indonesian, 12:00-14:00; Cambodian, 14:00-16:00; and Thai 16:00-18:00.

In 2004, in Taipei City, the brides go to Mandarin classes on weekends. The happiest thing for them is to meet friends from the same nation. They learn Mandarin by Mandarin Phonetic Symbols. One bride also hopes to learn Taiwanese, yet no such places exist (http://www.tvbs.com.tw/news/news_list.asp?no=tzeng20040306172932).

One Taiwanese physician of aborigine extraction, specializing in diseases of ear, nose and throat, took the initiative to learn patients' native languages like Vietnamese, Thai, Indonesian, Malay, etc. He is a popular physician in the Taichung Area: a physician willing to learn 'inferior' groups' language is admired, loved and respected. When I talked of language phenomena in 2017 in Taiwan, undergraduates in the mainstream culture felt puzzled about my overheated enthusiasm to urge Taiwanese to learn tongues of foreign female spouses, one reason being that the USA has never done so.

All the above shows the sporadic and unsystematic efforts of organizations to help the influx of immigrants preserve their own and adjust to Taiwanese culture. In

October 2004, statistics from MOE show more than 20,000 elementary school children with parents from Southeast Asia, a number constantly increasing. MOE thus has a project of 'Promoting Cultures of Southeast Asia' to let Taiwanese students understand their in-laws' cultures. Besides, MOE is going to practice compulsory education to foreign brides 34 years old and under, so that they become literate in Chinese. To let people from Southeast Asia be absorbed into Taiwanese culture, MOE is also planning to let elementary, junior and senior high school have courses in 'Understanding Southeast Asia' starting in February 2005. MOE also urges overseas Chinese from such nations to form 'Service Groups for Immigrants' to give professional psychiatric counseling (Hsing Bao, October 13: C4; Min Sheng Bao, October 13, 2004: A2). However, I later interviewed an elementary schoolmaster and got an answer of "I have not heard of it."

6. Interview Elementary School Children and Teachers

Tuesday, April 20, 2004, I went to Wenchang Elementary School in Taichung City, to interview three elementary school teachers and their four students (1 female, 3 male), one with a Vietnamese stepmother, the other three born of one Malaysian and two Thai mothers. Students were interviewed when their mentors were present. Once the students returned to their classroom, I interviewed the mentor for two minutes.

The first boy was a second grader with a Vietnamese stepmother expecting a baby in May. The stepmother, at the beginning of joining the family, spoke Vietnamese with the stepchildren. Later on, she changed to talk with them in Taiwanese and Mandarin. He spoke fluent Mandarin with no weird accent, a little Taiwanese, and understood Vietnamese speech. His father spoke a little Vietnamese before; now he speaks with the wife in Mandarin or Taiwanese. The boy spoke Mandarin, not Taiwanese, with peer students and never visited his stepmother's parents in Vietnam. Given an option to learn English or Vietnamese, he would choose English. The teacher believed that the student had no sense of inferiority because of his stepmother. He even told the teacher and peers that his stepmother was Vietnamese and was about to have a baby. He preferred a male baby.

The second boy, a six-grader, was born from a Thai mother. He spoke Thai with his mother until age four, when the family moved to Taiwan from Thailand, after which his mother spoke with him in Taiwanese and Mandarin. He forgot all Thai language. He was very good in the subject of Mandarin. His father spoke with his mother in Mandarin or Taiwanese. Only his mother, not other members of the family, went back to Thailand to visit her parents. Between two languages–English and Thai–for him to choose, he would learn Thai, because English could be learned everywhere. Few places offered classes for Thai language. He lived in an extended family, where his paternal grandparents spoke Taiwanese to him. The child had no inferiority complex, was a good student fond of school, because he had never been absent from class.

The third, a fourth-grade girl, indicated her mother spoke Mandarin or Taiwanese with her. On rare occasions she spoke Thai. Her father spoke Mandarin and Taiwanese with her. She spoke four languages: Mandarin, Taiwanese, English and Thai. Her father spoke with her mother, mainly in Mandarin and on rare occasions, in Thai. She interacts with peers in school in Mandarin and a little Taiwanese. She would like to learn Thai, if she could choose between English and Thai, Thai being her mother's language. She was attending complementary school of piano and English.

The fourth one, a fourth-grade boy, is a little introverted. His mother studied in university in Taiwan, fell in love with a Taiwanese man and got married. She spoke Mandarin and a little Malay to the boy. He spoke Mandarin the best, followed by English, Taiwanese, and Malay. His father spoke with his mother in Mandarin, not Malay. When he visited his maternal grandparents, he used gestures to communicate with them, not understanding their language. If he could choose, he would learn Malay, not English. The mother was a voluntary worker at school, helping children.

During the interview, I tried educating children and teachers to encourage the children to speak their mother's language and ask their mothers to speak to them in L1. It was well received. The teachers told me, "I've never thought of asking the children to master their mother's native language, Mandarin and Taiwanese to be assets for future. It is a good idea."

At the elementary school level, three children out of four are quite healthy and choose to learn their mothers' L1, not English, which is supposed to give one an easier access to global power. The first child interviewed might be targeting at the global market, while the other three are more concerned of the future local community.

In April 2004 when I used the search engine for 'Taiwan' and 'foreign brides' on http://www.google.com.tw to find most entries emphasized foreign brides and their children bringing big problems for educating the next generation due to great cultural differences and language barriers. Yet the interview does not show these problems. It might be that (1) our subject number is not big enough, or (2) the mass media are especially fond of reporting negative side of things (Lin 2004). Perhaps both reasons are correct. When interviewed, children told us their Thai, Malay, Vietnamese (step)mothers speak with them in Taiwanese and Mandarin, motivation unknown. The kindergarten teachers' observation: mothers are reluctant to speak with them in Vietnamese, Thai, Cambodian, Myanmar, Indonesian, etc. (being afraid to reveal their identity). I worry about misconceptions existing in Taiwanese as well as in foreign spouses and talked about this with my students. Many were also interested in problems I raised in class. Their replies to my question, "Will you, male students, marry a Southeast Asian lady in the future?" showed one or two men in each class willing. About the same number indicated uncertainty. This gives us a hint: students have to cultivate healthy attitudes toward the unpredictable future. At present, in universities, so we must offer courses of 'Understanding Southeast Asian Nations.'

7. Undergraduates' Intuition about Foreign Female Spouses

As an episode pertaining to foreign brides in Taiwan, in October 2004, I asked 154 undergraduates (97 female, 57 male) a question: "Do you know any foreign brides in your neighborhood or among your relatives? If so, is she in your neighborhood or among your relations? What nation is she from? What are your impressions about her?"

A total of 64 (41.6%) had known foreign brides among neighbors or relations, while 88 did not know or notice any. Among the 58 who knew the native nations of foreign brides, Vietnamese are a majority (39; 67.2%—see Table 2). Most students (61.6%) had good impressions about them: they are kind, friendly, humble, obedient, good housewives and cooks, devote their time to household chores. They study Mandarin diligently. Compared to Taiwanese women, they are more willing to tend household trivia. They value filial piety even more than Chinese/Taiwanese, who often boast about their filial piety. Foreign brides may marry Taiwanese for paying the debts of her parents' family. Most of them are young. They run very good ethnic restaurants.

Table 2. Native nations of the foreign brides

Cambodia	4	6.9%
Indonesia	8	13.8%
Philippines	3	5.2%
Thailand	4	6.9%
Vietnam	39	67.2%

Some bad impressions: they are from poor families, simple and innocent. They are miserable because they get married for money, and their husbands are generally very old or handicapped. They are dirty and rustic. They can only speak simple Mandarin or Taiwanese; thus we worry about education for their children; some are passive in approaching people; it is hard to communicate with them. They along with children had heavy accents in speaking Mandarin and/ or Taiwanese. They live a hard life in Taiwan, a foreign country. It is easy for us to distinguish between local ladies and foreign brides, because they are generally dark-skinned and rustic. They are unkind to Taiwanese, but talkative on phone (perhaps to their friends and/or family members in native lands). They sell themselves by marrying Taiwanese. Many of them are maltreated by husbands, who bought them and thus did not respect them.

Some observations/intuitions may be hard to categorize: they are very tolerant of in-laws, swallowing all bitterness. They marry Taiwanese men to improve their financial lives. They force themselves to adjust to the new environment. They are good at doing manual jobs Taiwanese women would avoid. I categorize them in the positive side.

I put some items in the neutral category: though they live in Taiwan for a long time, I can still feel their dissimilar modes of behavior and thought. Like Taiwanese couples, some are happy, some not. I have no bias against foreign brides: they are disgusting if they misbehave. They generally have dark skin.

Of the 99 Ss (70 female, 29 male) who expressed their hearsays, observations and intuitions about the foreign female spouses, 61 (61.6%) held positive views, 24 (24.2%) bad impressions, 7 (7.1%) both good and bad, 7 (7.1%) neutral; gender does not play any role in observations. Languages in Taiwan today is much more complicated than when Huang, Tse and Liao wrote papers for International Journal of the Sociology of Language to discuss Mandarin, Taiwanese, Hakka, and aboriginal tongues.

8. Interview Foreign Brides (April)

The interviews below imply that by 2017 it ought to be easy to find English, Tagalog, Vietnamese speakers in Taiwan, together with the longer-lived languages of Mandarin, Taiwanese, Hakka and aboriginal languages.

8.1 Basic Data

Twenty-four undergraduate sophomore students interviewed five Philippine ladies, thirteen Vietnamese, one Thai, one Mainland Chinese, and four Indonesians married to Taiwanese. Only one Southeast Asian lady married a Taiwanese for love only; she is also the only one not sending money regularly to her parents' family and the only one who is two years older than her husband (all others much younger). Four were married to Taiwanese for both love and improving the finances of her parents' family; they have sent money home since marriage. Nineteen married for improving their parents' economy and sent money home regularly. Two hoped their parents' economy can be improved and their own lives can be better in Taiwan. While Taiwanese like to say they value filial piety, here we find Southeast Asian ladies are better daughters.

Of the four Philipine wives, they were married for 3-6 years, average 4.5 years. Four Indonesian wives had been married for 3-8 years, average 6 years. The 13 Vietnamese wives had married for 1-7 years, average of 3.2 years. The Mainland Chinese has been married for 3 years, husband 8 years older. The Thai wife was married for 4 years, her husband being 8 years older. The husbands of the Philippine wives were 9 to 12 years older, average 10.3 years older. Husbands of Indonesian wives were –2 to 17 years older, average 9.8 years older. The husbands of the Vietnamese wives were 5-20 years older, average of 11.5 years. The fact that husbands were 5-31 years older than their wives tells us these Taiwanese husbands might have first tried finding a wife in Taiwanese families and were rejected or divorced. Later on, they got a wife from international matchmakers.

8.2 Languages in the Family

We have five Philippine wives; #12 (age 47) spoke with her husband in English and vice versa. She spoke with her son in Tagalog and English. #18 (age 37) spoke with her husband in English, and her husband spoke with her mainly in English, sometimes in Mandarin. #28, only 27 years old, spoke with her son (one and a half years old) in Hakka, with some code-switching to Mandarin. She and her husband spoke to each other in Hakka. She is less adept at Mandarin than Hakka. #32 spoke Tagalog before marriage, having a two-year-old son to whom she spoke Tagalog and a little English. Her husband spoke to the son in Mandarin and Taiwanese. The son can speak Mandarin, Taiwanese, Tagalog, and English. She and her husband spoke English to each other. #34, 24 years old, had a 3-year-old child. She spoke with the child in Mandarin, and the child spoke only Mandarin. She and her husband spoke Mandarin to each other also. Before marrying in Taiwan, she spoke English in the Philippines.

Five of the 13 Vietnamese bride interviewees have no child yet. One claimed she would speak with children in Vietnamese; one said half Vietnamese, half Mandarin. The other three did not answer. Seven Vietnamese brides had children: four talked with their children in Mandarin only, one in Vietnamese and Mandarin, one in Vietnamese and Taiwanese, one in Mandarin, Taiwanese, and Vietnamese. Finally, one had no child of her own, but had a stepchild born of her husband's Taiwanese ex-wife. She spoke Mandarin to the child. #2 had a one-and-a-half-year-old child, with whom she talks in Mandarin. Before she got married, she spoke Vietnamese. She and her husband spoke with each other in Mandarin. #10, married for only two years, had no child. When she does, she will speak to it half in Vietnamese and half in Mandarin. She and her husband spoke with each other in Mandarin. #22 had a ten-year-old stepson, with whom she spoke in Mandarin. Her stepson spoke Mandarin, Taiwanese and some English. She and her husband spoke with each other in Mandarin and Taiwanese. #24 came to Taiwan for only a year, speaking to her 6-month-old child in Vietnamese and Mandarin. She and her husband spoke to each other in Mandarin. #25 had been in Taiwan for seven years; she, the two children, and husband spoke only Mandarin to one another. #30 had been in Taiwan for five years, having a 4-year-old child. The three family members spoke to each other in Mandarin. #38 spoke to her 2-year-old child in Mandarin, Vietnamese and Taiwanese. Her child spoke only Mandarin and Taiwanese. She and her husband spoke to each other in Taiwanese. Her Taiwanese was better than Mandarin. #40 had been in Taiwan for six years, having a four-year-old son. She spoke to her son in Vietnamese and a little Taiwanese; her son spoke both. She and her husband spoke to each other in Taiwanese. #42 had been in Taiwan for five years, having two children, ages three and one. She, children and husband spoke to each other in Mandarin. #44 had no child; she and her husband spoke Mandarin with each other. #48 spoke with husband in Mandarin. #50 also had no child; she and her husband communicated in Mandarin. #52 spoke with her child in Mandarin, and her child only spoke Mandarin. Yet she and her husband spoke with each other in Mandarin and Taiwanese. #56 had no child and would speak to her child in Vietnamese. She and her husband communicated in Mandarin. Most Vietnamese mothers do not speak Vietnamese with their children born in Taiwan because they think their children do not need to learn Vietnamese. Most of them choose to speak with Children in Mandarin, because it is good for their education. While the Philippine brides may teach children the mother tongue, English because it is highly valued in Taiwan.

We have four Indonesian brides: two overseas Chinese and two Indonesians. In their families, no Indonesian was spoken. Mandarin was the major language, Taiwanese minor. #2 was an overseas Chinese from Indonesia. She spoke Indonesian outside the family in her maiden hometown; at home she spoke Hakka (her husband is

Hakka). She and her husband spoke with each other in Mandarin. #16, also an overseas Chinese, had been married with a Taiwanese for 8 years. At the beginning she was a laborer in Taiwan, then she fell in love and got married. She spoke with her two children and husband in Mandarin and Taiwanese. No Indonesian was used in the family. #54 talked to the two children in Mandarin; they spoke Mandarin and some Taiwanese. She and her husband spoke in Mandarin and some Taiwanese. #36 had two children with whom she spoke Mandarin. They spoke Mandarin and some Taiwanese. She and her husband spoke in Mandarin and Taiwanese.

One overseas Chinese in Thailand married a Taiwanese four years ago. At home in Thailand she spoke Cantonese to family members and friends. She had no children. She and her husband communicate in Mandarin. One Mainland Chinese bride had a two-year-old child. She spoke with the child and husband in Mandarin. The child spoke only Mandarin. Still, the husband spoke with her in both Mandarin and Taiwanese.

9. Interview Foreign Brides (November)

Table 3. Distribution of the 92 foreign brides' nations

Cambodia	5	5.4%
Indonesia	11	12.0%
Malaysia	2	2.2%
Myanmar	1	1.1%
Philippines	11	12.0%
Singapore	4	4.3%
Thailand	10	10.9%
Vietnam	48	52.2%

Ninety-two foreign brides were interviewed, including 48 Vietnamese (52.2%, see Table 3). Of the 86 brides responding to a specific question, 53 (61.6%) also converse with children in L1, some in secret; some in-laws also learned a foreign bride's L1. A majority (59.3%) stated that their husbands liked them to speak with children in L1, 41 (47.7%) indicating that both husbands and in-laws did. 29 (33.7%) that neither husbands nor in-laws did; 10 (11.6%) had happy husbands with unhappy in-laws to hear a foreign bride to speak L1 with children. A few (7%) indicated neither husbands nor in-laws mind. Viewing from this standpoint, we will surely find that about half people believe that one more language means an asset for children. A total of 27 (29.3%) was able to speak Taiwanese or learned it in her own country, 64 (69.6%) Mandarin, 14 (15.2%) Hakka, and 20 (21.7%) none of the three major languages in Taiwan. Four (4.3%) Singaporean people spoke all three tongues before immigration, 25 (27.2%) two languages (either [Mandarin + Taiwanese] or [Mandarin + Hakka]).

Among brides with children, none stick to the principle of 'one parent, one language' in talking with children. Most opt for three languages to speak with children: their L1, plus the major languages in Taiwan, Mandarin and Taiwanese. Each mother has her unique experience of language use with her children. For example, (*a*) K1 is from the Philippines; her husband and parents-in- law are very unhappy to hear her speak with children in L1. However, she hopes very much the children to speak her L1; she talks with children in L1 and Mandarin. C36 hails from Vietnam and has the same problem as K1; she talked with children in L1 only when she took them to visit her maiden family in Vietnam. (*b*) C14 was obedient: her husband and in-laws were unhappy to hear her talk Indonesian with children, so she used Mandarin only. (*c*) C43's husband and in-laws were unhappy to hear her use L1 with children, so she learned Mandarin and spoke nothing else with children, believing Mandarin better for their future.

(*d*) K2 and K15's husbands were very happy to let the mother speak with the children in Vietnamese, but K2's mother-in-law (responsible for teaching children Taiwanese) was unhappy, afraid that they may not learn Taiwanese well with the interference of Vietnamese. Here grandmother of the children sticks to the principle of 'one adult one language' in hoping a child can speak Taiwanese well. K15's husband hopes the child can speak mother's L1 to build intimacy, while the in-laws were afraid the child might reject Taiwanese or Mandarin due to the habit of speaking Vietnamese. Hence she spoke only Mandarin with the child for his/her socialization in the environment.

(*e*) C28, K3, K4 and K17's husbands and in-laws were happy to see Philippine wives talking with children in L1, since it is English. Still, at times they choose to talk with children in Mandarin and/or Taiwanese. (*f*) Although C4's L1 is Thai, her in-laws and husband are happy to let the children speak Thai; she thus speaks Thai, Mandarin and Taiwanese with children. (*g*) C18's husband would like her to speak with children in Indonesia; but she speaks only Mandarin because children easily forget Indonesian. As for C40, from Vietnam: the whole family is happy to let her teach them her L1, but her father-in-law gave up because it was too difficult. She also gave up speaking to her daughter in L1 after finding her unable to remember well.

(*h*) K10 sometimes speaks Vietnamese to children out of intuition. However, most of the time she speaks Taiwanese, a main language in the community. She is afraid that the children may be confused between languages. (*i*) Though K12's husband believed that if children can speak many languages it is a very good asset, the mother speaks with children mostly in Mandarin. (*j*) C12 chose not to speak Indonesian because it is not the lingua franca in Taiwan. As an overseas Chinese speaking Hakka in Indonesia, she thus spoke Mandarin and Hakka with children in Taiwan. C32 chose not to speak Cambodian, for it is not the language in Taiwan. (*k*) C23, K20 or K27 have no child yet; however, they plan not to speak with children in Thai or Vietnamese, using Mandarin instead. They believe their husbands and in- laws would not mind what language they talk with children. C29 also said she would not speak with children in L1 of Indonesian. Their reasoning is that Mandarin is more useful in Taiwan, which seems to imply a fear that L1 might interfere with children's Mandarin acquisition. (l) Neither C30 nor C33 has spoken with her child in L1 of Cambodian or a language in the Philippines; both chose English, Mandarin and Taiwanese. Their husbands and in-laws were not happy to hear them speak L1 with children. However, English is all right. Both women received university education.

10. Discussion

Historically, for a man to keep his higher status is to marry a woman not so highly educated. For a woman to improve her social status is to marry a man higher in social status because she can easily borrow fame from her husband's family, or race. In the 1940s through 1960s, many Taiwanese women married American soldiers in Taiwan and were envied (Hsia; http://mpa.ngo.org.tw/message/6-17.html). Even today, Taiwanese might still envy women married to an American, Australian, British or West European husband, since these countries are in a higher economic status than Taiwan. To marry men in these countries, Taiwanese women first learn the language, then fall in love, and finally get married.

Likewise, Southeast Asian women might be envied in their own country, because they have husbands from a much richer society. In Taiwan, they always bear a derogatory label of 'foreign brides' because we see advertisements of "NT$200,000 (US$6000) for a Vietnamese bride, virginity guaranteed. One running away, another guaranteed." Blatant purchase of foreign brides and the husband coming from a low socioeconomic class in Taiwan makes them despised. However, children of these people will become new Taiwanese. After 2017 they will become the base of the economic pyramid. Taiwanese should be educated not to despise foreign brides, who are the mother of these new Taiwanese. We have to educate and help them.

11. Conclusion

Throughout history, when a people is in power or has better economy, his language is learned. For example, after 1066, when William the Conqueror, was crowned in England, his Norman-French became the royal language in England. People of higher social class began learning it. In 1204, when King John lost the land of Normandy, gradually people began to think that all people in England should be able to speak English (Baugh and Cable 2002).

When you talk with anyone in Taiwan, they generally agree that foreign brides are in Taiwan and should be able to speak Taiwanese or Mandarin. To help their children feel comfortable in Taiwanese society, they should teach their children in Taiwanese or Mandarin. Maybe these happen because Taiwan's economy does much better than that in Vietnam, Indonesia, Thai, Cambodia and Myanmar. As for fifty years hence, things are unpredictable.

It is true that languages are just different. None is more beautiful than another, though social status of speakers makes one language more preferred. To promote language equality in Taiwan, on October 6, 2004, MOE passed a law: from 2007 onward, if a student from some aboriginal tribe wants to apply for the bonus of 25% addition to a higher level educational institute entrance exam score, s/he must pass the criterion-based native language test. This policy of fostering native language learning should be passed to apply to native languages of foreign female spouses to let Taiwanese have a harmonious life. Since elementary school teachers felt revealed encouragement of the children of foreign brides to master their mothers' L1, this concept of language assets should be disseminated and promoted throughout the island.

12. Suggestions for Taiwanese Government and Interested Parties

Officers at the Taipei Cultural Center in Vietnam have said, "When Vietnamese ladies marry Taiwanese, they become mothers of new-generation Taiwanese. Taiwan should do its best to lessen cultural differences to let all its people live harmoniously with the Vietnamese brides. Taiwanese seeing Taiwanese husbands maltreat Vietnamese wives should contact a related organization to help them (http://www.greenpeace.com.tw/ board/soap/posts/635.html). They do not instruct how one can shorten the cultural distance between Vietnam and Taiwan. University Departments of Languages and Culture of Southeastern Asia should be established for a deeper understanding besides what is offered in travel guides. After graduation, students can serve in hospitals as oral and written translators between Taiwanese doctors and foreign wives. I remember going to Portugal in 1996 and told Portuguese that in Taiwan we did not (and still do not) have university departments of Portuguese and they were very surprised: Macao was ruled by Portuguese until 1999. Taiwan is so close to Southeast Asia, it is a shame and pity that we lack university departments of Vietnamese, Indonesian, Myanmar, Cambodian, Thai Languages, Literature and Culture. For the long-term welfare of Taiwan and its people, these departments should be established as soon as possible. At present, National University of Kaohsiung has its own department of Asian Pacific Department, whose aim is to develop economic ties with Southeastern Asian nations. We can imagine how they analyze Southeastern Asian nations as suitable for labor-intensive business. Taiwanese universities hope to establish departments devoted to non-economic items: language, culture, and literature of Southeast Asia.

From now on, if one wants to become an elementary school teacher, s/he should be required to speak Vietnamese, Indonesian, Thai, Cambodian or Myanmar. Each elementary school needs to have translators between the school, children and foreign parents. Children might be trained to serve as translators too. After their children go to school, foreign mothers should be urged to do voluntary or paid work teaching the community their native languages. They can work at hospitals, job agencies, etc. as oral and written translators to bridge the gap between newer foreign mothers and the Taiwanese workers, plus make themselves more comfortable and visible in the society. Only by cooperation with Taiwanese can these foreign spouses have the opportunity to build trust with Taiwanese and to smash the Taiwanese stereotypes about them.

Foreign mothers should be taught to build confidence in communicating with their children in L1. Never think communicating with children in L1 hinders Taiwanese or Mandarin acquisition. Encourage children to interact with Taiwanese- and Mandarin- speaking children in the community. Children can soon become trilingual in Mandarin, Taiwanese/Hakka, and the mother tongue. Foreign mothers can communicate with people in Mandarin and Taiwanese; however, to her own children, she should insist on speaking her L1. Use that 'One parent speaking one language' policy to communicate with children. At home, the husband can talk with children in Mandarin, the grandmother in Taiwanese or Hakka; within three years, children will master three languages. If sisters-in-law are from another nation, then in the extended family, children might master four or five languages in a natural setting. The language ability is an asset for future jobs. There should be (complementary) Cambodian, Myamarian, Vietnamese, Thai, and Indonesian schools established for these children; communities might help teach in these schools. Taiwanese in USA have complementary Mandarin/Taiwanese classes, since mothers are highly educated and have peer connections. The foreign brides in Taiwan can so too. They should be also encouraged to run for the position of legislators, to be influential at a higher level.

References

Baugh, Albert C. and Thomas Cable. 2002. A History of the English Language. Fifth Edition. New Jersey: Upper Saddle River.

Blom, Jan-Petter and John J. Gumperz. 1989. Social Meaning in Linguistic Structure: Code-Switching in Norway. In Directions in Sociolinguistics. Ed. By John J. Gumperz and Dell Hymes. Basil Blackwell.

Chang, Po-tong. 2003. Vietnamese Bride Mastering Taiwan Affairs Become Good Partner of Police. http://www.greenpeace.com.tw/board/soap/posts/312.html as of April 16, 2004.

Deutsch, B. M. 1967. What is the Optional Learning Environment for the Young Child? American Journal of Orthopsychiatry 37(1): 8-21.

Deutsch, B. M., Katz, I., and Jensen, A. R. Eds. 1968. Social Class, Race and Psychological Development. Holt.

Eckert, Penelope and Sally McConnell-Ginet. 2003. Language and Gender. Cambridge U Press.

Hsia, Hsiao-chuan. 1995. Foreign Brides in Meinong. http://ngo.formosa.org/mpa/min24.html as of April 10, 2004.

Hsia, Hsiao-chuan. Before 'Foreign Brides'. http://mpa.ngo.org.tw/message/6-17.html as of April 16, 2004.

Hsue, Cheng-tai. 2003. Changing Taiwanese Families—Foreign Female Parent Phenomenon. http://www.npf.org.tw/PUBLICATION/SS?092/SS-B-092-019. htm (as of April 10, 2004).

Huang, Shuanfan. 2000. Language, Identity, and Conflict: a Taiwanese Study. International Journal of the Sociology of Language 143: 139-149.

Jensen, A. How Much can we Boost IQ and Scholastic Achievement? Harvard Educational Review 39(1).

Li, Ping. Daughters from Neighboring Countries—YWCA's Counciling Group in Vietnam. http://www.wrp.org.tw/Conf/index3a10.htm

Liao, Chao-chih. 2000. Changing Dominant Language Use and Ethnic Equality in Taiwan since 1987. International Journal of the Sociology of Language 143: 165-82.

Liao, Hsue-chen. 2004. International Daughter-in-Law in Taiwan. Nui Hsuan Magazine Vol 344. http://pct.pct.org.tw/women/lusoan/lus_345_5.htm.

Lin, Chao-chen. 2004. I am not Stupid, I Ask for Fair Treatment. Common Wealth 172: 172-74. (Also see http://www.cw.com.tw)

Tse, John Kwock-ping. 2000. Language and a Rising New Identity in Taiwan. International Journal of the Sociology of Language 143: 151–64

Yang, Ching-ching. Abruptly Increasing Foreign Brides Brings Taiwan a lot of Social Problems. http://www.epochtimes.com/b5/3/7/31/n351144.htm

Yang, Hsing-ling. 2003. View 'New Taiwanese Children': Chiafu Begin Family Service to Foreign Brides. http://www.ccf.org.tw/index/9210-127/03tbch/02.htm as of April 16, 2004.

3

Recent Change and Development in Different Language Communities of Nepal

B.K. Rana

Introduction

The Himalayan kingdom of Nepal is one of the linguistically diverse countries in South Asia and is a home for different peoples who speak different languages, adhere to different religions, practice different cultures and live in harmony forming distinct identities among themselves from the ages. Spoken as lingua-franca by nearly 20 million people, Nepali is the first language of 48.61% of total population of 22,736,934 [2001] and also the national language of Nepal. Except for Burushaski, a language isolate which is still spoken north of Gilgit in Hunja, a remote part of northern Pakistan at the border of China; languages of the world's major language families as: Indo-European, Dravidian, Sino-Tibetan and Austro-Asiatic families are spoken in Nepal. There are at least three native speakers of Kusunda[1] which is a very unique language used to be spoken in the central hills of Nepal some 30 years ago.

Nepali falls into Indo-European family of languages. It has much closer affinity with Hindi and Sanskrit. However, there are script differences between Hindi and Urdu, they also have much closer affinities. Hindi is spoken almost by half a billion people as their mother tongue in India only. Millions others speak either Hindi or Urdu both in India and

Pakistan. These two major South Asian languages are spoken among the Indian population across South and East Africa. People in Indonesia, Malaysia, Mauritius and Fiji also speak Hindi.

Some people who have migrated to USA, Canada and United Kingdom also speak either Hindi or Urdu. The Hindi-Urdu community comprises one of the largest speech communities in the world. Scholars as well as language activists of India are prescribing Hindi in a broader national context as well as global perspective to play a major role and assert the existence of Hindi as a world language.

Likewise, Nepali is spoken by a perceivable portion of speakers in Hong Kong, Burma and England also. It is spoken by a larger mass of population in different provinces of India. It is therefore, the government of India has recognized Nepali as one of its 18 state languages which is used in schools and in office materials also. The recognition of Nepali as an official language in 1988 by the government of India was a major event for Nepalese linguistic communities to assert their linguistic rights. In this paper I will attempt to offer some insights into recent linguistic dynamism in Nepal from South Asian perspective where language communities are asserting their linguistic and cultural rights for development. Language issue has been one of the vital issues since a couple of decades in Nepal.

Growth of Nepali as National Language amongst Linguistic Diversity

Along with the rise of Gorkha Kingdom[2] in 1768, the state had to promote Hindu Culture and Nepali Language to unify the country with a policy of one language and one culture. National policy as such could have relative importance in those days. It could ease the process of unification of scattered small principalities into a greater sovereign nation. Nepal has always remained an independent nation in South Asia. Since the founding of Gorkha Kingdom, Nepali has become the national language of Nepal and general identity of Nepalese people. There is a vast literary treasure in Nepali - government papers, educational materials, news papers etc. are published in Nepali language.

It is still a matter of discussion as to how many languages are spoken in Nepal. Since, linguistic survey of Nepal has not been carried out until today, only it was lightly discussed by academic circles a couple of years ago; nothing can be said on how many languages are spoken in Nepal. Language data tend to differ from one entity to another and an author to another. As many as 48 different languages have been enumerated in the population census report of 1991. The National Language Policy Advisory Commission [1993] in its report mentions that there are 70 different languages in Nepal of whom 20 are the endangered ones. The report also cites Kusunda as a dead language. But, a number of 87 Kusundas [males 37 females 50] have been reported speaking Kusunda as their first language in the recent national population census report. According to the population census report [2001] there arc 99 different caste, ethnic and two other unidentified groups of peoples who speak 93 different languages as their mother tongues in Nepal. An Ethnologue report [2000] is that there are 128 different languages in Nepal.

In Nepal the larger number of different languages falls in Sino-Tibetan language family. The speakers of Sino-Tibetan languages are mostly indigenous by their origin. They are remotcly settled, fewer in number, economically disadvantaged, socio-politically weaker and unrepresented or under represented to the national life. Situation as such has led to an intense language endangerment in Nepal. After the restoration of democracy in 1990 and also by the concerns of United Nations about the indigenous peoples in the world, different language communities in Nepal have begun to preserve their languages. They have even begun to develop their own scripts, vocabulary, dictionary, grammar and literature etc.

Establishment of Mahendra Sanskrit University for Revival of Sanskrit language

To preserve and promote Sanskrit education in different sectors of Nepalese society and also develop the Kingdom of Nepal into a centre for teaching and learning through Sanskrit, the government of Nepal has established Mahendra Sanskrit University in December 1986. The university was opened amidst a sharp decline in Sanskrit language in the country. No speaker of Sanskrit has been enumerated in national population census reports. This is an indication that Sanskrit is not spoken as the first language in Nepal. Indeed the great teachings of Rshi Munis[3] of the early centuries, possibly even before the Greeks, are inscribed in Sanskrit language. The Vedas, Upanishads, Smritis, the great philosophy – the Bhagbat Gita etc. are written in Sanskrit. Whether Sanskrit is spoken by its speakers or not it has an immense impact upon not only Nepalese social life but upon the much greater population in India also.

The greatness of Sanskrit language is unquestionable, however, in recent decades, it has faced sharp criticism from among the indigenous language communities of Nepal. These communities have designated Sanskrit as a dead language. They blame the government to have wasted wealth over a 'dead language' and standing unresponsive towards the demands of language communities to preserve their 'living languages'. There is a kind of tug-of-war between two groups of intellectuals who either favor the promotion of Sanskrit language or other indigenous languages. Sometimes Sanskrit is made compulsory subject in schools and sometimes optional, depending on what type of government is functioning in the country. However, Sanskrit is not spoken as the first language by the general public; it is not a dead language. There is an ample opportunity for Sanskrit to become revitalized as native language of certain group of people in the country. It is like English which is also not spoken as the first language in Nepal.

Indigenous Peoples' Movement for Linguistic and Cultural Rights

The indigenous ethnic peoples are nowadays known as Janajatis[4] of Nepal. Before the restoration of democracy in 1990, right to freedom of speech or expression was unavailable in the country. Naturally in those days, it was very difficult in founding a social organization that could spell out fundamental rights of the people. However, Padma Ratna Tuladhar had been able to found 'Nepal Bhasha Manka Khala' - an organization for the preservation and promotion of Newar[5] language and culture in Kathmandu, the capital city of Nepal and other two activists Suresh Ale and Parshu Ram Tamang had also started underground-advocacy for linguistic and cultural rights by forming 'Nepal Langhali Association' from among the Magars[6] and 'Nepal Tamang Ghedung' - an organization of the Tamangs[7] respectively in the mid-seventies. Parshu Ram Tamang could present Nepal's indigenous peoples' issues to the outer world including the United Nations' different forums in recent times.

As soon as democracy was restored in the country, these three indigenous peoples' advocates together with other five indigenous peoples' organizations became able to found an organization - 'Nepal Federation of Nationalities'[8] in mid 1990 and Suresh Ale was elected Secretary-General of this newly founded federation. This was a landmark achievement in the indigenous peoples' movement of Nepal. The federation vigorously publicized and lobbied for inclusion of linguistic and cultural rights of indigenous peoples in the Constitution which was being drafted by a commission formed by the government of Nepal. As a result of which some of the recommendations from indigenous peoples' sector have been incorporated in the constitution.

After the restoration of democracy and also the promulgation of Constitution of Nepal in November 1990 there was an open atmosphere in Nepalese academic community. Krishna Bahadur Bhattachan, began critical advocacy louder and clearer than ever before for social reforms in the country. He classified 58 Janajatis of Nepal and also offered a definition for them which the government recognized later. However, his arguments for social reforms have facts and foundations, the conservative school of Nepal, as anticipated, show strong displeasure in them. Out of his enumeration, a number of 16 Janajatis[9] are not enumerated in the national population census of 2001.The government population census report is not widely accepted in Nepal.

Kamal Prakash Malla and Hark Gurung who were indulging themselves in scholarly creations before the restoration of democracy have also published a number of polished works in favor of language communities of Nepal. Gore Bahadur Khapangi has an outstanding record of reaching the outposts and speaking for the rights of indigenous peoples in the country. This tireless advocate for social change in Nepal has made a significant contribution to the preservation and development of endangered language communities in Nepal at a time when many of the world's precious languages are vanishing day by day.

Constitutional Provisions

After the restoration of democracy in 1990, Nepalese society has undergone a lot of unprecedented changes. The Untied Nations' concerns about the indigenous peoples' rights and subsequent declaration of International Decade of the World's Indigenous People [1995-2004] have been remarkable in the effort of preserving Indigenous peoples' cultural heritage across the globe. Nepal also received some kind of message from the declaration. Now, the government of Nepal has begun to preserve and promote indigenous as well as other languages and cultures across the country.

In the Article 4 [1] of Constitution of Nepal [1990] it is stated that Nepal is a 'multiethnic, multilingual, democratic, independent, indivisible, sovereign, Hindu, constitutional-monarchial' country. The constitution has accepted multiethnic and multilingual essence of the country but it is silent about a number of other religions and cultures of Nepal. Such a provision in the constitution has prompted indigenous people's activists to demand constitutional amendment guaranteeing their religious rights also. The indigenous peoples in the country realize that they were converted into Hindu religion following the rise of Gorkha Kingdom. Previously, as they believe their ancestors had professed either Shamanism or Buddhism.

Similarly, in another Article 6[1] of the constitution it is written that Nepali in Devanari script is the 'nation language' of Nepal and hence official language of the country. But, in the same article 6[2] it is also stated that languages spoken as mother tongues in different parts of the country are Nepal's 'national languages'. This provision is to specify that 'nation' and 'national' languages have different constitutional status and relevance.

Article No. 18 of the constitution provides right to every linguistic as well as cultural communities to preserve their language and culture, to offer primary education in mother tongues. Another Article No. 26 of the constitution offers a wide range of directives for the preservation and promotion of languages and cultures of Nepal. There has been some significant development in the area of language in compliance with the spirit of Constitution in recent years. Understandably, there are lots of other things left to be done in the years to come.

Supreme Court Bans Local Governments from Using Local Languages

As guaranteed by the Constitution of the land, local autonomous bodies known as - local governments - like the Kathmandu Metropolitan City began using Newari as its additional official language from July 25, 1997. Following the metropolitan city, Dhanusha District Development Committee on November 18, 1997 and Rajbiraj Municipality on November 25, 1997 also respectively began using Maithili as their additional official languages. The Supreme Court of Nepal issued an interim order to halt such usage and later on June 3, 2001 passed a verdict that the use of local languages in local governments is unconstitutional and unlawful.

The court does not give any ruling to cut the expenses on Sanskrit language, which does not have any single native speaker in Nepal. The Vedas and other Sanskrit scriptures are very highly revered by the lovers of Sanskrit. But, indigenous language communities do not pay much attention to them. The spirit of the Constitution and the Supreme Court verdict conflict together. They do not actually match. Therefore, to protest the event language communities of Nepal stage 'Black Day' program on every June 3 in front of the Supreme Court of Nepal in Kathmandu. As the crux twisted other way round, consulting with other indigenous peoples' experts, activists, language communities and lawyers, Parshu Ram Tamang through Nepal Tamang Ghedung, drafted a public bill on Language Policy for the consideration in the Parliament of Nepal. It was registered in the House of Representatives of the Parliament at its 20th Session in mid-2001. Unfortunately, as the climax of political unrest in the country, the house was dissolved prior to table for further discussion on the bill.

Maoists Propaganda to Allure Disadvantaged Communities

The existing ethnic, linguistic and cultural differences among Nepalese peoples have made Nepal a country of rich diversity. The beautiful country with pristine natural beauty and diversity is now badly engulfed by unrelenting conflicts and has faced a number of serious challenges in her socio-economic development. Once the peaceful and beautiful Himalayan country in the world has gone on the rampage nowadays. There is chaos everywhere. More than 12 thousand Nepalese have been killed and many others are unaccounted for during these years of conflicts. The Maoist insurgency surfaced from a monolingual rural part of western Nepal in 1996. The people of that part of the country can not speak Nepali and also do not practice Hindu culture. The Maoists have a major agenda of uprooting the monarchy and establishing radical communist government in the country. They have also made it public that they would offer right to self-determination or regional autonomy on the basis of origin, language and culture of particular group of peoples, primarily of the is advantaged section of peoples who form almost two-thirds[10] of total population of the country. Questions have been raised whether national sovereignty and unity of the country could be maintained with such an offer.

The start of Maoists rebellion was declared from the profound support of Kham Magar language community of Thabang in Rolpa, western district of Nepal. The rebellion has spread all over crossing boarders of other language communities in the country. There are many monolingual communities in Nepal. To address to their need for change, indigenous peoples' activists, started campaign for linguistic rights of the indigenous peoples. They also opposed Sanskrit education in the country. The reason being that Sanskrit is a classical language. Its morpheme or rules of word formation, syntax structure, phonology, vocabulary, grammar etc. are very complex. An indigenous learner cannot even utter a single Sanskrit word. Understandably, such a person can not compete with others to secure a position in the government.

Nowadays, among the earlier three activists who started language issues, Suresh Ale is under arrest as the government found him becoming a top ranking Maoist leader. The other Padma Ratna Tuladhar is a believer of communist principles and a human right activist. Sometimes he endeavors to restore peace in the country. He was one of the mediators during the two failed dialogues between the government and the Maoist rebels. Without showing any inclination to whatever political agenda, an independent Parshu Ram Tamang currently chairs the Indigenous Peoples' Permanent Forum [IPPF] at the United Nations.

The Maoist rebels are out there to abolish Sanskrit education and discard Hindu culture. They have forced many Sanskrit schools to close down. The government cannot stop them doing so. For quite a number of times Sanskrit examinations were cancelled as the Maoists entered examination hall and indiscriminately looted Sanskrit questions. This kind of opposition has been an on going process in the country. Contrarily, the government sometime does not hesitate to pronounce that it would make Sanskrit a compulsory subject in the country.

There are some practical reasons behind the Maoists to become violent against Sanskrit education. Firstly, Sanskrit and Hindu culture go hand in hand together. One is always complementary to another. All Hindu scriptures, rituals etc. are written in Sanskrit language. Also the king is revered as Vishnu, the preserver in the Hindu trinity. He adheres to Hindu religion. Without Hindu culture and tradition, a king cannot rule in Nepal. The Sankaracharya[11] of Kanchhi Kamkothi, India visits Kathmandu occasionally and the King goes to pay homage to him. This is how Sanskrit and Hindu King are intertwined together. Now both of them have become targets of radical Maoists rebels.

But the indigenous language activists disapprove Sanskrit education because only students born to Brhaman caste group are entitled to receive this education free of charge. This system was introduced by the Rana regime that ruled Nepal for 104 years until its overthrow in 1950 and is ongoing in Nepal today. This sort of education has also resulted in the access to the national resources by mostly the Brahman caste groups whose total population percentage is 12.74 in the country. Since the Brahman population is so small obviously, the number of students there is also always small. The payroll expense is much bigger. This is unproductive and discrimination against other language communities. Further to it, English has been made compulsory subject up to graduate level in the Mahendra Sanskrit University colleges. The language activists charge it as ridiculous education system. But Sanskrit does also deserve preservation as it is one of the ancient languages of the world.

Languages Endangered as the Process of Globalization Accelerates

As the process of globalization or Anglicization is in effect all over the world, Nepal cannot withstand it. The country has embraced English as another 'essential language' since the emergence of British East India Company, a major force in the history of India for more than 200 years. Contrary to the foreign policy and tradition of Gorkha Kingdom, the Rana regime, that ruled Nepal for 104 years until its overthrow in 1950, vastly relied on the British East India Company.

English has been another language which seems to be replacing Nepali itself. Essential official materials are prepared in English. It is a compulsory subject from primary to graduate levels of education. Most of the university or college education materials are in English language. The government has recently formulated a policy to replace education materials by publishing them in Nepali language. It is good for Nepali language. The other interesting thing to note is that a Nepali student will certainly not understand clearly poems like 'Dover Beach' or 'Lucy' etc. written by English poets, unless they have seen Dover Beach in English Channel or experienced snowy storm of Northern Hemisphere.

Political leaders also prefer mixing up few bizarre English words while they speak at formal programs. They seem not to be keeping in mind whether the rural people could grasp what they speak out there. Doctors also write prescriptions in English language but they also don't care whether patients can read and understand what medication they have been prescribed by the doctors.

Everyone in urban areas prefers speaking English in Nepal. Nowadays, urbanite people mix up half English and half Nepali when they speak a sentence. The frequency modulation radios [FM Radios] announcers mix up nearly 75% English and 25% Nepali words and phrases while they read aloud a sentence from radio microphones. Doing this they differentiate themselves from among other general public. Speaking English like this, young people feel they have attained an upper class social status, which is not true. English has become a popular language in Nepal but there is no constitutional provision for the official use of this language. The status of English language in not specified in the Constitution of 1990.

The indigenous and other language communities are trapped in between Nepali and English languages. Both English and Nepali are posing like the killer languages in the country. In such condition preserving indigenous languages is a very hard job. Since the past two three decades Nepal has adopted a policy that education should be provided by private institutions also. As soon as this policy was adopted a wave of English schooling came over and touched remotest areas across the country. Everywhere, one could see signboards hanging that read 'English Boarding School'. This may have some brighter aspects also as blocking national wealth from draining out to other countries in the name of better education. It also could produce some kind of manpower that the country needed there. But such education is much expensive therefore Maoists rebels began opposing this sort of schooling. They have forced many English Boarding Schools to a complete closure. Everyone is after English language in Nepal. If no effective measures are applied on time, the overwhelming popularity of English language will one day certainly kill Nepali language also.

Efforts for Mainstreaming Marginal Populations through Mother Tongue Education

Following the reasonable demands of language communities, the government radio airs news in 18 different languages[12] from different parts of the country. The national population census also reports that a number of 5473 peoples who communicate in Nepali sign language. The state TV airs news for the Nepali sign language community also. These are the remarkable changes in recent times in Nepal. Primary education is offered at least in 11 different mother tongues: Limbu, Tamang, Newari, Tharu, Awadhi, Bhojpuri, Maithili, Bantawa Rai, Magar, Gurung and Sherpa. The ministry of education has, one month ago, published five different mother tongues[13] in one primer book for the grade one students to reduce cost. This is also another remarkable achievement. Some mother tongue communities have begun to publish booklets, calendar, news papers and pamphlets in their mother tongues. They have even started to offer language classes in recent times.

Also there has been a noticeable change in King's language also. The king has his own type of language like the 'King's English' in Britain. The royal family members of Nepal are addressed by the people with some specific words like: 'maushuph'[he/him or she/her] 'gari+baksyo' [did], gari+baksanechha [will do], sukala [sleep], bhuja [lunch or meal] jyunar [eat food], darshan+bhet [seeing, meeting] etc. These terms are only used if one has to address the royal family members. Before the restoration of democracy in 1990, general public, except for King's relatives, were not entitled to use the King's Nepali. Nowadays, general people in urban areas copy King's Nepali and speak in it a kind of fashion. But there is restriction for the general public to formally or publicly speak this language for themselves. Instead, political leaders as well as others do not hesitate to address the king or the royal family members in general terms with media or others like: woha [him], garnu+bhayo

[did], bhet [seeing, meeting]. But they must use the King's Nepali when they are to speak in front of the king or any formal programs.

The capital city of Kathmandu, a hub for Nepalese peoples has undergone some language change in recent times. As the Maoist insurgency has intensified, people have no way other than to migrate to Kathmandu for safety. So, a strange language mix-up is taking place nowadays. For example people of eastern Nepal say 'niska+nu' [to enter] whereas people in the west say niska+nu' [to exit]. The latter say 'pas+nu' [to enter]. These two words are antonyms. The other noticeable usage is 'bhyau+nu [to finish or complete a piece of work, affirmative], bhyau +daina' [can't complete or finish, negative]. But nowadays, this verb is widely used to mean 'to become enough or less'. Let us check the sentences below:

'Tyo kam bhya+nu' [you finish the job/work]. Generally used by general public few years ago. But the Kathmandu people now a days say 'Timro paisle bhyau +daina' [your money is not enough to buy it] etc.

Conclusion

There has been an unprecedented linguistic dynamism in Nepal in recent times. It is the out come of Nepal's democratization in 1990 and the change that took place in Indian subcontinent also - for example the Gorkha Hill Council Movement in Darjeeling. The United Nations' preference for indigenous people's issues provided an enormous energy to the language communities of Nepal. The UN declaration of Indigenous Peoples' Decade [1995-2004] was also another event that also influenced Nepal. But the country is in a political mess nowadays. The unrelenting conflicts have paralyzed the country. Therefore, on February 1, 2005 the King has taken over and formed a government under his leadership. As there is no democracy and King's rule has prevailed in Nepal. – right to expression and the likes have also been curtailed drastically. Some people have welcomed the king's move and some others have protested as well.

During the king's rule in the past, Nepal followed the policy of one language one culture. So, in a democratic system peoples asserted their language rights. The Maoists radicals also exploited language issues of Nepal. It also became an important agenda for them. In the event of king's direct rule, it is now widely feared that Rights Movement in Nepal will halt for sometime. The concerned language communities will also experience a setback. But, those communities will continue endeavoring to preserve their languages and somehow slow down the process of language death in the country.

Note: This paper has been prepared on my own experiences and observations. Therefore, I have not been able to cite references to it. Important dates and other data are provided on the footnotes.

References

Bhattachan, Krishana Bahadur 2003: *Report on Indigenous Nationalities & Minorities of Nepal.* Submitted to *Minority Rights Group International 379 Brixton Road London SW9 7DE United Kingdom* http://nipforum.org/bhattachan_report.pdf

——————— 2004: *Social and Economic Conditions of Dalit Women-ii, Manav Astitwa - Voice of Humanity for Peace & Justice* http://www.ahrchk.net/ma/mainfile.php/0201/61/

Dahal, Ballav Mani et al 2000: *Multiethnicity and Bilingual Education in Nepal. Paper presented to the International Conference on Bilingual Education organized by Central University of Minorities, Beijing.*

————————— 2002: *Rastrabhasha ra Rastriya Bhasaharuko Sahayatra Yebam Bikaska Apechhaharu, (Nation and National Languages: Journeying Together and Expectations of Development) Paper presented to a* National seminar organized by Rayal Nepal Academy, Kathmandu , Pragya, Royal Nepal academy Vol. 32 No.95

Grierson, G. A. 1909. *Linguistic Survey of India.* New Delhi, India.

Grimes, Barbara, Ed. 2000. *Ethnologue: Languages of the World.* Dallas: SIL.

Gurung, Hark.1998. *Nepal Social Demography and Expressions. New ERA, Kathmandu, Nepal.*

Gurung, Hark.2003. *Trident and Thunderbolt, Cultural Dynamics in Nepalese Politics* Mahesh Chandra Regmi Lecture, 2003 Kathmandu, Nepal.

Hodgson, Brian H. 1857. *Journal of Asiatic Society*. Bengal and Asian Educational Services. New Delhi.

His Majesty's Government of Nepal, National Planning Commission Secretariat, Central Bureau in collaboration with UNFPA Nepal 2002: Population Census 2001, National Report, June 2002.

Mahendra Sanskrit University Act 1986, His Majesty's Government of Nepal. & Mahendra Sanskrit University: http:/ /www.msu.edu.np/ue.php

Nepal Adhirajjyako Sambidhan 2047 [The Constitution of Nepal 1990]: His Majesty's Government of Nepal, Ministry of Law Book Management Committee, Babar Mahal, Kathmandu 2053.

Nepal Gazette Part 2, 2002: *Act to Establish a Foundation for the Development of Indigenous Nationalities Indigenous,* His Majesty's Government of Nepal, Ministry of Law, Justice and Parliamentary Affairs, Kathmandu, Nepal Section 51, Extra-number 67, Part 2, 2058/10/25 [March 8, 2002] http:// nfdin.gov.np/1/content/view/13/9/

News Report 2005: *Thap Dash Bhasha Addyapankalagi Prsatab* [Government of Nepal Proposes 10 More Different Mother Tongue Courses for college level education. Kantipur Daily, Kathmandu April 15, 2005 http://www.kantipuronline.com/ kolnepalinews.php?nid=37162

Pradhan, P. N 2004: *Assassinantion of King Birendra to Encourage Maoists to Nepal*

Daily Excelsior [June 1, 2004] http://www.dailyexcelsior.com/ 01june04/edit.htm

Rana, B. K. 2000. *An Ethnographic Study on the Shaukas of Byas Valley.* Janajati, Vol. 2, No. 1 Journal of Nationalities of Nepal: Kathmandu.

———— 2000. *The Lone Kusunda: Struggles for survival.* Report submitted to National Committee for Development of Nationalities, Kathmandu, Nepal.

———— 2000. *Writing on a Dead Language.* The Kathmandu Post, April 16, 2000.

———— 2001: *Bhashako Ghati Nayalayale Nimothda* [While the Court Strangulates Necks of Languages]. Kantipur National Daily, May 18, 2001

———— 2001. *Kusundaharuko Aanubanshik Parichhan Kina? (Why are we required to have genetic tests of the Kusundas?)* Kantipur National Daily, May 31, 2001.

———— 2001. *A short note on Kusunda language.* Janajati, Vol.2, No. 4. Journal of

Nationalities of Nepal, Kathmandu.

———— 2001. *Loponmukha Kusunda Jati, Ek Manab Bhasashastriya Adhyan (The Endangered Kusundas: A Linguistic Anthropological Study).* Report submitted to His Majesty's Government of Nepal, July 5, 2001.

———— 2001. *Note on the Kusunda Language.* OGMIOUS, Summer 31, August 2001. Foundation for Endangered Languages, Bath, England.

———— 2001: *Revitalizing Kusunda Language in the Himalayas.* Paper presented to a Symposium on Linguistic Perspectives on Endangered Languages, Linguistic

Association of Finland, Helsinki University, August 29 - September 1, 2001.

———— 2002: *Mainstreaming Marginalized Populations Through Mother Tongue Literacy and Education.* Report Submitted to World Education Nepal, Community Literacy Project, Supported by Department for International Development, United Kingdom [DFID, UK], July 2002.

———— 2003 :*Rastra Ra Rastriyata [Nation and Nationality]:* Comments on a National Symposium on National Crisis and its Solution. Tanka Prasad Acharya Memorial Foundation, Kathmandu, Nepal.

———— 2002: *The Kusunda language* Paper presented to the Harvard University – Department of Sanskrit and Indian

Studies - 4th Roundtable on Ethnogenesis of South and Central Asia. May 11-13, 2002. http://www.fas.harvard.edu/~sanskrit/RoundTableSchedule.html

——————et al 2003: *Recently recorded materials on the Kusunda language*. Paper presented to the Harvard University – Department of Sanskrit and Indian Studies - 5th Roundtable on Ethnogenesis of South and Central Asia http://www.fas.harvard.edu/~sanskrit/RoundTableSchedule03.html

—————— 2005: *Death of a Democracy,* Nepal-US Indigenous Peoples' Forum, *Somerville, MA 02143* http://nipforum.org/death_of_a_democracy.pdf

—————— 2005: *Additional Data and Analysis on Kusunda (Nepal),* Mother Tongue, ASLIP - Journal of the Association for the Study of Languages in Prehistory Issue X 2005.

Rastriya Bhasa Niti Sujhav Ayog. BS2050. *Rastriya Bhasha Niti Sujhau Ayogko Prativedan*. 2050 (Report of the National Language Policy Recommendation Commission, 1994, Kathmandu Nepal.

Reinhard, Johan. 1968. *The Kusunda: Ethnographic Notes on a Hunting tribe of Nepal*

Bulletin of the International Committee on Urgent Anthropological Ethnological

Research, No 10.

—————— 1976. *The Bana Rajas – A Vanishing Himalayan Tribe* Contribution to

Nepalese Studies. Journal of the Institute of Nepal and Asian Studies, Tribhuvan

University, Kathmandu.

Risely, H. H, George Grierson, and William Crooke. 1931/1975. The Ethnology,Language, Literature and Religions of India. Delhi: The Academic Press.

Skutnabb-Kangas, Tove 2002: *Language Policies And Education: The Role Of Education In Destroying Or Supporting The World's Linguistic Diversity* World Congress in Language Policies, Barcelona http://www.linguapax.org/congres/plenaries/skutnabb.html

Tamang, Parshuram et al. 1994: Indigenous Peoples of Nepal Towards Self-Identification and Re-Establishments, *Proceedings of the National Consultation on Indigenous Peoples of Nepal* held in Lapsiphedi, Kathmandu, and March 23-26, 1994.

Tamang, Parshuram et al. 2000, The 20th Session of the Parliament: *Draft Bill to Legislate the Languages Management,2000* (Submitted for adoption by the 20th session of the Parliament), Kathmandu: Nepal Tamang Ghedung & Newa Rastriya Aandolan , NTG & NRA.

United Nations, Indigenous Peoples' Permanent Forum & High Commissioner for Human Rights, Geneva, Switzerland *Indigenous People: International Decade of the World's Indigenous People 1995 – 2004*

http://www.un.org/rights/indigenous/mediaadv.html

Wattters, David E. et al 2005 : *Notes on Kusunda Grammar [a language isolate of Nepal].* National Foundation for the Development of Indigenous Nationalities, Kathmandu Nepal http://www.nfdin.gov.np/

Whitehouse, Paul. 1997. *The External Relationships of the Nihali and Kusunda Languages.* Mother Tongue 3: 4-49.

Witzel, Michael: *Early Sources for South Asian Substrate Languages*. Mother Tongue, Extra Number 1999 pdf http:// www.people.fas.harvard.edu/~witzel/mwpage.htm>

References

1. I could discover only three fluent Kusunda speakers in remote parts of western Nepal in the year of 2000. No other Kusunda speakers are reported to have been found until today. The government of Nepal has allocated some money for the preservation of Kusundas.

   Some linguists regard Kusunda and Burushaski as language isolate. Divergent views have emerged on whether Kusunda is a language isolate. Analyzing some 150 years old data, which often have inaccuracies, some western linguists have recently classified Kusunda as Indo-Pacific language. This new classification can not be accepted because it is not a complete study which lacks information on recent development on Kusunda language.

Only pronominal studies will not suffice. It is understandable that some linguists as well as anthropologists are out there to establish a theory that first human being evolved from Sub-Saharan Africa. Those scholars argue human beings evolved from Africa and migrated via Indian sub-continent to the Pacific region. Be it whatever, the recent classification of Kusunda as Indo-Pacific language is not accepted by other prominent linguists.

2. 'Gorkha Kingdom' also suggests the political process and development that happened in Nepal. The much preferred name in the history of modern Nepal, King Prithivi Narayan Shah, fore father of the current king Gyanendra, annexed Kathmandu valley into Gorkha in 1768. At that time Kathmandu Valley was known as 'Nepal' and Newari was its language. King Prithivi discarded Newari , introduced 'Gorkha language', gave the kingdom another name –Nepal and made Kathmandu capital of his kingdom. The king, Nepali language and Hindu culture are perceived as symbols of national unity.
3. Vedic Scholars [sages]
4. Indigenous ethnic peoples with their own mother tongues, traditions, distinct cultural attributes and social structures and who also do have written or unwritten histories are designated by law as Janajatis of Nepal.
5. Newars are one of the most advanced indigenous peoples of Nepal. They form 5.48% of the total population of Nepal.
6. Magars are the largest indigenous group by 7.14%. They are third largest population group after Chhetri [15.80%] and Hill Brahman [12.74 %] in Nepal. No individual caste/ ethnic group is over 16.00% of total population in Nepal.
7. Tamangs form third largest among indigenous population after Magar and Tharu [5.64%].
8. i) Nepal Langhali Sangh, ii) Nepal Tamang Ghedung, iii) Nepal Bhasa Manka Khala, iv) Tamu Baudha Sewa Samii, v) Kirat Yakthung Chumlung, vi) Kirat Rai Sanskritic Sangh vii) Sunuwar Sewa Samaj viii) Sagarmatha Sewa Kendra (Sherpa Association) were the signatories of the federation in 1990.

9. The 16 unmentioned Janajatis in the recent census report are Kushbadiya, Chhairotan, Tangbe, Topke Gola, Thudam, Fri, Mugali, Lhopa, Surel, Dolpo, Teen Gaule Thakali, Bankaria, Barah Gaule, Marphali Thakali, Larke and Lhomi [Shinsawa].

10. In Nepal Janajati [indigenous peoples], Dalit [so called water untouchables] and Muslims are treated as disadvantaged section of peoples. They altogether form 63.44% of the total population of the country. It may be argued there are some others who also are economically disadvantaged.

S. No.	Group	Population Percentage
1.	Janajati [so called lower caste]	37.38%
2.	Brahman, Chhetri and Others [so called upper-caste]	36.56%
3.	Dalit [so called water-untouchable]	21.79%
4.	Muslim	4.27%
	Total	100%

Source: His Majesty's Government, Central Bureau of Statistics, National Population Census Report 2001 pp. 72-73.

11. The highest ranking Hindu Guru [preacher /teacher]

12. Radio Nepal airs news in Nepali, English, Sanskrit, Hindi, Urdu, Newari, Maithili, Bhojpuri, Tamang, Abadhi, Tharu, Magar, Kham Magar, Gurung, Sherpa, Bantawa and Dotyali [Nepali dialect].

13. Maithili, Awadhi, Tharu, Sherpa and Magar.

4

The Plural Markers of Kui-Kuvi Revisited

Panchanan Mohanty

1. The categories of gender and number are "inseparably connected in Dravidian" (Caldwell: 1974:221). In other words, one cannot discuss either of them without taking the other into account, and therefore they "...have to be treated as a single system." (Krishnamurti 2003:206). Kui and Kuvi are no exception to it. Kui and Kuvi together with Ku:bi (or Koòda) are three tribal languages belonging to the South-Central or South Dravidian II branch of the Dravidian family (Zvelebil 1990:56, Krishnamurti 2003:25-6)). The names of these three languages consist of /*ku*/ `hill' and the suffix /-i/ denoting 'man', and thus, each of them mean `a hill man'. Previously, scholars were of the opinion that these "... three are very closely related languages." (Israel 1979:XXI) and "... the similarity in the three native names

Telugu Kui (Zvelebil 1990)

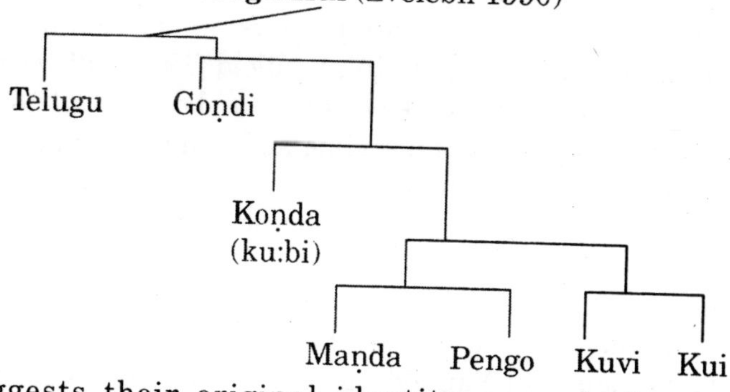

suggests their original identity as a single speech community, perhaps also culturally homogeneous." (Krishnamurti 1969a:3). But according to Subrahmanyam (1969a:133) and Krishnamurti (1969b:327), Kui and Kuvi are sister languages and Ku:bi is their cousin whereas Zvelebil (1990:57) and Krishnamurti (2001:381, 2003:21) determine Ku:bi is a distant cousin of Kui and Kuvi. It is clear in their subgrouping of these languages given previous page[1] :

Proto-South Dravidian II (Krishnamurti 2001, 2003)
(South-Central Dravidian)

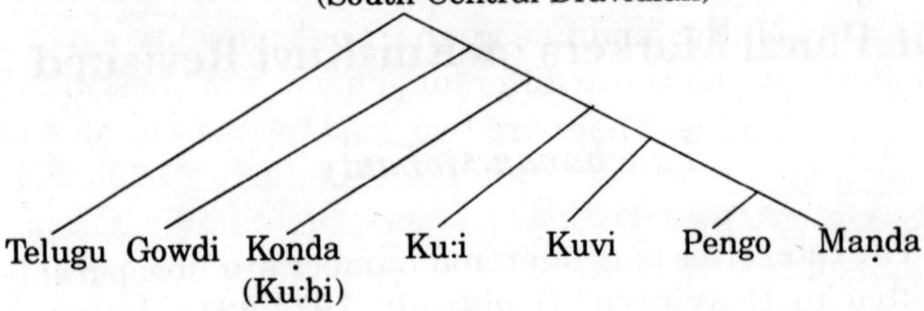

Thus, there is a difference of opinion regarding the relationship of Ku:bi with Kui and Kuvi. An analysis of the plural markers of these three languages support Subrahmanyam (1969) and Zvelebil (1990), not Israel (1979) and Krishnamurti (1969).

Kui, Kuvi and Ku:bi each has two numbers, i.e. singular and plural like other Dravidian languages. The former is generally unmarked whereas the latter, marked. That means the plural nouns are formed by adding plural markers to the singular stems. Scholars like Andronov (1979), Krishnamurti (1975), Shanmugam (1972), Subrahmanyam (1969a, 1969b), and Zvelebil (1977, 1990) are unanimous on the point that Kui, Kuvi and Ku:bi have two genders, i.e. masculine and feminine. With reference to Kui, Winfield (1928) follows the same line of argument in the beginning and divides all nouns into two categories, like masculine and non-masculine. But immediately after that he tends to recognise "... a feminine gender as forming a separate section of the other-than-masculine class. For example, the simple nouns denoting female human beings have a somewhat different plural ending (*/-ska/* instead of */–ka/*) from the rest of the non-masculine nouns." (Winfield 1928:12). Thus, he postulates three genders, i.e., masculine, feminine, and neuter in his grammar of Kui; and other scholars like Dash (1981) and Chetty (1984) follow him.

While discussing the category of number in Kuvi, Israel (1979:47) recognises three genders in this language and states: "The plural nouns are mostly marked and the plurality is represented by three different groups of suffixes, of which the first one is exclusively for masculine nouns, the second one is mainly for the neuter nouns and the third one is exclusively for the feminine nouns. Thus plurality may be discussed under the above different genders, viz. masculine, neuter and feminine. There are two genders, masculine and non-masculine or neuter." But Krishnamurti (1969a:224) clearly states: "There are two genders, masculine and non-masculine or neuter" in Ku:bi. Interestingly, when */-ska/* is recognised as the feminine plural suffix in both Kui and Kuvi by the scholars mentioned above and it is widely attested in these two languages, Krishnamurti (1969a:226) cites only one instance, i.e. */ko°onali/* `a nursing mother, a woman in birth pollution' which takes */-sku/* in the plural, i.e. */ko°onal-sku/* in Ku:bi. This is a striking difference between Kui and Kuvi, on one hand, and Ku:bi, on the other. For this reason, I have chosen to discuss the plural markers Kui and Kuvi together in this paper.

It should be noted here that Andronov (1977, 2001), Krishnamurti (1972, 2003), Subrahmanyam (1969a) and Zvelebil (1977, 1990) among others are of the opinion that Kui and Kuvi have only two genders, i.e. masculine (or high class) and non-masculine (or low class). But according to Chetty (1984), Dash (1981), Winfield (1928), and Israel (1979), there are three genders, i.e. masculine, feminine, and neuter in these languages. Thus, the views of both the groups of scholars are contradictory. The compelling reason for the latter to recognise the feminine as a gender is obviously the feminine plural marker */-ska/* which they could not account for in any other way. So the present paper aims to reexamine the existing data and analyses of Kui and Kuvi and give a more acceptable solution to the problem outlined above.

2. Let us now look at the plural markers of the languages concerned. There is an agreement among the scholars that there are only four plural morphemes in Kui and they differ

from each other with respect to their individual shapes. According to Grierson (1963:460), they are */-ru, -wi, -ga, -ska/*. Winfield (1928:13-18) and Dash (1981:62) state that they are */-ru, -ka, -nga, -ska/*. In the data collected by me, the plural makers are the same as those given in Winfield (1928) and Dash (1981). Notice that Grierson's */-wi/* is not attested in anybody else's data. Again, even though */-ga/* is found, it is only a conditioned variant of */-ka/*. That is, if there is a nasal in the stem-final position and */-ka/* is added to it, the [k] of */-ka/* changes to [g] by assimilating the feature [+voiced] of the preceding nasal. For example:

*penu + k*a ——> *penga* 'gods'

mi:nu +ka ——> *mi:nga* 'many fish'

k*anu + ka* ——> *kanga* 'eyes'

It should be pointed out here that Kui retains the archaic Dravidian characteristic of not allowing a word to end in a consonant. Therefore, an enunciative vowel, viz. [u] is found at the end of certain nouns which end in consonants, and it gets deleted when the plural morpheme */-ka/* is added to these nouns to get the plural forms. Thus, deletion of this enunciative [u] and voicing of the [k] in */-ka/* are in feeding order.

The only other difference is that Chetty (1984) has */-ra/* whereas all others have */ru/*. This difference is most probably dialectal, because, unlike others, Chetty has collected data from Koraput district. So I will take only the plural markers */-ru, -ka, -ska, -nga/* of Kui for consideration.

The situation in Kuvi is quite similar. It is reported to have */-ri, -ka, -nga, -na, -n, -yâ, V~* (nasalisation), *-ska/* as plural markers (Israel 1979:46-60). Out of these, */-ri/* and */–ska /* are employed to pluralise only the masculine and the feminine stems respectively; and among others */-ka, -nga, -yã/* are quite frequently used as the neuter plural markers, though sometimes they are added to the masculine stems also. As it can be easily seen, */-na, -n, -yã, V~* (nasalisation)*/*

are variants of */nga/*. In fact, */-na/* is realized by dropping [g] in */-nga/*. Then, */-n/* is formed by deleting /a/ in */-na/* whereas */-yã/* is the surface realisation of the underlying */-ã/* that is formed due to deletion of [n] in */-na/* and nasalisation of the following [a]. As Kuvi does not allow 'vowel clusters' (Israel 1979:8), the [y]-glide is inserted between the final vowel of the stem and /ã/ and thus, it becomes */-yã/*. This marker is an innovation in Kuvi as it is not attested in any other South-Central Dravidian language. Finally , */- V~ /* emerges due to deletion of the marker */-n/* which leaves its trace in the form of nasalization of the preceding vowel in the stem. For these reasons, I will consider only */-ri, -ka, -nga, -ska/* among the plural markers of Kuvi in this paper. Notice that except the vowel /i/, in */-ri/*, all these markers of Kuvi are identical with those of Kui.

3. First, let us look at the plural markers of Kui. According to Winfield (1928:13), "The plural of masculine words is formed by adding */-ru/* to the singular form..." and he lists four exceptions in which either */-ka/* or */-nga/* is used in the place of */-ru/*. Regarding the feminine nouns, he states that "The plural of feminine is formed by adding */-ska/* to the singular form." (Winfield: 1928:14), and there is no exception to it. He divides the non-rational beings and inanimate objects into five classes according to the final vowel of the singular stems and formulates rules for the distribution of */-ka/* and */-nga/*. But all these rules except the two concerned with the stems ending in [o] and [e] have so many exceptions that one would hesitate to call them rules.

On the other hand, Dash (1981:72) states "The plural morpheme suffixed to nouns has four variants (allomorphs) */-ru ~ ka ~ska ~ nga/*.

The distribution is as follows:

1.Masculine plural	*/-ru ~ ka ~ ska ~ nga/*
2.Non-masculine (+ human)	*/-ska/*
3.Non-masculine (- human)	*/-ka ~ nga/*."

Following Winfield (1928), he tries to determine the distribution of */-ka/* and */-nga/* on the basis of the stem-final vowels of singular nouns, and concludes, "... the distribution of the plural allomorphs */-ka/* and */-nga/* is unpredictable." (Dash 1981:72).

Chetty (1984) also follows a similar line of analysis. Like Winfield (1928) and Dash (1981), he states that */-ra/* and */-ska/* are masculine and feminine plural markers respectively though some masculine noun stems are found taking the neuter plural markers */-ka/* and */-nga/* and describes the distribution of */-ka/* and */-nga/* based on the syllabic structures of the neuter noun stems, the vowels that occur at the end of those stems, and the composition of the ultimate syllables (Chetty: 1984:89-105). But taking the exceptions into account, he concludes that "*/-ka/* and */-nga/* are to be taken as morphologically conditioned (or lexically specific) allomorphs as they occur in the same phonological environment." (Chetty 1984:105)

Israel (1979) illustrates that Kuvi, like Kui, uses the plural markers */-ri/* and */-ska/* exclusively for the masculine and the feminine nouns; and the remaining ones like */-ka/* and */-nga/* along with the other variants are added to both the neuter as well as the masculine nouns.

What is significant here is that Kui and Kuvi are almost identical with respect to the use of the plural markers. All the above scholars agree that */-ru/* of Kui and */-ri/* of Kuvi are added only to the masculine stems and */-ska/* is added only to the feminine stems; and */-ka/* and */-nga/* are used with both the masculine and the neuter stems.

The masculine markers */ru/* of Kui and */-ri/* of Kuvi can clearly be related to the Proto-Dravidian plural marker for human nouns *-Vr. According to Subrahmanyam (1969b:94), "The restriction of the –r Pl. suffix in the C(entral) Dr(avidian) nouns must be secondary since the alignment of the fem. with neu. in the Pl. category has to be interpreted as an innovation." Then, a comparison of all other plural markers, viz. /*-ka, -ska, -nga*/ clearly shows that all of them have /*-ka*/ in common. This, in fact, vindicates the position that originally there were only two plural markers in the proto-stage of the languages concerned, i.e. */*-rV*/ for masculine stems and */*-ka*/ for non-masculine stems, and "The separation between the feminine and the neuter genders seem to be later." (Zvelebil 1977:11). If /*-ka*/ is accepted as the retention of the proto-stage non-masculine plural marker, then we will have to account for the /*-s*/ of /*-ska*/ and the /*n-*/ of /*-nga*/. Let us now discuss them one by one.

4. Though the /*-sk*/ plural marker is found in Brahui, e.g. /are:/ 'man', /arisk/ 'men' (Andronov 2001:115, Bloch 1954:11), it is claimed to be a characteristic of the South-Central Dravidian languages (Krishnamurti 1972:258). According to Krishnamurti (2003:214), "A female human plural *-*si-kk* has developed as an innovation in all these (South-Central Dravidian) languages, except Telugu." In the related Central Dravidian languages like Kolami, Naiki, Ollari, and Parji, the most common feminine plural marker is /*cil* ~ *sil*/ (Subrahmanyam 1968:177, 1969b:98; Tyler 1975:101). If we compare the so-called feminine plural markers of both these groups, we will notice that the common element between them is /*-c-*/ or /*-s-*/. While talking about the plural markers of the said languages, Subrahmanyam (1969b:99) states, "Even though it is not certain, it is just possible that –sk and –cil are combinations of two original plural suffixes *-*c*, and *-*k* and *-*c* and –*l* respectively. *-*c* might have been the plural suffix in such nouns originally and *-*k* or *-*l* have been tacked on to them because of the fact that the latter were more predominant in the respective subgroups." But it must be mentioned at this point that "The plural in Dr(avidian) nouns and pronouns is not an obligatory category (except for most C(entral) Dr(avidian) languages which have developed it later.)" (Zvelebil 1990:21-22) So, one can ask, this being the case in Dravidian in general, why should the said languages have double plural markers at all? Thus,

Subrahmanyam's explanation does not seem quite convincing, and we will, have to look for some other explanation.

In his analysis of Kolami data, Emeneau (1961:39, 42, 48-49) posits */-si-/* as a feminine gender marker and states, "All nouns with these suffixes denote female persons; the suffix *–al*, or rather the complex *–a-l*, with its allomorph –*a-si*, therefore means female person." Again, Tyler (1975:100), while talking about Goòdi, observes that "... a more productive analysis would set up **-ac-* as a separate feminine marker ... before plural suffixes." Extending the same argument to Kui and Kuvi, it can be argued that */-ska/* consists of two morphemes like */-s-/* which is the feminine gender marker and */-ka/* which is the non-masculine plural marker. First, this */-s-/* is added to form the feminine stem, and then the stem takes the plural marker */-ka/*. In other words, here */-s-/* should be treated as a part of the stem whereas */-ka/*, as a suffix.

Regarding */-nga/*, scholars like Andronov (1977, 2001), Çaldwell (1974), Krishnamurti (1972, 2003), Winfield (1928) and Zvelebil (1977, 1990) hold the view that it is a variant of the plural marker */-ka/*. Let us first discuss it with reference to Kui.

Winfield (1928:16) states that "*-ka* is nasalised to *–nga* after roots ending in a vowel." Such a rule is highly unmotivated and there are many exceptions to it. Dash (1981:72) remarks that the distribution of */-ka/* and */-nga/* cannot be predicted. Chetty (1984:104-105) observes, "The plural suffix –<u>nga</u> generally occurs after disyllabic singular nouns which end with *–a̲*, *-i̲*, *-e̲*, and *–o̲*. *–<u>ka</u>* generally occurs after disyllabic singular nouns which end with *–u* (which will be elided before it) and after trisyllabic singular nouns ending with *–i̲* (which will be elided before it)". Again, as there are plenty of counter examples to his observation, he concludes that "*-ka* and *–nga* are to be taken as morphologically conditioned (or lexically specific) allomorphs as they occur in the same phonological environment."

Then, a careful look at the Kuvi data given in Israel (1979:46-60) makes it clear that the most frequently used neuter plural markers are */-ka/* and */-yã/*. "Broadly speaking, **-k* appears after nouns ending in a consonant and **-nk* after those ending in a vowel" in the South Central Dravidian languages (Subrahmanyam 1969b:98). The point to be mentioned here is that */-yã/* occurs only after vowels in Kuvi and this certainly strengthens our claim made above that it is a changed form of */-nga/*. Now, I want to argue that */-nga/* , like */-ska/*, consists of two morphemes, viz. */-n-/* and */-ka/*, and the latter becomes */-ga/* by assimilating the feature [+voice] of the preceding nasal. Further, this */-n-/* can be taken as the neuter marker in Kui and Kuvi.

In his discussion on Ku:bi, Krishnamurti (1969a:225) recognises */-n(u)/* as a non-masculine plural marker. Similarly, Subrahmanyam (1968:177) states that the non-masculine plural morpheme in Goòdi "... has two principal allomorphs, */-k/* and */-n/*." Thus, the */-n-/* of */-nga/* in both Kui and Kuvi can be related to the */-n/* of Ku:bi and Goòdi. What is important here is that all non-masculine nouns, whether feminine or neuter, take the marker */-ka/* whereas the masculine nouns take */-rV/*, i.e. */-ru/* in Kui and */-ri/* in Kuvi.

5. A pertinent question can be raised now: What was the cause behind the bifurcation of the non-masculine nouns into feminine and neuter in South Central Dravidian? Subrahmanyam (1971:104) remarks that "The neuter plural suffix in Dravidian is an optional category in both S(outh) Dr(avidian) and N(orth) Dr(avidian). It is obligatory only in C(entral) Dr(avidian) and there it seems to be an innovation." If we can determine the factor that caused the emergence of the neuter plural suffix in South-Central Dravidian, that will be the answer to the question regarding bifurcation of the non-masculine into feminine and neuter.

On the separation of the feminine from the masculine and its merger with the non-human or neuter, Subrahmanyam (1969a:109) states "... the Central Dravidian languages other than Telugu separated the feminine category from the masculine and joined it with the non-human in the plural on the analogy of the distinction – masculine versus non-masculine that was already existing in the singular." But, our concern is to account for the emergence of the feminine plural marker in the group of languages under discussion. There seems to be two possibilities. First, it is the result of an effort to make a distinction between the feminine and the non-human which originally belonged to one class. It should be mentioned here that the Neo Indo-Aryan (henceforth NIA) languages spoken in India used separate plural markers for neuter nouns. For example, in Oriya, the most frequently used plural marker for non-human and inanimate nouns is */-guṛa/* whereas */-mane/* is used for the epicene or human nouns. The following instances are illustrative [2]:

kOlOmOguṛa/*kOlOmOmane	'pens'
gOchOgṛa/*gOchOmane	'trees'
mOsagṛa/*mOsamane	'mosquitoes'
kukurOgṛa/kukurOmane	'dogs'
??? lokOgṛa/lokOmane	'men'
??? jhiOgṛa/jhiOmane	'girls'

Sometimes */-guṛa/* can be used with human nouns in Oriya. But, its use expresses a strong pejorative sense for those human nouns to which is is added. In other words, it can be said that human nouns are demoted to the non-human category if */-guṛa/* is added to them. For this reason, */-guṛa/* should be taken as the non-human plural marker in Oriya. So, it is quite possible that the South-Central Dravidian languages have made the neuter plural markers compulsory under the influence of the surrounding NIA languages like Oriya. Secondly, there was a pressure to retain a particular Dravidian structure and hence, the introduction of the said marker became necessary. This point needs elaboration. Krishnamurti (1972:171-172), while discussing the phonological structures of the Proto-Dravidian verb-roots, observes that two main types of verb-roots can be established for Proto-Dravidian and each type has sub-types like the following:

Type	*Sub-type*	*Possible number of occurrences*
I	(a) (C) V	44
	(b) (C) VC	760
II	(a) (C) V	44
	(b) (C) VC	760

The statistics clearly indicate that the verb-roots in Proto-Dravidian were predominantly consonant-ending. The same is true about the nouns also. Thus, Zevebil (1990:13-14) rightly observes, "The Dravidian root has generally been recognized as being monosyllabic of the pattern (C) V (C)" and "The typical stem be CV C, too, but is commonly rather disyllabic and triconsonantal, CVC-VC". It is significant here to note that whether a root or a stem, it is normally consonant-ending in Dravidian. The second point to be mentioned here is that the South Central Dravidian group is quite conservative and that is why it retains many archaic characteristics. The following remark of Zvelebil (1977:11) lends support to this view: "The problem of reconstruction of the situation in P(roto) Dr(avidian) has not yet been satisfactorily solved. Final opinion has not been expressed either, whether P(roto) Dr(avidian) has the category of gender at all. It seems, however, that the situations as reflected by the Kui-Kuvi sub-family (plus Goòdi Koòda Kôl (ami) Pâ(rji) may be considered as the preservation of the original state of affairs". Emeneau also considers himself to be "...on the right track as far as the archaic nature of Kui-Kuvi is concerned..." (Zvelebil 1977:53, f.n. 13).

The important points here are that roots and stems in Proto-Dravidian are predominantly consonant-ending, and Kui and Kuvi are quite conservative languages. Given these facts, it is natural to expect that Kui and Kuvi would make an effort to retain the said Proto-Dravidian characteristics in their roots and stems. For this reason, my contention is that whenever there is a non-masculine noun ending in a vowel, first of all a consonant, i.e. either /-s-/ or /-n-/ in this case, is added to it so that it confirms to the Proto-Dravidian stem-structure, and after that it takes the plural maker /-*ka*/.

7. To sum up, the main points discussed in this paper are the following: (1) Kui and Kuvi have only two plural markers, viz. /-*rV*/ for the masculine and /-*ka*/ for the non-masculine stems. (2) /-*s*-/ and /-*n*-/ should be treated as the feminine and the neuter markers respectively in these languages. (3) These markers developed most probably under the influence of the surrounding NIA languages which employ separate plural markers for the neuter nouns and also due to a pressure to retain the archaic consonant-ending Proto-Dravidian stem-structure in these languages which are quite conservative by nature.

Notes

1. Though Andronov (2003:67) classifies the Dravidian languages into seven groups i.e. Southern (Tamil and others), South-Western (Tulu and others), South-Eastern (Telugu), Central (Kolami and others), Gondwana (Goòdi, Kui, Kuvi etc.), North-Eastern (Kurux-Malto), North-Western (Brahui), his view regarding the relationship between Kui-Kuvi and Koòda is similar to Zvelebil's.
2. [O] stands for the half-open rounded back vowel that is represented by the upside down and inverted C.

References

Andronov, M.S. 1977. *Dravidian Languages*. Vijayawada: Visalandhra Publishing House.

——— 1999. *Dravidian Historical Linguistics*. Moscow: Institute of Oriental Studies.

——— 2001. *A Comparative Grammar of the Dravidian Languages*. Moscow: Institute of Oriental Studies.

Bloch, Jules. 1954. *The Grammatical Structure of Dravidian Languages*. Poona: Deccan College.

Caldwell, R. 1974. *A Comparative Grammar of the Dravidian or South Indian Family of Languages*. Madras: University of Madras (First published in 1856).

Chetty, N.T. 1984. *Kuttia Dialect of Kui*. Unpublished M.Phil. dissertation. Hyderabad: Osmania University.

Dash, G. 1981. *Structure of Kui : a Tribal Language of Orissa*. Unpublished Ph.D. dissertation. Santiniketan: Visva-Bharati.

Emeneau, M.B. 1961. *Kolami : a Dravidian Language*. Annamalainagar: Annamalai University. (First published in 1955).

Grierson, G.A. (ed. and comp.). 1967. *Linguistic Survey of India*, Vol.IV. Delhi: Motilal Banarasidass.

Israel, M. 1979. *A Grammar of the Kuvi Language*. Trivandrum: Dravidian Linguistics Association.

Krishnamurti, Bh. 1972. *Telugu Verbal Bases*. Delhi: Motilal Banarasidass. (First published in 1961).

——— 1969a. *Koòda or Ku:bi : a Dravidian Language*. Hyderabad: Tribal Cultural Research and Training Institute.

——— 1969b. "Comparative Dravidian Studies". In: T.A. Sebeok (ed.), *Current Trends in Linguistics*, Vol. 5, pp. 309-333. The Hague . Paris: Mouton. (also in Krishnamurti's 2001)

——— 1975. "Gender and Number in Proto-Dravidian". *International Journal of Dravidian Linguistics* 4, 328-350. (also in Krishnamurti's 2001)

——— 2001. *Comparative Dravidian Linguistics : Current Perspectives*. Oxford: Oxford University Press.

——— 2003. *The Dravidian Languages*. Cambridge: Cambridge University Press.

Shanmugam, S.V. 1972. "Gender-Number Sub-categorization in Dravidian". In S. Agesthialingam and S.V. Shanmugam (eds.), *Third Seminar on Dravidian Linguistics*, pp.383-415. Annamalainagar: Annamalai University.

Subrahmanyam, P.S. 1968. *A Descriptive Grammar of Gondi*. Annamalainagar: Annamalai University.

——— 1969a. "The Central Dravidian Languages". In S. Agesthialingam and N.K. Raja (eds.), *Dravidian Languages*

(Seminar Papers), pp. 107-134. Annamalainagar: Annamalai University.

——— 1969b. "The Gender and Number Categories in Dravidian". *Journal of the Annamalai University (Humanities)*. Vol. XXVI, 79-100.

——— 1971. "The Characteristic Features of Dravidian Languages". In H.S. Biligiri (ed.), *Papers and Talks*, pp. 103-105. Mysore: Central Institute of Indian Languages.

Tyler, S.A. 1975. "Gondih. With Some Notes on Number and Gender in Proto-Central Dravidian". In: H.F. Schiffman and C.A. Eastman (eds.), *Dravidian Phonological Systems*. pp.86-113. Seattle: University of Washington.

Winfield, W.W. 1928. *A Grammar of the Kui Language*. Calcutta: Asiatic Society of Bengal.

Zvelebil, K.V. 1977. *A Sketch of Comparative Dravidian Morphoplogy (Part One)*. The Hague, Paris, New York: Mouton.

——— 1990. *Dravidian Linguistics : an Introduction*. Pondicherry: Pondicherry Institute of Linguistics and Culture.

5

The Case of Dakkhini Hindi-Urdu

Harbir Arora and Karumuri V. Subbarao

1. The purpose of this paper is to characterize the nature of syntactic reanalysis. We shall show that syntactic reanalysis of an existing category results, among other things, in **category change** and sometimes a **change in the syntactic position** of a constituent. Such changes, we demonstrate, may automatically bring in **change in the function** of a specific category. By reanalysis, we mean, a mechanism of syntactic change where a form loses its original function and is reanalyzed to perform various new functions. We shall show that complement constructions and relative participial constructions in Dakkhini are examples of such a reanalysis.

Lightfoot (1979) concludes that syntactic change is basically a **category change**. We shall show that there are syntactic changes (a result of syntactic reanalysis) which do not necessarily involve category change. There are cases where there is only either a **change of function** or an **extension of functions**, where an existing category is reanalyzed to perform a new set of functions without its category being changed. The syntactic changes that took place in the dative and the genitive construction in Dakkhini can be sighted as an example see section 3). We shall also show that in the assignment of functions of a particular grammatical category, there need not necessarily be any functional commonality between the particular lexical item of the source and borrowing language/languages. Syntactic changes in Dakkhini lend support to the principle of optimal utilization of a particular grammatical category. We finally conclude that syntactic reanalysis has to be characterized distributionally as well as functionally in addition to being characterized as a change from one category to another. We agree with Langacker (1983) that "though not all diachronic developments in the domain of syntax involve syntactic reanalysis, syntactic reanalysis is clearly a major mechanism of syntactic evolution". Reanalysis in case of Dakkhini becomes evident from the diachronic developments in syntax, as early stages of this process can be verified from the written records available to us. In support of the contentions made above, evidence will be drawn from the syntactic changes that took place in *kar ke, bol ke, sarka / sarikha* constructions, *ki* constructions, ***so*** constructions and dative-genitive constructions in Dakkhini.

2. We shall first consider the complement constructions which provide evidence to show that reanalysis results in (i) change in functions, (i) extension of functions and (ii) a change in the syntactic position of a constituent. Dakkhini has developed a complementizer system with five finite complementizers *sarka, bol ke, kar ke, ki* and *so*. All the five are used in the present-day Dakkhini. Note that all the complementizers had different functions to perform in Hindi-Urdu.

Originally, in Hindi-Urdu *kar ke* and *bol ke* (cf. (1) and (2) below were simply the conjunctive participial forms of the verbs *karna*: 'to do' and *bolna*: 'to say' respectively. *ki* was a disjunctive marker (cf. (3) below) and presentential complementizer, *so* was a correlative pronoun (cf. (4) below) and *sarka* was an adverb of manner (cf. (5) below) in Hindi-Urdu.

Hindi-Urdu

1. vah	kām	***kar***	**ke**	so	gayā
he	*work*	do	cpm	*sleep*	*went*

'Having done the work he slept.'

'Having done the work he slept.'

2.

vah	mujhe	***bol***	***ke/kar***	gayā	thā	ki	der se	āyegā
he	*me*	*say*	cpm	*went*	*past*	*that (comp)*	*late*	*will come*

'He left saying that he'd come late.'

3.

vah	āyegā	***ki***	nahīN
he	*will come*	*disj mkr*	*not*

'Will he come or not?'

4.

jo	karegā	***so***	bharegā
rel	*will do*	*cor*	*will pay for it*

'The one who does it pays for it.'

We shall now illustrate the various functions of the aforementioned complementizers in Dakkhini.

1. Reanalysis of *sarka/sarikha*

In old Dakkhini (Old Dak) *sarka/sarikha* was used as an adverb of manner (cf. (5)) and as a postposed complementizer (cf. (6)).

Old Dakkhini

5.

aurangzeb	Sivājī	***ku***	choTe	amīr	ke	sarīkhā	kaid	kiyā
Aurangzeb	*Shivaji*	*dat*	*small*	*rich*	*of*	*like*	*arrest*	*did*

'Aurangzeb arrested Shivaji (treating him) like a small rich person.'

6.

agar	tūN	merehamrāh	dillī	***ko***	caleNgā	to	tujh	***ko***	beijjetī	naiN	kiye
if	*you*	*with me*	*Delhi*	*to*	*will come*	*than*	*you*	*to*	*insult*	*not*	*did*

sarīkhā	maiN	terā	jawābdār	hoNgā
like that	*I*	*your*	*answerable*	*will be*

'If you come with me to Delhi then I will not let you down and I will be responsible for you.'

In the present day Dakkhini too *sarikha* is used as an adverb as well as postposed complementizer (unlike Hindi-Urdu which has only the preposed complementizer *ki* (cf. (7), (8) and (9)).

Note that when *sarka* complementizer occurs, the verb of the embedded sentence is always finite and the verb of the matrix sentence is always a nonfactive verb such as *hona* 'to appear', *malum hona* 'to appear', *dikhna / lagna* 'to appear', *karna* 'to see to it' / 'to make it'. The following sentences are illustrative:

Dakkhini

7. pāni paRe sarkā ai
   water fall+perf comp is
   'It appears as though it is going to rain/it has rained'

8. memānā āye sarkā mālum horā
   guests come+perf comp appears
   'It appears as though guests are coming/have come.'

9. unoN yāNku kabhi bhi naiN āye sarkā kar dyo
   he here any time not come comp do it
   'See to it that he never comes here.'

2. Reanalysis of *kar* and *bol*

Another piece of evidence to show that Dakkhini has developed new finite complementizers by reanalysis comes from the grammaticalization of the two verbs *kar* 'do' and *bol* 'say'. *kar* as a main verb occurs both in early Dakkhini as well as in present-day Dakkhini. Notice that *kar* 'do' is reanalyzed as a postsentential complementizer in earlier Dakkhini as can be seen from the texts of Banda Nawaz (1388), Wajahi (1636) and Hussain (1819).

Old Dakkhini

10. muhammad maiN muhammad hūN kar kahe
    Mohammad I Mohammad am comp said
    'Mohammad said that he was Mohammad'

11. hameN bhi kuch the kar samjhe
    we also something were comp thought
    'We thought that we were also something.'

Notice that in sentences (10) and (11) *kar* is used as a complementizer in constructions where the embedded clause is in direct speech. A similar case has been noticed in Tok Pisin (Woolford, 1979) and in Buang (Sankoff, 1979). In Buang *na* 'be', an adverb, is used as an introducer in direct speech. Emergence of *kar* as complementizer in constructions where the embedded clause is in indirect speech is evident in the following examples from Sabras in Mulla Wajahi (1636).

Old Dakkhini

12. khudā hai ***kar*** bolyā jātā hai
God is comp said go is
'It is said that God is there.'

13. hazrat ali kahe haiN allā ko ek ***kar*** jānnā
Hazrat Ali said present god dat one comp know
'Hazrat Ali said that one should consider god as one.'

In the above examples we observe that in some earlier stages of syntactic reanalysis a verb has become a complementizer. What is crucial to note is that such a reanalysis results in a complementizer which is POSTSENTENTIAL in consonance with the type SOV that Dakkhini belongs to. That is, the preference in reanalysis is to move towards 'consistency'. Subsequently, there was a further development and in addition to the verb *kar*, its conjunctive participial form *kar kar* was also reanalyzed as a postposted complementizer in later Dakkhini as is evident from the following examples:

Old Dakkhini

14. bād ālam us mubārak zāt ku moye **kar kar**
after situation that sacred soul dat dead comp
samj ke kudāRi fāvaRe le ke cikkaR haTāye
understand cpm spade spade take cpm mud removed

'After that incident having thought that the sacred soul has passed away, he took the spade and removed the mud.'
(Mohammad Sharif, 1700)

15. vahāN jā apnī mrauvvat pāv ***kar kar*** khudā kahā hai
there go your mercy get comp god said is

God said 'go there, and get mercy.'

16. nandāN ãteiN ***kar ke*** uRte uRte sunī
sisters-in-law will come comp flying flying heard
'(She) heard sisters-in-law are coming.'

It is interesting to note that at this period preposed (left peripheral) complementizer *ki* as well as the reanalyzed post posed (right peripheral) complementizer *kar* and its conjuntive participial form *kar kar* coexisted. The coexistence of three complementizers indicates that syntactic change is in progress and the language is in a transitional stage. However, in the written texts of the subsequent period and in present day Dakkhini, it is only the conjuntive participial form *kar kar* that is retained as a complementizer along with other extended functions which we shall discuss later (cf. section 2.2). We shall notice that some of the functions that are performed by *kar kar* in present day Dakkhini were already present in old Dakkhini. These functions included naming-labelling and purposive functions. The following examples are illustrative.

(I) Purposive

Old Dakkhini

17 apne ūnt kā patā mileNgā ***kar kar*** ā kar kyā dekhte haiN ki ...
own camel of information will get comp come cpm what see is comp
'He came in order to get the information about his camel and what he saw was that.....'

(II) Naming-Labelling

Old Dakkhini

18. ab-dullā bin falāyā ***kar ke*** ek bujurg the
Abdullā Bin Falāyā comp one old man was
'There was an old man called Abdulla Bin Falāyā.'

19. yo abdul hai jo dakhani meN ise toshā ***kar ke*** boltā hai
this Abdul is who Dakkhini in this tosha comp say is
'It is Abdul who calls it 'toshā' in Dakkhini.'

Another such complementizer which is the result of grammaticalization of a lexical item is the past participial form of the verb *bol* 'say', reanalyzed as a postposed complimemntizer. This complementizer does not exit in the written records available to us. It is syntactically similar to the *kar ke* complementizer. The following examples where both the complementizers can occur alternatively are illustrative.

Dakkhini

20. rām ātāa **bol ke/kar ke** bolā pan naiN āyā
Ram will come comp/comp said but not come
'Ram said that he would come but did not come.'

Such reanalysis in addition to category change (from verb to complementizer) resulted in extension/change in functions where an existing category is reanalyzed to incorporate new construction types in order to perform new functions.

1. In addition to acquiring the status of a postposted complementizer, *bol ke* and *kar ke* in Dakkhini have extended their semantic and syntactic domain to many more functions which are not found in Hindi-Urdu. Some of the main functions are: as a reason marker, as a purposive marker, as a quotative marker in constructions expressing desire, intentions, thought, as a question word complementizer to express deliberateness, for naming and labeling, as an introducer and in onomatopoeic expressions etc. The following examples are illustrative. Both *bol ke* and *kar ke* are used to express the reason function.

(*i*) As a reason marker

Dakkhini

21. āp nahiN āye **kar ke/ bol ke** merā ittā nuksān ho gɛ
you neg came comp comp my this much loss occu
'I ran into a great loss because you did not come.'

(*ii*) As a purposive marker

22. yāN pe kām karnā **bol ke/kar ke** āyī ūN
here loc work do+inf in order to have come
'I have come here to work.'

(*iii*) As quotative marker

23 mohan kām kartāun ***bol ke/ kar ke*** bolā pan naiN kiyā
Mohan work will do comp/ comp said but not did
'Mohan said that he will do the work but did not do it.'

(*iv*) In constructions expressing desire, intention and thought

24. mere ku bhot sā paisā honā ***bol ke/ kar ke*** khāish ai
I dat lot of money need comp/ comp desire is
'I have a desire to have a lot of money.'

(*v*) As a question word complementizer

bol ke or *kar ke* occurs with a question word in Dakkhini where the verb has potential to take a complement.

25. rām kyā ***bolke/kar ke*** likhā
Ram what comp/comp wrote
'What did Ram write?'

(*vi*) To express deliberateness

26. rām honā ***kar ke / bol ke*** gilās toRā
Ram needed comp /comp glass broke
'Ram broke the glass deliberately.'

27. sudhā ***bol ke/kar ke*** baccī tumku mālum kyā
Sudha comp /comp girl you dat know what
'Do you know a girl named Sudha?'

(*vii*) As an introducer

28. ye ich ai rādhā ***bol ke / kar ke*** merī frenD
this emphatic is Radha comp / comp my friend
'This is my friend Radha.'

(*ix*) In onomatopoeic expressions

29. thakk ***bol ke/ kar ke*** zor se āvāz huī
knock comp/comp loud from sound happened
'There was a loud thud.'

Not only in Dakkhini but other Indo-Aryan languages such as Konkani, Marathi, Bengali, Oriya one can see that the participial form of the verb has been lexicalized and it performs a number of new functions. Similarity in the extended usage of verb *say* in these languages is still explainable as Marathi, Konkani, Dakkhini and Oriya have been in contact with Telugu and Kannada. (Emeneau 1969, Kachru 1979, Subbarao 1989,What is more surprising and worth noticing is a similar kind of development in languages belonging to different language families such as Yoruba and Ewe of the Kwa group and other Niger Congo languages such as Swahili, Effik and Lugande (Lord, 1976). One of the common features of **say** in these languages is its use as a generalized complementizer. In the other functions too these languages show similar developments to the ones found in South Asian Languages which lead us to believe that there is a general tendency of certain categories or lexical items moving towards grammaticalization in the process of syntactic reanalysis. Supporting evidence come from different studies such as Washabaugh (1975) who makes similar claim regarding the development of *fi* complementizer from a preposition in Providence Island Creole in Columbia. According to Washabaugh development of the complementizer is not a unique process for a distinct language, but rather this development is creolization, and perhaps in all cases of grammar elaboration proceeds generally along the same route. A somewhat similar view is expressed by Woolford (1979) in case of Tok Pisin which developed complementizer system by the mechanism of change; quite a ordinary process of change namely, syntactic reanalysis. In such a reanalysis, there is no special process unique to creolization involved and it is general type of change.

Some other languages where the verb is reanalyzed to the grammatical category of the complementizers are Thai, Japanese, Burmese and Jamaican Creole (Lord, 1976). In some languages however, the occurrence of verb as complementizer is restricted only to the verbs of saying, for example, in the languages belonging to Uto-Aztec group (Munro 1974). This process goes beyond the development of a new category of complementizers alone.

It is further reanalyzed in relative constructions too. For example Ewe (Westermann 1930), a Niger-Congo language of the Kwa, has it in relative clauses. In Kere (Ebert 1973) too the *say* complementizer appears in complement as well as in relative clauses. Although Dakkhini does not have a form of the verb *bol* 'say' in relative clauses, we observe the occurrence of the complementizer *ki* as a linker in complement constructions where the embedded sentence expresses doubt and as a linker in relative constructions. A similar development can be seen in Konkani (Nadkarni, 1970) and Konyak (Nagaraja 1984).

To sum up, in the above discussion, we have demonstrated that the syntactic change involved in the shift of a preposed complementizer to postposed complementizer in case of *bol ke, kar ke, ki* and *sarka* is a case of syntactic reanalysis which involves a category change as well as a change in syntactic position of a constituent. On the basis of the postposed *ki*, its various functions in addition to functioning as a generalized complementizer, (cf. 2.3) it is argued that as a result of reanalysis an existing construction or category in the language is reanalyzed to incorporate new construction types (of the language with which it comes in contact) into its system. As the language undergoes a process of syntactic change or reanalysis, it expands its structure and functions and there is an emergence of an additional device to express certain new construction types. We have observed that the development of *kar ke* and *bol ke* as well as *ki* complementizer along with their multiple syntactic functions provided an example of such a device and it proves that reanalysis involves change in function as well as *extention* of functions. The postposed complementizers *kar ke, ki* and *bol ke* performing varied functions indicate the optimal utilization of a particular category where an existing category or lexical item is grammaticalized and exploited to the maximal possible extent to perform a new set of functions instead of having a new lexical category.

The existence of *kar/kar ke*, as a postposed complementizer in earlier Dakkhini (texts) and absence of *bol ke* in the written texts available to us leads us to believe that *kar ke* might have acted as a catalyst in accelerating the borrowing and reanalysis of *bol ke* complementizer with various functions from Telugu into Dakkhini which in turn might have introduced its own various functions to *kar ke* (as these functions, except a few, did not exist in earlier Dakkhini). We therefore, hypothesize that the earlier presence of *kar ke* could have been instrumental in the borrowing of *bol ke*. This type of change also leads us to conclude that a particular syntactic change may have the effect of triggering the syntactic change of another element. We shall now discuss the *ki* construction in Dakkhini to further demonstrate our claims concerning reanalysis.

3. Reanalysis of *ki*

ki which functions as a presentential (left peripherial) complementizer in Hindi-Urdu has been reanalyzed in Dakkhini as a postposed (right peripherial) complementizer along with many other functions. We do not have any evidence of *ki* as a postposed complementizer in earlier Dakkhini as is clear from the following examples, where *ki* is a preposed complementizer.

Old Dakkhini

30.	bāje kaite	haiN	ke	khudātālā	ku	kyāmat	ke	din	dekheNge
	a few say	*are*	*that*	*God*	*dat*	*day of judgement*	*of*	*day*	*will see*

'A few people say that they will see the God on the day of judgement.'

31.	uske	māNe	ye	haiN	ke	tamām	jamīn	ke	jhāroN	ke	kalam	banānā
	his	*means*	*this*	*are*	*comp*	*all*	*land*	*of*	*trees*	*of*	*cuttings*	*make*

'He meant that he cut all the trees of the land.'

ki functions as a postposed complementizer in present day Dakkhini. The following examples are illustrative:

32.	rām	kab	āta $_{S2}$	***ki***	mere	ku	kyā	mālum
	Ram	*when*	*will come*	*comp*	*to me*	*dat*	*what*	*know*

'How do I know when Ram will come?'

33.	[$_{S2}$anjeyya	kitte	paise	le	ko	āyā $_{S2}$]	ki	apan	ku	naiN
	Anjayya	*how much*	*money*	*bring*	*cpm*	*came*	*dat*	*to us*	*dat*	*neg*

'Anjayya did not tell us how much money he brought.'

Syntactic behavior of *ki* is different from that of *bol ke* and *kar ke*. There are syntactic constraints on the distribution of these complementizers. The *ki* complementizer in Dakkhini has also been reanalyzed to acquire a number of new syntactic functions in addition to functioning as a postposed complementizer.

As a disjunctive marker

(*a*) Clausal

34.	rām	kal	ātā	***ki***	āj	ātā	***ki***	mere	ku	naiN	mā
	Ram	*tomorrow*	*will come*	*disj mkr*	*today*	*will come*	*disj mkr*	*I*	*dat*	*not*	*kn*

'I don't know whether Ram will come today or tomorrow.'

(*b*) Phrasal

35.	inoN	***ki***	unoN	***ki***	kon	jātā	***ki***
	this one	*dis mkr*	*that one*	*dis mkr*	*who*	*go*	*dis mkr*

'Either he (distant) or he (proximate) or who will go?'

In dubitative constructions

ki along with question word *kya* 'what' and finite form of verb *hona* 'be' is used to convey the meaning of 'perhaps' or 'might'.

36.	kamlā	ātī	kyā	ai	***ki***
	Kamla	*will come*	*what*	*is*	*dub mkr*

'Kamla might come.'

As a staller

In conjunction with *phir* 'then' and *kya ai* 'what is' *ki* is used as staller.

37. phir kayā ai ***ki*** naiN āyā
then what is ki not came
'(he) did not come.'

ki with embedded questions – *ki* occurs in the postverbal position with embedded questions expressing doubt.

38. kon āyā ***ki*** mere ku naiN mālum
who came ki I dative not known
'I don't know who came.'

Indefiniteness when used with question words.

39. kon ***ki*** āyā
who ki came
'Some one came.'

40. hamāre abbā kisku ai ***ki*** leko āye
our father what is ki has brought
'My father brought something.'

41 uno kaisa ***ki*** kar rā
he what ki do being
'he is doing something.'

We shall now discuss the case of *so* in Dakkhini in the following section.

4. Reanalysis of *so*

The archaic Hindi-Urdu correlative marker *so* has been reanalyzed in Dakkhini to perform an entirely a new set of syntactic functions, such as **complmentizer, adjectivalizer** in prenominal and predicate position, as well as with **conjuntive participles** and **negative relative participles** (whether prenominal or predicative), **linker** in negative verbal participles and reason adverbial clauses. As a consequence the functions that *so* performs in Dakkhini are entirely distinct from those of *so* of Hindi-Urdu. The use of *so* to perform so many varied functions represents the optimal utilization of a grammatical category. The reassignment of functions of **so** in Dakkhini, we claim, shows that in syntactic reanalysis there need not necessarily be any functional commonality between particular lexical items of the source and the borrowing languages.

Hindi-Urdu (and other Indo-Aryan languages) have two correlative pronouns *vo/vah* and *so*.

Hindi-Urdu

42. jo mehnat kar-tā hai vah tarakkī kartā hai
who hard work do.imperf pres he progress does is
'Whoever works hard, progresses.'

43. jo sotā hai so khotā hai
who sleep pres he lose pres
'Whoever sleeps, loses.'

Dakkhini *so* has been reanalyzed and performs a new set of functions which are as follows:

(*i*) *so* is used as a **complementizer**. This use as a complementizer is found with verbs such as **malum hona** 'to come to know', **batana** 'to tell' and **dekhna** 'to see', etc.

Dakkhini

44. bālammā gayee so mere ku naiN mālum
Balamma went comp I.dat neg knowledge
'I don't know that Balamma has gone.'

45 tum ku ye janānā hai so naiN dikh rā kayā
you dat this ladies place is comp neg appear progr q mkr
'Don't you know that this is a place exclusively meant for ladies?'

(*i*) In addition to being used as a complementizer, a very productive use of **so** as a reanalyzed category is that of adjectivalizer.

The reanalysis of *so* as an adjectivalizer in the prenominal position can be noticed in the following examples:

Dakkhini

46. kal āye so usku pūcho
yesterday came adjr him ask
'Ask the person who came yesterday.'

47. kal āye so unoN mere ku bhāī honā
yesterday came adjr he my to brother be
'The one who came yesterday is my brother.'

(*ii*) The adjectivalizer **so** can be used to convert a conjuntive participle into a modifier. In the following example Dakkhini conjuntive participle of the type *V-ke* can be made into a nominal modifier by addition of the adjectivalizer *so*. It should be emphasized that the presence of a tense marker is obligatory.

Dakkhini

48. ghar meN ā ke hai so (vo) logāN mere ko dost honā
home in come cpm is adjr those people I dat friend to be
'The people who have come home are my friends.'

49 rām us ku de ke ai so paisā abbī talak naiN milā ai
Ram he dat give cpm is adjr money now until not got is
'Ram did not get the money till date, which he gave to him.'

Notice that the presence of the tense marker *ai* 'is' obligatory.

(*iv*) In Dakkhini an adverbial of **reason, time, manner** or **quality can be modified** by a participle. Examples of **so** occurring as adjectivalizer in reason clauses are given in (50) and (51).

Dakkhini

50 tum bulāye so usku āyī ūN
you called Adjr it+dat come be
'I came because you called me.'

51 āp jaldī āye so usku pūchrī ūN
you early came adjr it+dat asking am
'I am asking you because you came early.'

Examples (52)-(53) illustrate Dakkhini sentences in which a relative pronoun *jab* 'where' and two correlative pronouns *vaisa* 'like that' and *utta* 'that much' are modified by *so.*

Dakkhini

52. āp bulāye so jab ātī ūN
you called adjr when come will
'I will come when you call me.'

53 āp bole so vaisā kartī ūN
you said adjr like that adv (manner) do will
'I will do as you say.'

54 āp bole so uttā dī ūN
you said adjr that much adv (quantity) gave be
"I have given as much as you asked me to give.'

Notice that *so* in reason clauses (as in (50) and (51) modifies a third person pronominal followed by a reason marker in the same way as it modifies the adverb of time (52), adverb of manner (53) or adverb of quantity (54).

(*v*) *so* functions as an adjectivalizer also with negative relative participles both in prenominal and in predicate position. The following examples are illustrative.

Dakkhini

55. tum naiN kare so kām maiN kar detī ūN
you neg did adjr work I will do be
'I will do the work which you did not do.' (Prenominal

56. unoN yāNku paile naiN āye so ai bolke āp ku kaise mālum paRā ?
he here before neg came adjr is comp you dat how know felt ?
'How did you come to know that he had never come here before.' (Predicative)

(*vi*) *so* also functions as a *linker* in negative sentences linking negative adverbial clauses with the main clause.

Dakkhini

57. rām mere ku naiN bole so cale gayā
Ram I dat neg said adjr went away
'Ram went away without telling me.'

58. maiN naiN āye so tum kaisā jāte
I neg came adjr you how will go
'How could you go without my having come?'

Note that the negative occurs with verbal participles in sentences (57) and (58). A wide variety of negative participles (Arora, 2004) emerged in Dakkhini due to its contact with Telugu.

(*vi*) *so* as a gap filler or explative is used in rhetorical questions which suggest that the questioned proposition is not likely to happen..

Dakkhini

59.	yāN	kon kon	ātā	so
	here	*who who*	*will come*	*expletive*

'Who will come here?' = (No one will come here.)

To sum up the discussion so far, we have shown that in Dakkhini *so* functions as an adjectivalizer. A variety of new functions has been added as a result of reanalysis thus, demonstrating that change involves a category change, extension in function and maximal utilization of a particular lexical item. The reassignment of a wide range of new functions to this single lexical item clearly shows that there need not be any commonality between the functions originally performed by the item in the source language and thc functions performed by it in the new contact variety. (For example the case of *ki* complementizer in Dakkhini).

3. In this section we shall discuss the syntactic change that took place in the dative-genitive constructions in Dakkhini in order to prove that syntactic changes do not necessarily involve category change. It might be either a change in function or extension of function where an existing category is reanalyzed to perform a new set of functions without its category being changed.

The domain of the dative in Dakkhini has extended its range to several other constructions such as adverbials denoting time, purpose, direction, constructions denoting possession, comparison and kinship relations. etc. It is also used as an expletive marker with question words and in nonfinite complements.

The dative *ku* in Dakkhini replaces the genitive of Hindi-Urdu in most of the cases which are as follows.

1. In possessive constructions expressing kinship relation and a person to person relationship.

Hindi-Urdu

60 rām us kā kyā lagtā hai

Ram she gen what related is

'How is Ram related to her?'

Dakkhini

61. rām us ***ku*** kon honā

Ram she dat who related

'How is Ram related to her>

Hindi-Urdu

62. uskā is duniyāN meN koī nahīN hai

his this world in somebody neg is

'He has nobody in this world.'

Dakkhini

63 us ***ku*** ye duniāN meN koī bī naiN ai

he dat this world in somebody emphatic neg is

'He has nobody in this world.'

2. Inalienable Possession

In case of inalienable possession too, where Hindi has a genitive, Dakkhini and Telugu have a dative.

Hindi-Urdu

64 kutte ***ke*** cār pāNv hote haiN

dog gen four feet exist are

'A dog has four feet.'

Dakkhini

65 kutte ***ku*** cār pairāN raite

Dog dat four feet exist

'A dog has four feet.'

3. In Concrete and Abstract Possession

It is worth mentioning that in the case of concrete as well as abstract possession the dative occurs with the logical subject whereas Hindi-Urdu has the compound postposition *ke pas* 'near'.

Hindi-Urdu

66. us ***ke*** pās bahut paisee haiN
he gen near a lot of money are
'He has a lot of money.'

Dakkhini

67. us ***ku*** bhot paisee ai
he dat a lot of money is
'He has a lot of money.'

Hindi-Urdu

68. rādhā ***kī*** chuTTiyāN haiN
Radha gen holidays are
'Radha has holidays.'

Dakkhini

69. rādha ***ku*** chuTTiāN ai
Radha dat holidays are
'Radha has holidays.'

4. In conjunct verb Constructions

The genitive links the infinitivalcomplement with the conjunct verb in Hindi-Urdu. Dakkhini has a dative in place of the genitive.

Hindi-Urdu

70 rām ***kā*** ghar jāne ***kā*** dil kar rahā hai
Ram gen home to go gen feel do being is
'Ram feels like going home.'

Dakkhini

71. rām **ku** ghar jāne **ku** dil bolrā
Ram dat home to go dat heart saying
'Ram feels like going home.'

The genitive of Hindi-Urdu linking an infinitive verb with nouns such as *jaldi* 'quickness', *khwaish* 'desire' is replaced by the dative *ku* in Dakkhini.

Hindi-Urdu

72. mujhe ghar jāne **kī** jaldi hai
to me home to go gen hurry is
'I am in a hurry to go home.'

Dakkhini

73. mere **ku** ghar jāne **kī** jaldī horī
I dat home to go dat hurry is
'I am in hurry to go home.'

In addition to replacing the genitive in the constructions mentioned above the dative is used in the following constructions.

5. To express Directionality

Hindi-Urdu

74. kahāN jā rahe ho ?
where go being ?
'Where are you going?'

Dakkhini

75. kāN **ku** jāre ?
where dat going ?
'Where are you going?'

Notice that there is no corresponding dative in Hindi-Urdu.

To express the Purposive Function

Dakkhini

76. tum ***ku*** khānā banāne ***ku*** kittī der honā ?
you dat food to make dat how much time needed ?
'How long do you need to make the food?'

77. ye davā kis ***ku*** lāye ?
this medicine who dat brought ?
'For whom did you bring this medicine?

Hindi-Urdu

78. *ye davāī kis ***ko*** lāye
this medicine who dat brought

3.7 Yet another instances where the new functions are assigned to dative in Dakkhini are constructions where the difference between two objects is measured:

Dakkhini

79. tum ***ku*** us **ku** kitta farak ai
you dat he dat how much difference is
'What is the difference between you and him?'

Hindi-Urdu, on the other hand, does not permit the dative in such a construction. For example:

Hindi-Urdu

tum meN/ *ku aur us meN/ *ku kitnā farak hai
you in dat and him in dat how much difference is
'How much is the difference between you and him?'

In Capabilitative Constructions

Dakkhini

81. mere ***ku*** ye pen se likhne ***ku*** naiN ārā
I dat this pen with to write dat neg is coming
'I am not able to write with this pen.'

Hindi-Urdu does not have a dative marker in such constructions. To sum up, such a wide range of functions performed by dative *ku* in Dakkhini where it either replaces the genitive or extends its domain to perform variety of functions in different constructions demonstrates how an existing category is exploited to maximam possible extent. The additional occurrence of dative in comparative constructions, in capabilitative constructions in Dakkhini and dative with time adverbials in Dakkhini is a case of **extention of functions** without its category being changed.

3. To conclude, we have demonstrated in this paper that the syntactic reanalysis of an existing category results among other things in (*i*) categorychange (*ii*) change in function (*iii*) extention of functions as well as (*iv*) change in the position of a constituent. The syntactic change that took place in the above mentioned syntactic constructions in Dakkhini provides insights into the nature of syntactic change.

Abbreviations

Acc-accusative, adjr- adjectivalizer, adv-adverb, comp-complementizer, corr- correlative, cpm-conjunctive participial marker, dat- dative, disj-disjunctive, dub-dubitative mkr, emph-emphatic, gen- genitive, hon-honorific, imp-imperfective, inf-infinitive, npi-negative polarity item, perf-perfect, perfect participial marker, pres- present, progr- progressivem q mkr-question marker, quot-quotative, rel-relative.

References

Ahmed, I. 1986. *Dakkhini Sahitya Ka Itihas*. Lokbharti Publication,

Allahabad.

Arora, H. 1986. Noune Modification In Dakkhini, *Working Papers in*

Applied Linguistics. ISDL, Pondicherry.

————. 1987. *Some Aspects of Dakkhini Hindi-Urdu Syntax with*

Special Reference to Convergence. Ph.D Dissertation, University of Delhi.

————. 2004. *Syntactic Convergence – The Case of Dakkhini Hindi-Urdu*. Publication Division, University of Delhi, Delhi-110007.

Arora, H. and K. V. Subbarao. 1988. Convergence and Syntactic Change:

The Case of the Conjunctive Participle in Dakkhini Hindi-Urdu *Papers from the Conference on the Theory and Practice of Historical Linguistics. Chicago Linguistic Society,* Chicago, Illinois.

——— 1989. Convergence and Syntactic Reanalysis: The Case of **so** in Dakkhini. *Studies in the Linguitic Sciences*. Vol. 19. University of Illinois.

———— 1990. Contrastive Analysis and Syntactic Change. *Papers and Studies in Contrastive Linguistics,* Vol. 27, Adam Mickiewiez University, Poznan, Poland.

———— 2002. The Case of Non- Nominative Subjects in Dakkhini and Konkani; in: Non-Nominative Subjects 61, (eds) P Bhaskararao and K. V. Subbarao. In John Benjamin; Amsterdam.

Chatterji, S.K. 1963. *Language and Literature of Modern India.*

Bengal Publishers Private Ltd. Calcutta.

Ebert, K. 1973. Field Notes in Files of E. Keenan. UCLA (Original not consulted)

Emeneau, M. B, 1969. Onomatopoetics in the India Linguistic Area. *Language* 45:2. 274-94.

Kachru, Y. 1973. Some Aspects of Pronominalization and Relative Clause Constructions in Hindi Urdu. *Studies in the Linguistic Sciences*. 3:2. 87-103.

————. 1979. The Quotative in South Asian Languages. *South Asian Language Analysis*. 1. 63-77.

———— 1986. The Syntax of Dakkhini: A Study in Language Variation and Language Change. Eds. Bh. Krishnamurti et al, *South Asisn Languages: Structure, Convergence and Diglossia. 165-73.*

Langacker, R. W. 1977. Syntactic Reanalysis' Li, C. N. (ed.).

Mechanisms of Syntactic Change. University of Texas Press, Austin.

Lightfoot, D. 1979. *Principles of Diachronic Syntax*. Cambridge University Press, Cambridge.

_______ 1983. On Restructuring a Proto Syntax. In Rauchet et al. (eds.) *Language Change*. Indiana University Press, Bloomington.

Loro, C. 1976. Evidènce for Syntactic Reanalysis from verb to Complementizer in Kwa. *Paper from the Parasession on Diachronic Syntax*. C. L. S.

Mohammad, V. P. 1988. *Dakkhini Hindi ka Sufi Sahitya*. Lokbharati Prakashan, Allahbad.

Munro, P. 1974. 'Chemehuevi 'say' and the Uto-Aztecan Quotative Pattern.' (ms.) UCLA, revised version appeared in *The Procedings of 1974* Great Basin Anthropological Conference.

Nadkarni, M. V. 1970. *Noun Phrase embedded Structure in Kannada and Konkani*. Unpublished Ph. D. Dissertation. University of California, Los Angeles.

Nagaraja, K. S. 1984. Relativization in Konyak *Indian Linguistics* 45.

Panchal. 1978. *Dakkhini Hindi: Vikas Aur Itihas*. Alankar Prakashan, Delhi.

Rai, A. 1984. *A House Devided –the Origin and Development of Hindi / Hindavi*. Oxford University Press, Delhi.

Romaine, S. 1983. Syntactic Change as a Category Change by Reanalysis And Diffusion. Some Evidence from The History of English. In Devenport et, al. (eds.) *Current Topics in Historical Linguitics*. Odense University Press.

Sankoff, G. 1979. The Genesis of a Language. In Hill, K. (ed.) *The Genesis of Language*. An Arbor: Karome Publishers.

Sankrityayan, P. 1959. *Dakkhini Hindi Kavyadhara*. Bihar Rashtriyabhasha Parishad. Patna.

Sharma, S. 1954. *Dakhiuni ka Padya aur Gadhya*. Hindi Prachar Sabha, Allahabad.

_______ 1955. *Sabras*. Dakhini Prakashan Samiti, Hyderabad.

_______ 1962. *Dakkhini Hindi Ka Sahitya*. Dakkhini Prakashan, Hyderabad.

_______ 1964. *Dakkhini Hindi ka Udbhav Aur Vikas*. Dakkhini Prakashan, Hyderabad.

Subbarao, K.V., K. Vishwanath Rao, N. Rao, & A. Saxena. 1989. Verb 'say' in South Asian Languages. In: (ed.). A. Mukherjee,

The proceedings of *The Conference on Language Changeand Variation.* Osmania University, Hyderabad.

Subbarao K. V. and Harbir Arora. 1989. On Extreme Convergence.

In: (ed.). A. Mukherjee, *The Proceedings of the Conference on Language Change and Variations.* Osmania University, Hyderabad.

Takahashi, A. *1975. Mullah* Vajahi Krit Sabras Ki Dakkhini Hindi ka *Bhasha Vishleshan.* Sambhavna Prakashan, Hapur.

Telang, B. R. 1975. *Hindi Banam Dakkhini* Padmakar Anushandhan Shala, Aurangabad.

Washabaugh, W. 1975. On the Development of Complementizer in Creolization, *Working Papers on Language Universals,* Vol. 17, pp. 109-140.

Wazahi, M. 1609-1635. *Kutubmushtari* (edited by Vaghre and Hashmi (eds.) 1954. Dakkhini Hindi Prakshan Samiti, Hyderabad.

Westermann, D. 1930 *A Study of the Ewe Language.* Oxford University Press, London

6

Language Variation and Change Among the Bangladeshis in Manchester

Salman Al-Azami

Introduction

Bilingualism is a thriving discipline in contemporary academia, but there is no clear-cut definition of the term. Bloomfield (1933:56) terms it to be 'native-like control of two languages', though Baker, C. and Jones, S.P. (1998:12) call this claim to be a myth. David Crystal (1992:362) opines that command over the two languages is not equal and feels that one language is more fluent than the other. Hockett (1958:16) uses the term 'semibilingualism' for those whose second language is at the passive or receptive stage. Contemporary sociolinguists use the term 'language shift' to correlate it with bilingualism. It is observed that immigration initially leads to bilingualism, but later moves towards language shift. Susan Romaine (1995:39) calls bilingualism a type of 'transition' to a new language. Wardhaugh (1986:99) disringuishes between *stable bilingualism* and *unstable bilingualism* and says that the latter is prevalent in the situation of immigrant communities.

The present research aims to look at the state of Bilingualism among the Bangladeshi community in Manchester in order to examine the changes in the Bengali language due to local influence. There are a large number of first generation Bengali speakers in Manchester, and these first generation speakers are the main bilinguals among the community. Bilingualism among the second generation Bangladeshis is moving towards 'language shift', because younger speakers lose fluency in their native language and the dominant language becomes their first language (Baker & Jones, 1998:151). The research intended to undertake a comparative study of the changes in linguistic habit from that of the origin between first and second generation Bengali speakers in that area and to analyse the linguistic manipulations done by both generations in their code-mixed and code-switched expressions.

Bangladeshis in the UK

According to figures published a couple of years ago by the Office for National Statistics (ONS), almost half of the ethnic minority population in Britain are South Asians, with Bangladeshis being the third highest among them. The Bengali Speech community in Britain consists of two groups – speakers belonging to the Eastern Indian state of West Bengal and speakers belonging to Bangladesh. Most of the Bengali speakers in UK are from Bangladesh, and the present study concentrates only on the Bangladeshis.

A recent survey by BBC shows that the Bangladeshi community has increased by more than 79% in the last ten years. ONS says the number of Bangladeshis in UK was 283,063 in April 2001, of which 260,000 were Muslims. Being one of the fastest growing immigrant communities in the country, the Bangladeshis constitute 6.1% of the 4.6 million ethnic minorities in UK (ONS 2001). Majority of the Bangladeshis here belong to Sylhet, and are scattered all over the nation with the maximum (153,893) living in London (ONS).

The socio-economic condition of Bangladeshis in UK is among the worst in the country. According to ONS, in 2001/02, Bangladeshis had the highest unemployment rate among men in Great Britain at 20 per cent. Over 40 per cent of young Bangladeshi men were unemployed. Nearly half (48 per cent) of Bangladeshi women and 40 per cent of Bangladeshi men has no qualifications. Bangladeshi women have the highest female economic inactivity rates (78 per cent). The majority of these women are looking after their family or home.

The majority of Bangladeshis are settled in the East End of London. They live in London's poorest borough: Tower Hamlets, where around 37% - 123,000 - of the borough's population is Bangladeshi. Households headed by a Bangladeshi person were the largest of all with an average size of 4.5 people in April 2001.

Economically, the restaurant business is the most successful entrepreneurial activity in the Bangladeshi community. It is true that Bangladeshis were not the pioneers in this business, but the restaurant business is now largely dominated by them and has become the single largest business sector for Bangladeshi community in Britain. Two thirds of Bangladeshi men in employment work in the distribution, hotel and restaurant industry. Two in five Bangladeshi men are either cooks or waiters. A Guardian report published on 21 June 2002 says that according to the Curry Club of Great Britain, there are 8,500 Indian restaurants in the UK, of which roughly 7,200 are owned by Bangladeshis. Initially, as part of undivided India, they were called Indian restaurants, but after 57 years of separation from India, they are still called so.

Literature Review

In a background context, a discussion on three aspects that are closely related to the present study seems pertinent. They are:

- History of immigration in UK, particularly that of Bangladeshis;
- Works on the linguistic minorities in different countries;
- Researches on linguistic minorities in Britain

History of Immigration in UK

According to historians, the earliest inhabitants of this land were the Celts. Then in the fifth century AD, three

Germanic tribes, the Angles, the Saxons and the Jutes migrated here and gradually became the dominant community from then on (Crystal, 1995: 7). The entry of other nationalities into this land mostly began in the 19th century, though there have been a number of migrations before. Panikos Panayi (1994:10) categorises those early migrations into four periods. Firstly, the age of invasions until the 11th century; secondly, continental tradesmen, craftsmen and Jews during the high and late Middle Ages; thirdly, religious refugees, economic newcomers and slaves during early 16th century till the middle of the 17th century; and fourthly, a combination of various groups from the mid-17th century till 1815.

Panayi observed that as many as a million Irish migrated to Britain during the 19th century. During the later stage of this century, a large number of German, Russian and Jewish Poles came to Britain. One of the most concentrated immigration in the history of Britain took place during the First World War when 240,000 Belgian refugees entered the country escaping German invasion, although almost all of them went back after the war. After relative decrease in the coming of immigrants between the two World Wars, the influx of foreigners started again when the Second World War broke out as 200,000 European refugees made their way into Britain with half of them being Poles. Apart from these major immigrants, Panayi observed that a small number of Italians, French, Spaniards, Greeks, Indians, Africans and West Indians, collectively numbering approximately 300,000, moved to Britain in the years 1815-1945. He opines that most of these immigrants came here because of either economic or political reasons.

One of the most prominent immigrant communities in Britain, the black communities, first arrived here from West Africa in the 16th century as black slaves (James Walvin, 1984:33). Walvin, in his *Passage to Britain,* gave a detailed account of the black immigration in UK, one that was not much discussed in Panayi's book. According to him, by 1764 there were 20,000 black slaves in London alone. Walvin highlighted that the immigrants from different cultural backgrounds and the host race got influenced by each others' cultures and turned the nation into a *'mosaic of communities'*. He also touched upon the problems of British born Diaspora communities who are severely confused for falling in the crossfire between two diverse cultures.

Since 1945, there has been increasing influx of Asian immigrants into this country and they now constitute the highest number of immigrant communities in Britain (2001 Census). However, coming of Asians in Britain is not that recent. It dates back to early seventeenth century when the first Indian existence in Britain was recorded on 22 December 1616 (Visram, 2002: 1). This happened after the Charter was granted by Queen Elizabeth I to a group of London merchants on 31 December 1600, establishing 'The Governor and Company of Merchants in London, Trading into the East-Indies', leading to the establishment of the 'East India Company (EIC)', which ultimately affected the fate of the entire Indian sub-continent.

The most systematic early arrivals in Britain were the sailors who got the job to fill the gap of British sailors who died. Known as 'lascars', these Indian sailors were mostly from the district of Sylhet, which is now under Bangladesh (Adams, 1987). Apart from sailors, another group who migrated to Britain during this period were the Indian wives and children of English men. During their stay in India, many Englishmen either married Indian women or lived with them. A good number of them brought their partners with them to Britain. Besides servants, sailors and women, people from diverse backgrounds and social origins also came to Britain during the 18th & 19th centuries (Visram, op cit).

From the middle of the 19th century to the beginning of the First World War, several hundred Asians lived in Britain. Some were born here, a few came from Africa or the

Caribbean, but the majority came from the Indian sub-continent. As need in the labour market increased, every year thousands of sailors and hundred's of ayahs were brought in Britain. Many students also arrived to study at universities. There also were exiled Indian nobility. But, as Visram observes, between the First and the Second World War, there were attempts by the British Government to bar Indian working-class people into Britain. Yet, the migration continued. She categorises these migrations into various reasons, such as, needs of labours in British industries, a sense of adventure and the lure of the West among some Indians, and of course economic – looking for a better life. The scenario changed after the War ended in 1945. During the 1950s, the British labour industry was desperately in short of labourers. So, the arrival of Indians was encouraged by the government.

Visram concludes that the Asians' arrival in Britain was of diverse nature. Some were working class just managing to survive in the society, some mingled with the upper class English people and some were professionals active in medicine, education, law, business, politics and so on. Even there were ministers of religion, sportsmen and entertainers. Indian immigrants were largely economic migrants, unlike East-European migrants of that time who were mostly political refugees. Visram opines that the Indian immigrants had a significant influence on British society and culture, but unfortunately, that influence did not receive the attention they deserved.

Adams (1987) described that many of the seamen lost their lives after British ships were bombed by Germans. According to Indian records, 6,600 Indian seamen were killed during the Second World War and 1,022 were injured. Among them were seamen from Mirpur and North West Frontier (now in Pakistan), Goa (now in India), and Chittagong and Sylhet (Now in Bangladesh). It is assumed, according to Adams, a large proportion of them were Sylheties as they were mostly engine room crews. Adams found that among those who survived, a good number deserted the ships and fled into different parts of England. They mostly settled in London, though some stayed in Birmingham, Manchester, Coventry and some other areas.

Caroline Adams, in her *Across Seven Seas and Thirteen Rivers* (1987) gives some historical facts in her book. We know from here that the first known Sylheti to come to Britain was one Syed Ullah who came in the middle of the nineteenth century as the servant to the son of a vicar who came from India. Yet it is not until the early 1920s that we see a regular trend of Sylheti ex-seamen settling in Britain. The first known Sylheti seaman to settle in the UK was Mr. Munshi who came in 1922. Though there were one or two seamen from other districts like Noakhali and Chittagong, the seamen were more than 90% from Sylhet and this proportion is still maintained among the Bangladeshis living in UK.

Works on the linguistic minorities in different countries

Hannah Slavik (2001), Al-Khatib (2001), Dweik (2000), Holmes (1992), David, Naji & Kaur (2003), Fishman (1985), Modarresi (2001), Yagmur & Akinci (2003), Milroy (1987), Mukherjee (2003), Tabouret Keller's (1978), Remennick (2003), Nercissians (2001), Kamwangamalu's (2003), and Webb (1995) – all studied the language of immigrant communities in different parts of the world. Their studies show that whenever immigrations take place, there is obviously a cultural and linguistic amalgamation between the host and the immigrant communities. In most cases the dominant, i.e., the host culture and language influence those of the immigrants and the language of the immigrants slowly changes from its original form. The first generation immigrants tend to maintain their own language, but as years go by, their next generation adopts the language of their birth as their own language and a gradual language shift starts to occur. These researches show some common characteristics of immigrants' language, which are described as below:

1. The first generation speakers use a lot of code-mixed expressions between their own language and the language of their adopted country.
2. The first generation speakers strongly feel that their next generation should know the language of their origin. Yet, very few of them speak to the next generation in that language.
3. The second generation mostly understands the language of their origin but is not fluent in it.
4. Some parents talk to their children in their own language, but do not ensure that the children use the same language with them. As a result, parents and children are often found speaking in two languages while talking, each using the language in which they are fluent.

Second generation have very little emotional bondage towards the language and culture of their parents and adopt the linguistic culture of their land of birth or upbringing.

Research on Linguistic Minorities in Britain

Britain is without doubt a multi-ethnic and multi-lingual country. But as Michael Stubbs (1985) observes, the linguistic diversity in UK is something which is subject to widespread ignorance. Whether the majority community accept it or not, "In reality", says Stubbs, "The languages of the different linguistic minorities are now part of everyday life in multilingual England". His edited book entitled, *Other Languages of England* was written by members of the multi-disciplinary 'Linguistic Minorities Project' based at the University Of London Institute Of Education from 1979 to 1983. The book strongly supports the idea of continued and widespread bilingualism in England, which is potentially a valuable resource for individuals as well as the society as a whole.

Safder Alladina and Viv Edwards (1991) in their edited book *Multilingualism in the British Isles* illustrate the richness and diversity of linguistic usage and experience of modern Britain and represents a major survey of the bilingual and multilingual reality of the country in present time. The linguistic scenario of 33 speech communities in Britain has been discussed in as many chapters in the book written by members of respective communities. The studies showed that in almost all the communities, it was evident that there is a strong community feeling. The link with the country of origin in the form of letters, visits and investment in land and property; the maintenance of language and culture through community organisations; frequent community gatherings in religious places like mosques, churches, temples etc.; and maintaining a strong community network having a wide range of cafes, restaurants, travel agents, food shops, clothing shops and video outlets run by and for a given minority community – all help a great deal in maintaining the ethnic language. Finally, the community language schools play a vital role for controlling language shift among the younger generation.

According to ILEA Language Census (1987), Bengali speakers in Britain have the lowest level of fluency in English. The reason might be that almost 95% of the Bangladeshis come from the rural areas of Sylhet and mostly confine themselves within the community. Therefore language shift is less intense among the Bangladeshis. However, the trend is changing in recent times. Jyoti Husain (1991), in her article, "The Bengali Speech Community" in *Multilingualism in the British Isles* (1991), talked about the history and development of the Bengali speakers in Britain with a brief account of the changing patterns of language use, the culture and community factor, and education and language production. She observed that the Bangladeshis are coming out of the shell of their own community now and trying for jobs outside the community. The Tower Hamlet council is also facilitating different types of job opportunities for the Bengali speakers. Unlike most other authors in that book, Husain didn't take up language maintenance and shift among the Bangladeshi speakers. There has been a couple of works on Bangladeshis in UK, but they were mostly on literacy among children. No work on this aspect was found so far.

The Study

In spite of being one of the largest growing ethnic minority populations in Britain, there has been very little work on the sociolinguistic aspects of the Bangladeshis in Britain. We know very little about the state of Bilingualism among the Bangladeshis living in this country. A study of this nature may prove to be a starting point for further research in this field. According to figures published a couple of years ago by the Office for National Statistics, Britain's ethnic minority population are growing 15 times faster than the white population (The Guardian, September 21, 2001). The same research shows that nearly half the ethnic minority population was South Asian, with Bangladeshis being the third highest among them. As Bangladeshis are one of the largest growing immigrant communities in Britain, a study on their linguistic habit should be quite contributory in the sociolinguistic scenario of this nation.

Methodology of the Research

The present study revolves on the following two issues of the linguistic scenario of Bangladeshis in Britain.

(*i*) The types of bilingualism prevalent among the first and second generation Sylheti and non-Sylheti Bangladeshis in Manchester.

(*ii*) The changes in linguistic habit from that of the origin between first and second generation Bengali speakers in that area.

For analyzing types of bilingualism, semi-structured interviews were taken to observe the contrasting states of bilingualism prevalent among the two generations. To analyze the linguistic changes done by both generations from the original Bengali spoken in Bangladesh, a participant observation was undertaken.

A questionnaire was prepared and data were collected from 20 Bangladeshi British residing in the Longsight area in Manchester. The participant observation was done by recording the discussions of an informal family gathering consisting both first and second generation speakers.

Findings

The study showed that Sylheti second generation have more competence in their mother tongue than non-Sylheti second generation have in theirs. This is because there is a difference in approach between Sylhetis and non-Sylhetis. As evident from the data, the first generation non-Sylhetis are relatively more educated and they are able to communicate with their children in English. So, there is no compulsion for the children to learn Bengali if the parents do not make them use it. Still, the figure among the non-Sylhetis is relatively higher than was expected with 40% first generation non-Sylhetis using Bengali more than English to their children. On the other hand the data shows that all the first generation Sylhetis use Sylheti more than English while speaking to the next generation.

In most of the non-Sylheti houses, the parents use both English and Bengali to their children. They speak in Bengali while the children reply in English. In contrast, the linguistic environment among Sylhetis is mostly monolingual as both the parents and the children communicate in Sylheti. Many second generation Sylhetis are compelled to learn their mother tongue because Sylheti is the only possible medium to communicate with parents.

80% sylhetis said that at the time they came here, their initial condition of English was nil. Though most of the first generation Sylhetis feels that their English is reasonably well now, about 20% are still not confident to speak English with native speakers. Their English remain poor in spite of staying in this country for two or three decades. The reason is mainly twofold. Firstly, because of poor education, their inhibitions towards English are still prevalent. Secondly, living in a densely populated Sylheti community, these people have very little scope of using English. Perhaps this is another reason for the next generation Sylhetis to be more proficient in Sylheti. As their parents are not fluent in English, they are forced to speak with them in Sylheti.

As far as non-Sylhetis are concerned, they became bilinguals in Bengali and English relatively quicker than Sylhetis. The figure is completely opposite from Sylhetis as 80% non-Sylhetis knew English quite well at the initial stage. Non-sylhetis came here with better education and therefore had better skills in English. Among them, 40% first generation often (60% do it sometimes) use English words or phrases while speaking Bengali. They often use code-mixing and code-switching in their expressions. This aspect has been taken up separately in the present study.

It has been observed that most of the first generation Bangladeshis also knows a third language. And obviously the language is Urdu/Hindi (90%). There are several reasons for this extremely high percentage of Urdu/Hindi proficiency. Firstly, many first generation Bangladeshis were born when Bangladesh was part of Pakistan. Hence, many of them knew Urdu before coming to the UK. Secondly, the Bangladeshis in Manchester are surrounded by a huge number of Pakistani populations, particularly in the Longsight area. Because of their overwhelming number and frequent contact with the Bangladeshis, the respondents learnt the language. The interesting point to note here is that some Sylhetis are more proficient in Urdu/Hindi than they are in English. The third reason is the role of media. Indian movies and TV serials are extremely popular among the Bangladeshis. By watching these and also by listening to their music, these Bengali speakers find it easy to learn the language. This proves the assumption that many

Bangladeshis are multilingual, but the data does not show that the trend is only among the educated first generation speakers proving one aspect of this assumption wrong.

The Bangladeshis have been coming to the UK fore more than fifty years, though most of the immigration took place in the last thirty years. Naturally, the Bengali language now spoken here has undergone some linguistic changes, though the changes are not significant enough to be called as a variety. We will now discuss the linguistic changes in the Bengali language by the first and second generation speakers in the UK at different linguistic levels:

Word Level

There is a significant change in the lexical level among the second generation from that of the original Bengali in Bangladesh. Due to the influence of English, sometimes the difference is at the vocabulary level and sometimes at morphological construction. The following sub-points can be discussed under this category:

A. Collocation

Here, a word is used in a different context than its usual usage. For example, to ask someone if he or she wants tea, some second generation Bangladeshis say: /apni cha chan?/ In English we say, 'Do you want tea?'. So, 'want' has been translated here as /chan/. But a native Bangladeshi would say, /apni cha khaben?/ Generally, /cha/ 'tea' does not collocate with /chan/ 'want'.

B. Word Ending

Some second generation Bangladeshis create new forms of word endings while talking to fellow generation Bangladeshis. For example, once one of them was heard saying to the other:

'I know that you were *adda maraing*' meaning 'I know that you were chatting'. The phrase /adda mara/ 'chatting' has been ended by the present continuous marker /-ing/ to create a unique type of expression. Similarly, plural marker word endings are also used like the expression: 'I think there are a lot of *shubidhas* in it'. The Bengali word /shubidha/ 'advantage' has been given English plural word ending in this case to match with the English construction. This type of plural use is also found among first generation non-Sylheties. In a family discussion, one of them was heard saying: 'There are lots of *chachus* and *chachis* around'. Here, /chachu/ 'uncle' and /chachi/ 'aunty' both have been inflected by English plural marker /-s/. In the same programme, one first generation member also used the term /ukils/ 'lawyers' to mean the plural of /ukil/.

But the first generation mostly tend to use Bengali suffixes with English root words. In the participant observation, they were found using words like /friend-er/ (possessive), /support-tai/ (emphatic), /family-r/ (possessive), /life-e/ (possessive), /late-o/ (emphatic), /desire-er/ (possessive), /rest-to/ (possessive), /break-gulate/ (plural), / feelings-ta / (article), /outcome-ta/ (article) where Bengali inflections have been used with English words.

C. Generic pronouns

One common problem some second generation Bengali speakers face is the use of second person generic terms / apni/, /tumi/, /tui/ which have only one equivalent in English word 'you'. As English does not have this distinction, they often make mistake by calling elders as /tumi/ whereas in Bengali, the elders are supposed to be called /apni/. Some second generation also make mistakes in the subject-verb agreement as they say: /tumi bhat khabo?/ 'Will you have your meal?'. /khabo/ agrees with /ami/ 'I' and /khabe/ agrees with /tumi/ 'you'.

D. Code Mixing

Code mixing refers to transfer of linguistic elements from one language to another. In other words, code mixing is a process where a word or a phrase of a second language is used in the syntax of a language. Wardhaugh (1992) defines code mixing as "The deliberate mixing of two languages without an associated topic change." Wardhaugh opines that code mixing is not a haphazard combination of two languages, rather, "it requires conversants to have a sophisticated knowledge of both languages."

First generation non-Sylheties are the ones who use code-mixing very frequently. Some examples are given below:

1. /unar ja dorkar she bepare amra FULLY AWARE kina/ 'Whether we are fully aware what she needs.'
2. /bektigoto EXPERIENCE theke bolchi/ 'I am speaking from personal experience.
3. /jokhon shujog ashe tokhon shotosfurtobhabe MAXIMUM SUPPORT dewata ESSENTIAL/ 'When opportunity comes, it is essential to give maximum support spontaneously.'

The second generation does exactly the opposite. They use Bengali words in English sentences while code-mixing. For example:

1. Where did you put the TORKARIR BATI? (Where did you put the curry plate?)
2. He enjoys giving ADDA. (He enjoys chatting.) The interesting thing to notice here is the use of the English word 'giving' to make way for the Bengali word ADDA.
3. He has become a BACCHA! (He has become a baby!)

Sentence Level: Code-Switching

At sentence level the only and the obvious manipulation found is code-switching. 'Code-switching' emphasizes movement from one language to another, i.e. the movement takes place at sentence level. To be more precise, sentences of another language is inserted while using a language. Here again, the approaches towards code-switching is different among the two generations. The first generation use English clause or sentence while using Bengali while the second generation use Bengali sentence in their English expressions.

A. First Generation

The following code-mixed expressions were found in the participant observation:

1. /ami bollam THAT'S GOOD NEWS/ 'I said that's good news.
2. /AT THE SAME TIME er mane ei noy je ———/ 'At the same time it doesn't mean that ————
3. /hothat kore ekla hoe gele SHE MIGHT FEEL LONELY/ 'If she suddenly becomes alone, she might feel lonely.'

B. Second Generation

As mentioned already, the second generation tend to base their conversation in English and use a clause or a sentence in Bengali in between while speaking to first generation. Following are some examples:

1. /Even though we have our own works, AMMU AMADER SHATHE THAKLE that will be the easiest thing/ 'If mother stays with us, that will be the easiest thing even though we have our own works.'
2. /I don't know how it's been because AMI ETO GHONO ASHTEO POCHONDO KORINA because it will create a lot of inconvenience/ 'I don't know how it's been because I don't like to come so often, because it will create a lot of inconvenience.'

Summary and Conclusion

The study aimed at investigating the changes in the Bengali language from its standard form among the Bangladeshis living in this area at phonological, lexical and syntactic levels. It tried to find the similarities and dissimilarities between the Bengali spoken by the first and second generation speakers in the community. The research intended to see how actually the two groups are different from one another in terms of bilingualism; what differences are there between Sylheti and non-Sylheti speakers in terms of language maintenance and shift; and what linguistic manipulations are done by both the generations in their conversations. To obtain results, a semi-structured interview and a participant observation were undertaken.

The study found that the Bengali language is undergoing some changes in the UK due to local influence. The first generation frequently uses English words, phrases and even clauses while speaking in Bengali. The second generation seems to do the other way round. They sometimes use Bengali expressions in their own idiosyncratic ways while using English syntax. The end result is that the language is gradually changing from its original form in Bangladesh. However, the change is still not enough to be called a variety.

Both the first and second generation made some interesting manipulations in the Bengali language at word and sentence levels. There are phonological changes, collocational novelties, inflectional innovations, grammatical errors etc. but the most noticeable phenomena are the code-mixing and code-switching from two separate perspectives by the two generations.

The study is a humble beginning of a vastly unexplored area of sociolinguistic research in the UK. There can be many more researches in this field from different dimensions. A big-scale similar study is extremely important in the Borough of Tower Hamlets in East London where most of the Bangladeshis in the UK are concentrated. The results of such a study will carry much more weight and authenticity.

There can be many future studies in the field of sociolinguistics from different dimensions. A similar large-scale study can be useful in the Borough of Tower Hamlets in East London where most of the Bangladeshis in the UK are concentrated. The results of such a study would carry much more weight and authenticity. A qualitative analysis of the code-mixing and code-switching by second generation Sylhetis could also be an interesting study.

As a pioneering work in this area, the study makes a number of contributions in the field of Sociolinguistics in the UK. Some of the contributing areas are discussed below:

1. Very little research can be found about the language of the Bangladeshi community in any part of the world. The present research may inspire researchers in other countries to work on Bangladeshis living in that country.
2. Research on a linguistic minority community needs to be carried out by a member of the community itself. The present study might inspire native speakers of Bengali, particularly those from Bangladesh to work in this field.
3. There has been very little research on code mixing and code switching among the immigrant communities due to the mixture of two languages. This study might lead to more studies in this area.

References

Alladina, S. & Edwards, V. (Ed.), 1991. Multilingualism in British Isles: Africa, The Middle East and Asia, edited by Alladina, S. and Edwards, V., Longman Group UK Ltd.

Baker, C. and Jones, P.J. 19 98, Encyclopedia of Bilingualism and Bilingual Education, Multilingual Matters Ltd., Clevedon, UK

Bloomfield, L. 1933, Language, Holt, New York.

Carvel, J. 2001, *Minority Groups Grow by 15%* in "The Guardian", UK.

Crystal, D. 1992, The Cambridge Encyclopedia of Language, Cambridge University Press, UK.

Crystal, D. 1995, The Cambridge Encyclopedia of Language, Cambridge University Press, UK.

Hockett, C.F. 1958, A Course in Modern Linguistics, Macmillan, New York.

Hudson, R.A. 1982, Sociolinguistics, Cambridge University Press, UK.

Husain, J. 1991, *The Bengali Speech Community* in Alladina, Multilingualism in the British Isles: Africa, The Middle East and Asia, edited by Alladina, S. and Edwards, V., Longman Group UK Ltd.

Prideaux-Brune, K. 1985, A Kind of Love Affair (From Brick Lane to Bangladesh), Toc H, Bucks, UK.

Rampton, B. 1995, Crossing Language and Ethnicity among Adolescents, Longman, UK.

Romaine, S. 1995, Bilingualism (Second Edition), Blackwell Publishers Inc., USA.

Stubbs, M.W. (Ed.), 1985. The Other Languages of England (Linguistic Minorities Project), Routledge & Kegan Paul, UK.

Sufian, A.J.M. 1998, Methods and Techniques of Social Research, University Press Limited, Dhaka, Bangladesh.

Trudgill, P. 1983, Sociolinguistics: An Introduction to Language and Society, Penguin Books.

Visram, R. 2002, Asians in Britain: 400 Years of History, Pluto Press, London, UK.

Walvin, J. 1984, Passage to Britain: Immigration in British History and Politics, Penguin Books, UK.

Wardhaugh, R. 1986, An Introduction to Sociolinguistics, Basil Blackwell Ltd, Oxford, UK.

Wei, L. 1994. Three Generations Two Languages One Family: Language Choice and Language Shift in a Chinese Community in Britain, Multilingual Matters Ltd., UK.

Williamson, R.C. 1991, Minority Languages and Bilingualism, Ablex Publishing Corporation, New Jersey, USA.

7

Patterns of Code-Switching among Sinhala/ English Bilinguals in Sri Lanka

Manel Herat

Bilingual studies examining specifically the area of English-Sinhala code-switching in relation to its diverse patterns do not happen to be many. Although much has been written on Sri Lankan English as a variety of New English, little attention has been devoted up to now to ascertain how this variety of New English, little attention has been devoted up to now to ascertain how this variety in association with Sinhala, the majority language of Sri Lanka, has continuted to influence the speech of Sinhala-English bilinguals in the 21st century, during which the number of these bilinguals has increased substantially. In this paper, I examine the patterns of code-switching used by 18 Sinhala-English bilinguals and discuss the significance of these patterns to Sri Lankan English speech. On the basis of this data I argue that these patterns go a long way in explaining how the different languages are appropriate and extended in ways which are creative and sophisticated. It is suggested that in-depth analysis of this kind is necessary for showing that code-switching is one of the many linguistic choices available to bilinguals in Sri Lanka and for understanding how 'mixed' language is used for negotiating a distinct identity in this context.

KEYWORDS: bilingual speech, code-switching, language mixing, Sri Lankan English.

1. Introduction

Although code switching is a commonly used phenomenon among bilingual speakers in Sri Lanka, as elsewhere, it has not given rise to many studies. Except for a few studies that briefly discuss the phenomenon, such as Passé (1948); C. Fernando (1977); S. Fernando (1985,1990); and Parakrama (1995), the only full-scale study is that of Sivasuriya (1993), which discusses the code switching behaviour of Sri Lankan Tamil/English bilinguals.

In his pioneering work on Ceylon English, Passé (1948:83ff) notes that in Ceylon conversations are often carried out in a mixture of English and Sinhala or Tamil. According to him,

> the struggle is most apparent in those who know English and one of the indigenous languages. Then Sinhalese or Tamil is liberally mixed with English words and phrases. The resultant speech is a rich mixture. A conversation is carried on in the vernacular and when the conclusion is reached, and the speaker wants to emphasize the point he slips into English. The converse is also true. The point of a conversation being driven home in homely Sinhalese or Tamil.

Like Passé, subsequent linguists working on language choice in Sri Lanka have tended to see code switching as a positive occurrence between bilinguals whereas speakers usually see it as 'improper linguistic behaviour'.

C. Fernando (1977:355) tells us that the influence of English on Sinhala is much more dramatic and striking than the influence of Sinhala on English. The tendency to introduce English words into Sinhala is much more marked than the reverse. The bilingual who chooses to talk English rather than Singlish or Sinhala will only introduce those

Sinhala words (names of local fauna, flora, etc.) that have become an accepted part of the Sri Lankan English lexis. But anyone who talks Sinhala will use a higher proportion of English words or words of English origin. C. Fernando (1977:355) says that lexical transfers are unidirectional from English to Sinhala or Singlish which is, as a linguistic system, more Sinhala than English based, i.e. Singlish would show a higher proportion of Sinhala phrases and sentences than English ones. In other words Singlish is a sub-variety of Sinhala, not a sub variety of English.

According to C. Fernando (1977:356) the code switching behaviour among older bilinguals in Sri Lanka generally approximates to the code switching behaviour of Weinreich's (1953:73) ideal bilingual, who switches from one language to the other according to appropriate changes in the speech situation (interlocutors, topics, etc.), but not in an unchanged speech situation. In her opinion, older bilinguals would use Sinhala generally to monolinguals or receiver bilinguals only in limited domains. In the case of younger bilinguals she notes that the complimentary spheres of English and Sinhala are not kept as clearly apart as they generally were for the older generation. She sees the code switching of younger bilinguals as 'ragged code switching' because it does not conform to what Haugen calls `a clean switch of codes' (1970:314) in terms of interlocutors and topics. The widespread use of this type of language behaviour has been called accharu bhasava, literally meaning 'mixed' or 'impure language' (S. Fernando, 1990) as well as Singlish (C. Fernando 1977) denoting the negative attitudes of speakers towards code switching prevalent in Sri Lanka.

Parakrama (1995:103) notes that while the argument to locate Singlish within Sinhala is entirely understandable in certain specific contexts, he has yet to come across any reference to Singlish in everyday conversation, which does not refer to the 'dilution' of English with Sinhala words and phrases. According to Parakrama, the absence of an analogous term for Tamilised English in Sri Lanka means that these utterances also get grouped together with examples of Singlish, which is of course, no accident and reflects the hegemony of Sinhala in Sri Lanka, since even non-Sinhala speakers use Singlish.

A similar phenomenon exists in Singapore. But, as Gupta (1999:61) notes the Sing- of Singlish in Singapore stands for Singapore not a language as in Sri Lanka. McArthur (1998:216) refers to Singlish in Singapore as a mixed variety, an Anglo-hybrid, along with Hindlish (Hindi+English), Spanglish (Spanish+ English) and Frenglish (French+English). Gupta (1999:61) notes that this is misleading, as the others are semi-institutionalised code mixed varieties. In Sri Lanka, Singlish is most often used to refer to the code mixed variety although it is sometimes also used to make reference to spoken Sri Lankan English. Whereas in Singapore English dominates the lexis of Singlish (Gupta 1999:61), in Sri Lanka, it is dominated by Sinhala. Nevertheless, in both countries the term Singlish is used predominantly to mean a sort of 'impure language' as opposed to the standard or 'pure' language. The low status of Singlish in Sri Lanka has led some Sri Lankan English speakers to refuse to use it in certain contexts, so as to prove that they are able to speak 'proper English'.

2. Definitions and Types of CS

In the literature on the speech patterns of bilinguals in Sri Lanka as well as elsewhere, the term 'code switching', along with similar terms such as 'code mixing' and 'code shifting' has been used in more than one sense. In 1972 the investigation of code-switching underwent a change when Blom and Gumperz gave this subject more serious treatment in a study describing code-switching between two Norwegian dialects in Hemnesbergt, a Norwegian fishing village. This treatment of code switching gave impetus to further interest in code switching, especially between different languages.

Blom and Gumperz (1972:421) say that code switching is triggered by social motivations that reflect the social fabric of the community and suggests that 'linguistic alternates within the repertoire serve to symbolise the different social identities which members may assume'. Their analysis also highlights the conclusion that linguistic choice conveys meaning of a socio-pragmatic nature and that it is not only a reflection of stable factors outside the speaker's control such as, age, sex, and education, but other dynamic factors related to the social relations between speakers.

Since Blom and Gumperz's ground-breaking article in 1972, code switching, has been variously studied in many bilingual and multilingual communities. Factors such as topic, participants, domains, for example, have been established as having an influence on code/style variant selection in all types of language communities. Kachru (1978), for instance, claims that the choice of code used by a bilingual is influenced by such factors as the nature of interlocutor, topic or setting, the speaker's mood. Hamers and Blanc (1989:148), point out that between the choice of one language or the other, there exists for the bilingual speaker a whole range of intermediary strategies which include the modification of either code and the relative use of both. Thus code switching can be seen as one of the most common and original devices used by bilingual speakers in facilitating effective communication.

Though code switching has been generally defined as the alternation between two or more languages in the same discourse, more precise definitions have also been attempted. According to Gumperz, code switching 'relies on the meaningful juxtaposition of what speakers must consciously or subconsciously process as strings formed according to the internal rules of two distinct grammatical systems' (1982:66). For Gumperz, then, CS involves the juxtaposition of at least two strings of dialectal difference.

Code switching has also been analysed according to its types, and Blom and Gumperz (1972) were the first to classify it. They differentiate between metaphorical and conversational code switching. Blom and Gumperz (1972:425) describe metaphorical code switching as being related to particular kinds of topic or subject matter rather than to a change in the social situation. In metaphorical code switching, the use of a certain variety of language alludes to the social values it encodes (Downes 1998:64). Thus, metaphorical switching involves a change in topic hinting to a special relationship between the speakers.

3. Attempts at Differentiating CS from Other Language Contact Data

Even though code switching is a common occurrence in bilingual communities, all instances in which two languages come into contact are not always seen as resulting in code switching. Poplack et al. (1988) as well as other researchers have pointed out some language situations which look similar to code switching, but which are said to be instances of code mixing. The term 'code mixing' is used to denote a category of code switching identified as intrasentential switching or switching codes within the same utterance. Hamers and Blanc (1989:152) define code-mixing as a process characterised by the transfer of elements from a language Ly to the base language Lx. Code switching, on the other hand, involves the presence of two languages in the discourse 'chunks of one language alternating with chunks from the other. Chunk /x/ belongs only to language Lx, chunk /y/ solely to Ly' (Hamers and Blanc 1989:148). Because code mixing is seen as taking place within sentence/clause boundaries with no apparent change in topic/interlocutor/ setting, etc., some researchers (Romaine 1995:123) feel that it is the best evidence of an individual's fluency in two separate languages, as it requires a high degree of fluency to mix codes. Although the terms 'code mixing' and 'code shifting' are sometimes used to distinguish intrasentential switching from intersentential switching most modern studies now use the term 'code switching' for all.

The Methodology used in Collecting Data

The data for this paper is taken from interviews with 18 Sinhala/English bilinguals. The spoken corpus used in this study contains 30,391 words. On an average speakers produced around 1,688 words per hour during an interview session. The analysis of code switching in this paper is based on patterns of structure and use found in the spoken discourse of these 18 respondents.

Although the interviews were conducted in very relaxed and comfortable surroundings, it must be noted that 'the possibility of interlocutor effect is virtually inescapable in the interview context' (Hannah 1997: 349). The occasional presence of laughter during the interview sessions, however, makes it possible to conclude that the informants' behaviour is, at times, 'casual' in Labov's sense. As well as laughter, the interviews contain jokes, a whole range of personal topics, references to social events, money, food, etc. This suggests that the informants were generally not very conscious of being recorded. As a result of the procedures used in gathering data, I feel the analyses have the benefit of being based on data which are close to conversation as reasonably possible. This methodological advance must increase the validity of the findings in terms of new areas and in replicating aspects of other studies. As Labov (1972:118) states 'the value of new data for confirming and interpreting old data is directly proportional to the difference in the methods used to gather it'.

As the interviews were designed to elicit large bodies of bilingual speech, a single interview generally lasted about one hour or a little longer and took place in the respondents' homes at their convenience. Prior to the interviews I had prepared a list of 25 interview questions. However, in an attempt to keep the tone of the interviews informal, I did not follow my printed questionnaire. Instead, I allowed my respondents' interests and work experiences to guide my questions, lingering long over topics that drew them in while passing over ones that seemed to hold little interest for them (Hannah 1997:349). The topics we explored broadly fell into two categories: (1) non-linguistic (work experience, , family, religious affiliations, etc.), and (2) linguistic (pronunciation, grammar, attitudes to language).

My interviews with the 18 participants vary considerably in the amount of CS they contain. The initials SG, HP, DP, etc. used throughout the paper identify the participants. Although all the participants were aware that I speak Sinhala not all of them code switched. From the responses of the respondents to the question 'In what instances do you use Sinhala or Tamil?' it was clear that choosing which 'voice' to communicate in was consciously strategic. Most of them claimed that they would try as far as possible to avoid Sinhala. However, they said that they would code switch into Sinhala when they did not want others to understand what they were saying. Most of the respondents voiced the belief that generally speaking 'proper' or 'correct' English should not contain any code switching.

Although most of the respondents claimed that code switching was 'bad' where performance was concerned most respondents code switched at least once. However, some interviews contain only a handful of Sinhala nouns as code switched forms; others have few sentences not showing extensive switching. The speakers who showed the most CS in my data belong to a similar age group but have varying levels of education. All the speakers were fluent in both Sinhala and English. For instance, in the example given below the speaker switches codes several times within the same sentence constantly changing the matrix language from English to Sinhala and Sinhala to English.

1. ***I took some foreigners to see a pan perehera. Meeka gamwala nithara 45 karana ritual ekak. Oya dannawa ethine. Now pen pereheras you get always in villages. This is a ritual that all villagers perform during the drought season. What they do is they buy new clay pots, fill them with water from tissa vewa and come in procession and pour water at the foot of bodhi tree Menna mee wage pennanakota unta hari pudumai. They love it when you take them and show things like that. Being Buddhist you must be knowing all these things. meewa apita nothing much wunata foreignerslata alien concepts ne.***

In this example, not only does the speaker code switch within the same sentence, but he also code switches across sentences. In line 46, there is an interesting use of the English plural –s, which is affixed to a Sinhala noun pen perehera (water procession). Likewise, in line 52 the speaker uses Sinhala morphology (the plural –la and the dative suffix –ta) with the English word foreigners. These examples show the syntactic patterns that may be emerging within Sinhala/ English discourse.

The examples analysed in this paper are taken from a corpus of interview data collected from 18 individuals. The entire corpus consists of 30,000 words. Altogether, the data from the interviews contain 38 individual lexeme types of CS forms. By code-switched forms I mean singly occurring lexemes. Lexemes within 'islands' entirely of English or Sinhala (referred to as Sinhala or English EL islands) are not counted as individual types; rather islands themselves constitute a form class.

5. Types of CS in the data

One of the most frequent types of code switching that is evident in my corpus is singly occurring code switches. Single lexical items used in code switching may feature grammar from the donor language or may be bare. When they are bare, the single lexical items are usually problematic because we cannot be entirely sure whether they are code switches or borrowings. Thus, unlike islands from the donor language, the status of which is easily discernible, since their structure is internally consistent with the morphological and syntactic rules of the language of origin, singly occurring words are inherently ambiguous as to their status as CS or borrowing.

Table 1 shows the types of code switching evident in my corpus.

Table 1. Types of CS in the data

Code –switch	*No. of switches*
English suffixes combined with singly occurring Sinhala words in English clauses	5
Sinhala suffixes combined with singly occurring English words in Sinhala clauses	10
Use of bare English verb stems with Sinhala verbs	17
Sinhala islands in English clauses	62
English islands in Sinhala clauses	25
Use of adjacent English words without grammar in Sinhala clauses	2
Use of singly occurring words with internal grammar	7

In my data singly occurring lexical forms consist of 38 words. Of these, 32 singly occurring forms are combined with English or Sinhala suffixes to make new lexical items, closely followed by islands, which account for the majority of CS in the corpus overall. Singly occurring lexical words are the top category out of the three categories. In a breakdown by subgroup, bare English verb forms account for the largest category within single lexical items with 17 instances.

'Single occurring' switches

When dealing with singly occurring lexical items many researchers have tended to look at single lexical items as slot fillers which are used to fill lexical gaps. For example Haugen (1956:39) describes this process as follows:

> The simplest possible form of linguistic influence is that in which a single item is plucked out of one language and used in the context of another.

In relation to Sri Lankan English, C. Fernando (1977:354) says that lexical transfers are an important feature of Singlish. Such lexical transfers would include not only loan words, loan translations, etc., that have been absorbed into Sinhala but also regular transfers peculiar to Sinhala even where there are common equivalents in Sinhala. Some of these transfers are single lexical items like husband, wife, man, etc. This leads us to ask a perfectly legitimate question, which would be: Why Sinhala speakers use English words when there are equivalent Sinhala words? C. Fernando suggests that it could be because Sinhala words may be strongly associated with monolingual use. In her view, the introduction of English words maintain the informal, colloquial dimension whereas the equivalent Sinhala words can sometimes sound artificial and formal. Another possibility that suggests itself is that the equivalent Sinhala words may not be adequate to convey the meaning intended by the speakers.

In my data, depending on the language which provides the grammatical framework to a clause, there are code switches into either Sinhala or English. When singly occurring lexical items are selected they are usually combined with grammar from either Sinhala or English. There are, however, instances where singly occurring words also occur without internal grammar from either language. Sinhala origin lexical items generally take on English suffixes such as the plural -s, and the verb derivational suffix fy, whereas English origin words take on Sinhala affixes such as those marking case, definiteness, assertion, and interrogation. These are usually combined with English lexical items to make new words. There are 10 instances in which Sinhala affixes are attached to English nouns in the data. These forms indicate the emergence of new words formed with Sinhala and English elements such as foreinersla, velenda's, which is fast becoming an important feature of Sri Lankan English discourse.

5. 1.1 English Suffixes with Singly Occurring Sinhala Words

There are 5 instances where English suffixes are affixed to singly occurring Sinhala words to form new words. These include the use of the English possessive suffix's and the plural suffix–s which are affixed to English words and the word derivational suffix fy+ing.

2. ***HP:*** *To all clients I have told the story of hatseller. You must be knowing* ***thoppi velenda's*** *story no because hatseller is related to the monks*
3. ***DP:*** *Now pen pereheras you get always in villages*
4. ***SG:*** *There's so many people who look down, especially women, always* ***kusukusufying*** *when they see guide with tourists*

    a. talk talk.

In example 2, the word thoppi velenda (hat seller) is combined with the English possessive 's to make thoppi velenda's and in 3 the English plural suffix-s is used with the Sinhala word pen perehera (water procession) to make the plural pen pereheras, compound type words described by Poplack et al. (1988:52). For them, words such as the ones given above represent 'the incorporation of individual L2 words or compounds functioning as single words into discourse of L1, the host or recipient language, usually phonologically and morphologically adapted to conform with the patterns of that language, and occupying a sentence slot dictated by its syntax'. Likewise, in example 4 the English derivational suffix –fy + ing is used with the verb kusukusu to make the new verb kusukusufying. The word combination using the derivational suffix fy+ing is a common feature in colloquial Sri Lankan English speech. For instance, I have heard the following being uttered at a cricket match between Sri Lanka and England by a Sri Lankan man who was annoyed with the batsman's performance at the crease.

5. **My god, is that bugger going to <u>thattufy</u> the whole day? If he's <u>thattufying</u> machang we'll go, no point no, watching?**

In this example the singly occurring Sinhala word thattu is combined with fy as well as fy+ing to make two new word combinations; thattufy and thattufying. In Sinhala thattu allanawa means just waiting at the crease and wasting time without scoring runs. This shows how Sri Lankan English speakers use code switching in pragmatically meaningful ways to convey their meaning. A similar use of code switching is evident in Sinhala clauses used by some of the informants where singly occurring words are combined with suffixes from Sinhala.

5.1.2 Sinhala affixes with singly occurring English words

(*i*) Words with the Sinhala plural *–la*

A similar occurrence to that of thoppi velenda's where a single lexical item is morphologically adapted to function as a single word in the recipient language, as mentioned by

Poplack et al. (1988:52) is when English plural nouns are morphologically adapted with the Sinhala plural inflection –la. Double morphology in this case is quite common in Sinhala and there are 5 such code switches in my data where Sinhala affxes are used to form new words, as in guidesla, marked with the English plural –s and -la, the Sinhala plural, as opposed to only one instance where double morphology is not used (touristla). Hays (1997:199) notes that the use of pluralisation of a noun is often not as simple as conveying only the additional information that there are more than one of these things referred to. Such valuable information is lost when individual lexemes are treated as loans in data regardless of their form as for example in Myers-Scotton's list of 'singly occurring switches' where 141 nouns are reported. The use of the Sinhala plural inflection –la with English words in the following examples is necessary in order for the sentences to be grammatical according to Sinhala. If the words were used without the plural inflection they would be odd in Sinhala, as they would not fit in with the rest of the sentence.

6. ***DP:*** *mata hithena widiyata* ***foreignersla*** *ekka* ***compare*** *karanawanan*

   I think way with do if

   we speak much better

   'The way I think if we compare with foreigners we speak much better English'

7. ***DP: so guidesla*** *hetiyata api denagana inna oona* ***how to use***

   as we know stay must

   indigenous expressions

   'So as guides we must know how to use indigenous expressions'

(*ii*) (Single switches with the inflection *eka/ekak*

Another highly frequent form in the speech of the respondents is the use of the Sinhala inflection eka/ekak

(Gair 1998:19) with singly occurring English words. As in Sinhala, English speakers in Sri Lanka tend to append eka/ ekak to English lexical items in order to indicate singularity. In Sinhala, the eka forms are treated as phrasal inflections, that is, as single units parallel to the singular forms of other nouns. Similarly, with English nouns the phrasal inflection eka/ekak is used to form a new singular lexical form. An English noun (singular) + eka/ekak + a Sinhala operator is used with mixed compound verbs. Similarly, an English verb+eka+Sinhala operator kara (e.g. research+ekak+ karanawa) can also be used to form verbal nominalisers.

8. ***ST:*** *eyaa loku researchekak karanawa.*
she big one doing
'She's doing a big research'

(*iii*) Sinhala particles appended to singly occurring English words

Other Sinhala forms which are frequently combined with English words include particles. If we look for particles in Sinhalese standing on their own we will find fewer in comparison with English, but a considerable number of particles are realised through suffixation, and the emphatic particle –ma, the dative suffix –ta, the use of the co-ordinating suffix uy or y and the interrogative particle da are some of them. There are 8 instances where Sinhala particles are realised through suffixation with English words.

For instance, in the following example the speaker combines the English word foreigner with the Sinhala emphatic particle –ma

9. ***DP:*** *hema* ***foreigne****rma ehema nemey*
every foreignerEMPH that like not
'every foreigner <is> not like that'

The Sinhala dative suffix –ta is also commonly used in

Sri Lankan English to form words like manta, girlta, as in the following example:

10. ***DP:*** *itin commentaries dena kota mee guide kiyana manta*
so give when this called man DAT
okkama ***briefly explain*** *karanna wenawa.*
all do has

'So when (we) give commentaries this man called guide has to briefly explain all this"

Some of the more difficult combinations with English words are formed by using the Sinhala co-ordinating suffix –y. The English co-ordinating conjunction and has no one word equivalent in Sinhala. In English while and occurs between co-ordinated clauses, in Sinhala the post-fix uy, –y and –t are suffixed to the clauses themselves at the end of each word being co-ordinated. Similarly, when single English nouns are used in Sinhala they are co-ordinated using –uy, -y or –t as in the following examples:

11. ***ST*** **:** ***wife****uy lamai ehema kohomada?*
children so how
'So how are the wife and children keeping?'

12. ***PJ:*** *legnedsuy* ***stories***uy *ape* ***culture****eke* ***part****ekak nee?*
legends stories our GEN one SING no?
'legends and stories are a part of our culture no?'

In example 11, the English noun wife is co-ordinated with the Sinhala noun children, characteristically, as in Sinhala, by adding the co-ordinating particle -uy to the ending of the English noun, which serves to co-ordinate the two nouns. Similarly, in example 12 where the two English nouns legends and stories are used these are coordinated by the use of –uy. A rather more difficult example is the one given below (13), where two adverbs are used adjacent to each other but where the coordinating particle –y is more difficult to distinguish.

13. ***DP:*** *ee kiyanne api****systematically grammatically*** *katha karanawa.*
that means we speak do
'that means we speak systematically and grammatically'

This example consists of a sequence of two grammatical words used adjacent to each other in a Sinhala clause which appears to have somehow developed the grammatical framework to accommodate their use. As can be seen the code switched words follow Sinhala word order although they are used to modify the verb katha karanawa (talk+doing) as in English.

The interrogative da particle, which is used in forming yes/no questions in Sinhala, is sometimes used in code switching instead of the tag question forms no or isn't it? These two tag forms are more common in English than the da form.The da particle is not restricted to use in Sri Lankan English, and is also commonly used by people of South Asian ancestry in Singapore/Malaysian English.

14. ***LB:*** ***sure*** da?
yes
'<are> you sure?'

15. ***ST:*** *thama* ***work*** *karanne ara parana* ***place*** *eke da?*
still do that old GEN yes?
'still working at that old place?'

In Sinhala, as Gair (1998:54) notes, if an utterance is focused, then it is usually followed by the *da* particle. In Sri Lankan English this question form is sometimes used with English words, although the tag question form *no* is more common than the particle *da*.

5.1.3 'Bare' English verb stems with auxiliary verbs from Sinhala

Another frequent form of code switching in Sri Lankan English speech evident in the data is English words that are used without inflections or modifying function words. Of particular interest is the way in which singly occurring English verb stems are combined with the Sinhala compound verb *kara* (to do). In this construction English verbs occur as uninflected stems accompanied by an inflected Sinhala verb (*kara*) that is the equivalent of ' to do' in English. My data contains 17 tokens of the kara construction occurring with English verb stems. In the examples given below (16-18), the English verbs emphasise, compare and explain are combined with Sinhala *kara*.

16. *DP:* *ithin api hematissema eeka* ***emphasise*** *karanna oona.*
so we always that do must
'So we must always emphasise that'

17. *DP:* *mata hithena vidiyata* ***foreignersla*** *ekka* ***compare*** *karanawanan*
I think way PL with do if
we speak much better
'I think if we compare with foreigners we speak much better English'

18. *DP:* *itin* ***commentaries*** *dena kota mee* ***guide*** *kiyana* ***man****ta*
so give when this called man
okkama ***briefly explain*** *karanna wenawa.*
all do has
'So when (we) give commentaries this man called guide has to briefly explain all this"

Patterns similar to those with kara appear in other South Asian language contact data too. Chana and Romaine (1984:459) note that this general pattern of restructuring in the verb system is a well known hallmark in cases of language contact involving the languages of South Asia. Kachru (1978:36), for example, shows how in Hindi different styles drawing on Sanskrit, Persian and English are demarcated at least in part through the use of mixed compound verbs:

	Sanskritised	Persianised	Englishised
'to pity'	daya karna	raham karna	pity karna

Chana and Romaine (1984:459) give examples from studies of transplanted Hindi in Fiji and Trinidad, which also show the creation of a new class of compound verbs using the kara construction e.g. phonam karna 'to telephone', and trabal karna 'to make trouble'.

Romaine (1995) examines a number of similar compound verb constructions in Punjabi. In her description, these constructions are formed by a verb, noun or adjective and an 'operator':

> The operators comprise a small class of simple verbs with lexical meaning in their own right. The main ones are *karna* 'to do' and *hona* - 'to be/become'. The basic meaning of the compound is determined by the first element and modified by the verbal operator" (Romaine 1995:131).

The operator karna is particularly susceptible to being used in the construction of new compound verbs. In Panjabi, the verb karna is used with English verbs not only in cases where the equivalent Panjabi meaning would be expressed with a compound verb, but also in cases where the Panjabi equivalent would be a simple verb. Thus, while Panjabi has khelna 'to play', mixed Panjabi English has created the new compound play karna 'play do'.

Sinhala also allows the use of various kinds of phrasal verbs composed of a verb stem bearing the main inflection preceded by another form that may or may not be verbal. For example weda karanawa 'work to do' (noun stem plus verb), hitaa gannawa 'decide' (verb stem plus verb), hamba wenawa 'to meet' (indeterminate stem plus verb), saara wenawa 'become fertile' (adjective plus verb), and so on (Gair 1998:19). Although these by no means exhaust the possibilities, they demonstrate how Sinhala uses compound verbs with main inflectional verbs. The main inflectional verbs comprise a class of basic verbs with lexical meaning in their own right. These are kara (to do) and wena (to become/happen). The basic element of the compound construction, as noted by Romaine (1995:131) for Punjabi, is determined by the first element and modified by the verbal inflection (see Romaine 1995:131ff for a extended discussion of VPs in code switching involving uninflected English verb stems and Panjabi auxiliary type verbs).

As in other South Asian languages, the kara construction is definitely productive in English/Sinhala code switching, as can be seen by the examples given above. In all the examples, the English bare verb is used as the preverbal element compounded with the Sinhala operator kara. These examples indicate that English verbs plus kara can be used with different inflections to express tense/aspect. Gair (1998:40ff) notes that the verbs kara and wena are the most commonly used verbalisers which are used to form phrasal verbs, and that such pairs can be used to seek a correlation between verbalisers and their purposive/reactive distinction. In addition to the examples given above where singly occurring bare English verbs were combined with kara, there are also two instances where the preverbal constituent is an English phrasal verb.

19. *HP:* *oyaa apiwa* ***let down*** *karanna epaa*
you us do not
'don't let us down'

20. *DP:* *itin apita puluwan mee widiyata ape* ***knowledge***
so we can this way our
eka lassanata ***show off*** *karannna.*
one nicely do
'So in this way we can nicely show off our knowledge'

These examples indicate 4 main types of delexicalised verb constructions with kara.

(1) describe	karanawa	(English verb plus operator)
(2) show off	karanna	(English verb plus particle and operator)
(3) accounts settle	karanna	(English noun plus verb plus operator)
(4) briefly explain	karanna wenawa	(English adverb plus verb plus operator+operator)

When phrasal verbs are combined with kara as in the case of Type 3, a construction of Type 1 can be used followed by an object which may be in either language. In other words, the preverbal element can be in either language.

When it is in English, it takes the form of a verb or an –ing form of the verb. But, the operator must always be in the recipient language. In the context of language contact, the major function of compounding uninflected English verb stems with kara seems to be to inflect the uninflected EL verb stems.

5.2 'Islands' or mixed code utterances?

In Myers-Scotton's (1993a:2) words, code switching utterances conform to the grammars of the participating languages though they are subject to the constraints of her Matrix Language Frame model (MLF model). At the centre of Myers-Scotton's model is the theory that the matrix language (ML) plays the main role and that the embedded language (EL) plays a minor role. This is one of the controversial issues in language contact and in particular in Myers-Scotton's model as there have been and still are strong reactions to the assignment of a base language to switches. Sankoff and Poplack (1981) argued that language assignment of code-switched sentences is impossible and inappropriate, partly because switches take place between constituents whose order is shared by the two languages. More recently, Auer (1998) questioned the need to establish a base language.

This point is particularly important in Myers-Scotton's MLF model because once the matrix language is set, it is the one that prepares the sites into which EL content morphemes are inserted (1993a:137). In doing so Myers-Scotton's approach tends to ignore the relationship between the mixed elements and the main focus is on what participating language is lending the structure. In recent years the point has been raised as to whether the mixed code itself can be seen as the starting point from which to determine grammatical acceptability. Le Page and Taboret-Keller (1985) consider the mixed code as an independent code bound by its own grammar. In such cases CS can be seen as governed by its own grammar rather than that of either of the contributing languages. In her study of mixed Hindi English, Pandit (1986:86-93) mentions that there are no speakers who acquire Mixed Hindi English as their native language; there are only speakers of English who learn English and later become 'users' of the mixed code. Since traditional linguistic analysis relies on the intuitions and performance of native speakers she discusses the problem of deciding whose judgements may form the basis for such a grammar. Myers-Scotton (1993b:157) mentions a grammar based on the mixed code in connection with German/English data from Australia and the United States. Her discussion on this concept comes in the context of convergence between the matrix language and the embedded language which results in an interlanguage that predominantly reflects the order of the recipient language but with incursion from the embedded language.

Whether the mixed code can be considered a separate code or not, mixed utterances usually contain chunks of language which are sometimes referred to as islands. By definition, an 'island' from the embedded language consists of at least two lexemes in a hierarchical relationship (Myers-Scotton 1993a:137), that is, it must show internal dependency relations. After singly occurring words, utterances in which the two languages are mixed are the second largest clause type in my data. Although the concept of islands is not in itself useful in determining how or why mixed language chunks are used, I will refer to chunks of language from either Sinhala or English as 'islands' for the sake of convenience. There are 62 Sinhala islands and 25 English islands consisting of clauses with internal grammar. According to Myers-Scotton, islands are generally used when there is incongruence between the two languages participating in CS.

21. **DP:** *so what I do is mama* ***[sinhalaeka maruata engriisieke daala]*** *I*
I one well EnglishGEN put
give it
'so what I do is I mix the Sinhala stuff well in the English and I give it'.

22. **DP:** *oyata hina yai un kathakarana vidiyata* ***[shall we have***
you laugh go they speak way
dinner] *kiyala ahanawa dawalta kana ekata*
say ask afternoon eat oneDAT
'You might laugh but they say shall we have dinner for the afternoon meal'

23. **DP:** *eekai mama kiyanne* ***[without (knowing the language)]*** *mee*
that I say/tell this
job*eka karanna bee kiyala*
oneSING do can't done
'That's why I say without knowing the language this job can't be done/ can't do this job'

In example 21 given above, the English island contains the clause knowing the language. The code-switch from Sinhala to English occurs with an English preposition without. Since Sinhala does not have prepositions, the speaker has to continue the rest of the clause in English. The clause also contains the noun knowing which cannot be combined with kara or wena, as neither knowing karanava (know do) nor knowing wenava (know become) are grammatical according to Sinhala grammar.

An immediately visible aspect of 'islands' is that they are subject to varying degrees of syntactic modification. Nattinger and Decarrico (1992:8) note that when fixed phrases are co-selected from another language some phrases such as for the most part allows no modification while others like it's only in X that Y, allows a certain degree of modification. This theory is also valid for the data discussed above. When 'islands' are selected from Sinhala in an English sentence a fixed interrogative form like shall we have dinner (example 22) cannot be modified as then it would violate the grammatical order of English. Nattinger and Decarrico connect the notion of lexical phrase to the notion of pragmatic competence: "although grammatical competence encompasses the knowledge of the lexical forms and their internal syntax, pragmatic competence accounts for the speaker's ability to continue to access these forms as pre-assembled chunks, ready for a given functional use in appropriate context." (1992:13).

According to Myers-Scotton 'islands' are embedded elements within a matrix language, typically consisting of a matrix (receiver) language determiner + an NP from the embedded (donor) language. Myers-Scotton cites cases of double determiners, as in this example from Moroccan Arabic/French:

24. dak la chemise
that the shirt

(Bentahila and Davies 1983:317, Myers-Scotton 1993b:154)

A more common pattern is an matrix language determiner and an embedded language NP consisting of a noun and adjective, as in

25. C'est le highest class French

A similar pattern can be seen in my data where a Sinhala demonstrative, which acts as a determiner, is used before an English word. Sinhala demonstratives occur 20 times before English islands in mixed constituents. Demonstratives in Sinhala occur in the same order as in English; that is they usually precede adjectives or nouns. In addition, they can also occur adverbially in a limited number of environments. They also occur as subjects in clauses with a noun or noun phrase as predicator.

26. ***DP:*** *ee kiyanne mokakda mee [transfer of responsibility] kiyanne*
that means what this say
kiyala
'that means we have to say what this transfer of responsibility is'

27. ***DP:*** *[(mee verses)* ***(chant*** *karahama)* ***[automatically they get to know***
these done
our culture]
'when verses like these are chanted automatically they get to know our culture'

In example 26, the demonstrative mee occurs adjacent to an English island (mee transfer of responsibility) whereas in 27 it occurs adjacent to an English plural noun (mee verses) in its characteristic position. This is a common use in my data. Sinhala determiners are often followed by English words. The following example demonstrates the use of ara (that).

28. ***DP:*** *hema welema api (ara* ***value*** *eka)* ***stress*** *karanna oona*
always time we that oneSING do must
'we must always stress that value'

5.3 Adjacent words

As discussed above, although English clauses are commonly used by speakers as 'islands' in code switching a much rarer phenomenon that can be observed in the discourse of the respondents is the use of pairs of words which are used together but which are not grammatically linked to any other words in the utterance (see example 29). A phenomenon similar to what I have labelled 'adjacent words' is mentioned in Myers-Scotton's (1993b:84) work. She observes that there are cases of two English morphemes which are not islands and that they are so identified by the fact that they follow the word order of the dominant language. She reports only five tokens of this phenomenon in her Swahili/English corpus, all consisting of a noun and descriptive adjective (for example *timing proper*).

These adjacent pairs of words differ from other 'islands' in that they are not 'islands' but are two words which are not related in any way but which are nevertheless used adjacent to one another within the same clause. In this respect, although these adjacent words resemble single lexical items they are more interesting because they can be seen as another strategy of incorporating English material into Sinhala discourse. More importantly, these adjacent words are arguably treated as compounds by their users.

29. *ee* *nisa* *api* *pennala* *denna* *oona* *ape* *rate*
that because we show give must our country
marriage concept*eka* *gena*
one about
'because of that we must show them about the concept of marriage in our country'

These adjacent words do not violate the syntax of either language; they categorically obey the grammatical structure of Sinhala. It will be noticed that these adjacent words appear at the boundary with Sinhala, a point where any equivalent Sinhala nouns could also occur. In this case the Sinhala equivalents for the words marriage (vivahaya) and concept (sankalpaya) would not convey the meaning of what is being said as economically as the selected English words do, and would also sound very formal and artificial. The use of the two adjacent words makes the utterance more colloquial. Since these words are used as lexical gaps, there is nothing to indicate that these are not code-switches into English. Words such as kinship terms can also be considered CS in certain cases, especially in written iscourse.

5.4 Cultural Borrowings

The phenomena of code switching are highly complex and there are many issues which have remained unresolved. A long-unresolved issue in the area of code switching is the distinction between borrowing and code switching, which has divided language contact researchers for several decades. Myers-Scotton (1993b), however, claims that unlike CS, borrowed forms are a part of the mental lexicon of the donor language. She considers the two phenomena to lie along a continuum where CS acts as the gate for core borrowing.

In her model, there are two types of borrowed forms which are cultural lexemes and core lexemes. Although this distinction is not new, in her analysis, Myers-Scotton disposes of cultural loans and emphasizes the importance of core lexemes:

> Core borrowed lexemes are taken into the language even though the recipient language already has lexemes of its own to encode the concepts or objects in question (e.g. town) (Myers-Scotton 1993b:5).

It is not always easy to separate core borrowings from cultural borrowings. In Myers-Scotton's theory the distinction between code switching and borrowing is measured in terms of frequency and widespreadness rather than on the basis of phonological and morphological integration. Hence one of the difficulties that arise in using this theory is to decide what criteria to use in drawing a distinction between code switching and borrowing. The theory does not make clear whether it is etymology or the function in a particular discourse utterance that is to be used in deciding whether a particular morpheme is a code-switch or loan word. According to Duranti (1997) firstly, once cultural loans gradually lose their cultural content they come to be seen as core borrowings. Secondly, a lemma has a variety of word forms. A particular form of a 'core lexeme' may be culturally significant and end up as a borrowed form in the other language. When this happens, it is not always the most frequently used form or the most common meaning that is borrowed (for instance, see the discussion of the use of the word 'diet' in Sinhala). Moreover, also cultural words form new lexical words in the matrix language. The use of 'bare' English verbs with Sinhala verbs (describe karanawa) and compound type words (foreignersla, velendas) are convincing examples in this respect. Thirdly, if the main issue is 'to reveal the internal operations of language' as Myers-Scotton claims, cultural forms likewise display patterns which are well worth observing. Thus, the fact that they are core or cultural is irrelevant as long as they provide insights into the way mixed code works.

In my data there are many single lexical items with internal grammar which are used in code switching. These are unadapted to Sinhala grammatical patterns although they follow Sinhala grammatical structure and are sometimes used with Sinhala possessives as in ape songs. As mentioned before, some researchers see such words as 'slot fillers' in sentences (Haugen 1956). However, what counts is the way in which the lexical items are used in their new environment. In the utterance given below the nouns idioms, songs and metaphors are all used in the plural form. As discussed before, in the case of single code switches the particle eka/ekak and the Sinhala plural form -la are used with English words to indicate singularity and plurality respectively. In the case of example 30 given below, the –la form cannot be used with the nouns idioms, songs and metaphors as its use would make the words ungrammatical according to Sinhala. In Sinhala the –la plural can only be used with animate nouns referring to people. The borrowed English words already have plural morphology and serve to emphasise the idiom kelala erala, which suggests something that has been done in an impressive manner. These utterances break new ground in creatively combining English plural words with Sinhala, and moreover, do so without violating the grammar of either language.

30. *DP:* *Sinhala idioms ape* ***songs*** *wala hondata hoyala beluwoth*
our in well find check

ingriisi ***metaphors*** *kelala arala.*
English used a lot

'if you check well you can find a lot of English metaphors in Sinhala songs and idioms'

In the literature on code switching, code-switches are generally distinguished from borrowings either phonologically or on the basis of a measure of frequency; forms with a more frequent occurrence in the data such as three or more instances are classified as borrowings, whereas forms appearing less than that are considered code switches. However my data suggests that code switched forms may become borrowed forms through their adoption by Sinhala monolinguals. Therefore, how frequently a word occurs in the data is not as important as how it is used.

The sources of the Sinhala vocabulary are many, including, along with words inherited throughout its development, forms borrowed from Sanskrit and Pali as well as from Dravidian, particularly Tamil, and from European languages, specifically Portuguese, Dutch, and English, together with a scattering of others. Sanskrit borrowings have taken place at various stages in the history of Sinhala with varying degrees of adaptation to the Sinhala speech habits of the time. Colloquial Sinhala has been particularly receptive, over the past few centuries, to borrowings from Portuguese, Dutch and English. Some examples are padiri (priest), kamise (shirt) from Portuguese; artapal (potatoes), kokis (cakes) from Dutch; saykale (cycle), miitima (meeting) from English (Gair 1998:218ff). These words can be seen as cultural borrowings which have been completely adapted to the phonological system of Sinhala, although some features of the original phonological system may be retained.

For example, the degree of phonological integration of the English verb diet in Sinhala can be seen by its adaptation as [dait] rather than [dai«t]. The most common pronunciation among Sri Lankan English speakers is the latter; nevertheless, personal observation has shown that the former appears to be the preferred choice among the majority of Sinhala speakers. The complete integration of the verb diet into Sinhala can also be seen in the changes it has undergone semantically, as it is currently used to mean 'having a hearty meal' instead of the standard connotation of restricting the intake of food in order to control one's weight (Parakrama 1995:120). The example given below illustrates the way the word diet is used with the new connotation in the data, which has reference to a hearty intake of food.

31. ***LB:*** *Appuhamy honda* ***fried rice*** *ekak danna mee nonata honda*
good oneSING make this ladyDAT good
diet *ekak denna oona*
oneSING give must
'appuhamy make a good fried rice. Must give this lady a good diet'

Borrowings from English into Sinhala may sometimes be classified on the basis of phonological and/or morphological integration as reflected in spelling, phonology and integration into the lexicon. However, as discussed earlier, it is not easy to distinguish between borrowed words and code-switched words. Although if access to the word in question can be seen as limited to speakers with bilingual competence, it is generally considered a CS, this is not always accurate.

Other frequent cultural borrowings in my data include names for items of food such as mologathanni, ambul thial, pittu, indiaappa and words like rekee-raksha. These are all words which express cultural concepts, and which are not available in English.

5.5 The significance of CS patterns in Sinhala/English discourse

Numerous motivations for code switching have been identified by researchers. Some of these are summarised below:

1. To signal ethnic identity and to probe for shared background knowledge (Gumperz and Hernandez-Chavez 1975:154, Gumperz 1982:72).
2. To express emotion, close personal relationships and solidarity, and to exclude a third person from part of a conversation (Harding and Riley 1986:57-60).
3. To identify with EL culture or at least aspects of it or with a prestigious person who uses them (Myers-Scotton 1993a).

The code switching behaviour of the respondents in my data suggests that code switching here acts as a means of reinforcing the speaker's ethnic identity. Gumperz (1982:72) reported that the direction of the switch has pragmatic value. Although I did not code switch nor (re) phrase my questions in Sinhala, most of the respondents frequently code switched within or across sentences. The alternation of the two languages can be seen as a metaphoric representation of their ethnic identity. As I did not speak in Sinhala it could also be seen as a way of challenging me to express my identity as a Sinhala speaker. The fact that I only spoke English may have been seen as a signal that I want to become Anglicized, and that I do not relate to the rest of the Sinhala/English bilingual community. In order to validate these claims it is necessary to empirically investigate what code switching means in this context. In a study on CS in Birmingham, Chana and Romaine (1984) played data back and asked speakers about why they code switched. By asking speakers to be introspective they found that people are evaluated in different ways depending on whether they speak more Punjabi or English. The public lives of the speakers who code switched in this study are grounded in English but they nevertheless have a deep-rooted attachment to Sinhala culture and values. Therefore, in this context, code switching can be seen as a tool for negotiating a distinct identity unique to Sinhala. By speaking in English and embracing Sinhala at the same time these speakers appeared to enact a kind of linguistic behaviour that was intended to mirror their identity as complex and creative individuals who draw from different linguistic and cultural resources at their disposal.

6. Conclusion

The use of suffixation to form new words and the creation of compound type words show speaker innovation within Sri Lankan English discourse. In the context of speech, code switching can be seen as another linguistic strategy used to enhance communication between speakers of the same languages. The use of code switching as a linguistic feature is of particular interest to research on sociolinguistic variation as different cultures react differently to the use of CS in speech. Most of the features of CS discussed in this paper are viewed negatively by Sri Lankan English speakers who see it as not being proper linguistic behaviour. Yet the use of code switching shows that in Sri Lanka code switching is one of many linguistic choices available to bilingual speakers. Code switching is used by speakers for its cultural value and adds creativity and sophistication to their speech.

References

Auer, Peter. (1998). Code switching in Conversation. London: Routledge.

Baetens Beardsmore, Hugo. (1982) Bilingualism: basic principles. Clevedon: Multilingual Matters.

Bentahila, Abdelali and Eirlys E. Davies. (1983) The Syntax of Arabic-French Code Switching. Lingua 59, 301-330.

Blom, Jan Peter and John J. Gumperz. (1972) Social Meaning in Linguistic Structure: code switching in Norway. In Directions in Sociolinguistics: The Ethnography of Communication, ed. John J. Gumperz and Dell Hymes, New York: Holt, Rinehart and Winston. pp. 407-434.

Duranti, Alessandro. (1997) Linguistic Anthropology. Cambridge: Cambridge University Press.

Fernando, Chitra. (1977) English and Sinhala Bilingualism in Sri Lanka. Language in Society, 6, 341-360.

Fernando, Siromi. (1985) Changes in Sri Lankan English as Reflected in Phonology. University of Ceylon Review, 24, 41-56.

Fernando, Siromi. (1990) Style Range in Sri Lankan English Fiction: an analysis of four texts. World Englishes, 8 (2), 119-131.

Gair, James W. (1998) Studies in South Asian Linguistics: Sinhala, and other South Asian Languages. Oxford: Oxford University Press.

Gumperz, John J. (1982) Discourse Strategies. Cambridge: Cambridge University Press.

Gumperz, John J. and Eduardo Hernandez-Chavez. (1975) Cognitive Aspects of Bilingual Communication. In El Lenguage de los Chicanos: regional and social characteristics of language used by Mexican Americans, ed. Eduardo Hernandez-Chavez, Arlington, Virginia: Center for Applied Linguistics. pp. 154-163.

Gupta, Anthea Fraser. (1999) Standard Englishes, Contact Varieties and Singapore Englishes. In Teaching and Learning English as a global language: native and non-native perspectives, ed. Claus Gnutzmann, Tübingen: Stauffenberg Verlag. pp. 59-72.

Hamers, Josiane F. and Michael H. A. Blanc. (1989) Bilinguality and Bilingualism. Cambridge: Cambridge University Press.

Hannah, Dawn. 1997. Copula Absence in Samana English: implications for research on the linguistic history of African-American Vernacular English. American Speech 72:339-372.

Harding, Edith and Philip Riley. (1986) The Bilingual Family: a handbook for parents. Cambridge: Cambridge University Press.

Haugen, Einar I. (1956) Bilingualism in the Americas: a bibliography and research guide. Alabama: Alabama University Press.

Haugen, Einar. I. (1970) The Stigmata of Bilingualism. In The Ecology of Language: essays by Einar Haugen, ed. Einar Haugen. California: Stanford Press. pp. 307-323.

Hays, Paul R. (1997).. Collocational Similarity: emergent patterns in lexical environments. Unpublished PhD dissertation, University of Birmingham.

Kachru, Braj B. (1978) Toward Structuring Code-Mixing: an Indian perspective. International Journal of the Sociology of Language, 16, 28-46.

Le Page, Robert B. and Andrée Tabouret-Keller. (1985) Acts of Identity: creole based approaches to language and ethnicity. Cambridge: Cambridge University Press.

McArthur, Tom. (1998) The English Languages. Cambridge: Cambridge University Press.

Myers-Scotton, Carol. (1993a) Building the Frame in Code-switching: evidence from Africa. In Current Issues in Linguistic

Theory: topics in African linguistics, Edited by Saikiko S. Mufwene and Lioba Moshi. Amsterdam: John Benjamins. pp. 253-278.

Myers-Scotton, Carol. (1993b) Duelling Languages: grammatical structure in code-switching. Oxford: Clarendon Press.

Nattinger, J. R. and J. S. DeCarrico. (1992) Lexical Phrases and Language Teaching. Oxford: Oxford University Press.

Pandit, Ira. 1986. English Hindi Code-Switching: mixed Hindi English. New Delhi: Ditta.

Parakrama, Arjuna. (1995) De-hegemonizing Language Standards: learning from (post) colonial Englishes about 'English'. London: Macmillan.

Passé, H A. (1948) The English Language in Ceylon. Unpublished PhD dissertation, University of London.

Poplack, Shana, David Sankoff, and Carol Miller. (1988) The Social Correlates and Linguistic Consequences of Lexical Borrowing and Assimilation. Linguistics, 26, 47-104.

Romaine, Suzanne. (1995) Bilingualism. Oxford: Blackwell.

Sivasuriya, Shivanthini. (1993) Attitudes to Tamil English Code Switching. Unpublished MA dissertation, University of Colombo.

Weinreich, Uriel. (1979) Languages in Contact: findings and problems. The Hague: Mouton.

8

Food Talk in Oriya

B.N. Patnaik

This paper deals with what may be called "food talk", and is organized in three parts: the first is devoted to food talk in the so-called standard dialect Oriya, which is the central concern of the paper, the second suggests that such talk may not be restricted to this language, and the third offers a brief and tentative account of how part of food talk has the features that it has.

Food and food codes in the Indian context are among the more well-discussed topics in Indian social anthropology and folklore studies, A.K. Ramanujan's being among the most insightful, as far as the latter is concerned. There is some interesting writing in Oriya language mainly by literary critics and folklorists on Oriya food and food codes, but to the best of our knowledge, food talk has not so far drawn the attention of the Oriya linguists, literary critics, and scholars working on this language from other perspectives. Food talk uses the vocabulary of food, and is seemingly about food, but is really not about it; thus descriptive terms belonging to the discourse on food such as "cooked / non-cooked", "sacred / non-sacred", "polluted / non-polluted", or the traditional Indian saatwik / taamasik etc. do not apply to it. In conversation it performs certain functions, such as conversation starter / facilitator, marker of informality, even indicator of good will in certain contexts, etc. Food talk is part of the informal use of language; more so of the rural population than of the urban, which may be one reason why it has not been noted for study. It does not find mention in the collections of Oriya folk literature, but it may be because these are not among the stuff the folklorist is generally concerned with, such as proverbs, riddles, wisecracks, tales, songs, etc. These do not occur in folk tales too – one place where one would expect them to occur, these being part of ordinary conversation. Food talk has also escaped the attention of the Oriya socio-linguists. Careful study of discourse in Oriya is yet to be undertaken, which may constitute yet another reason why food talk has not drawn the attention of the scholars so far.

Consider the following:

(1) khaailani / khiaapiaa helaani?
eat-perf-2p / eating-drinking - be-perf – 3p
(Have you eaten / Is dining over?)

This is part of the linguistic etiquette system, called kushala pachaaribaa (asking about the other's welfare) in Oriya; it's a form of responding to a customary greeting or a part of conversation starting strategy.[2] It can be used only after meal time, and would be inappropriate if used earlier, say, soon after sun rise, which is the time for worship, or to go to work, etc. "Meal time" is clearly not a fixed time concept; it is a matter, among others, of the economic condition of the family concerned, and the job requirements of a certain individual. The speaker of (1) is not really interested in or concerned about whether the hearer has dined. One advantage of (1) as conversation starter is its relative neutrality of tone; it isn't too personal, yet it isn't distant and formal.[3] It invites comparison with the polite, phatic "how-do-you-do" or weather talk in English. As far as the conversation starter and greeting features are concerned, these are equivalents, but there is a difference; there is a fairly fixed response to the phatic expression, but it is not so as far as (1) is concerned. It is interpreted both as a greeting expression and as a question requiring an affirmative or a negative reply, and is ordinarily answered in terms of any of the variants of "yes" or "no" or "not yet", "going to", etc.; in other words, the response is not fixed, although some response is required and null response is unacceptable. Either as a conversation starter or as a continuation of (1), one could use (2):

(2) kana tarakari heithila?
What – curry – be-perf
(What curry was made?)

The hearer interprets it correctly as a form of greeting, and could respond by either giving the information asked for or giving an appropriate non-committal and evasive reply. Both are considered acceptable responses, and either could give rise to some more talk. Worthy perhaps of attention is that the question is not framed about rice or pulses, which are part of a meal too, but about curry, which could be a cover term for a range of dishes - vegetarian, non vegetarian, fried, mashed - which need not even include what strictly speaking is curry – the preparation with rather thin gravy. It may be because in the traditional, ordinary, minimal Oriya meal at least in the villages, curry is the item that permits some variation, rice and black gram daal being the fixed ones.

A few decades ago, when a person returned to his village after visiting some distant place, he was sometimes affectionately asked by the village elders about what that place was like with the following:

(3) ...sethi kana dekhila? kana khaaila?
there – what – saw-2p? what – saw-2p?
(What did you see there? What did you eat?)

Seeing and eating constituted a cover term for a variety of the person's experiences in the place he had returned from. (3) was used somewhat more to express cordiality towards the person who had returned home than to really know from him what all he had experienced. But literalness is not completely absent in (3); that is why a brief answer giving some information about the kinds of food available or not available, cost of food, etc. even in a casual manner was quite acceptable.

It may be noted that food talk is conspicuous by its absence in literary texts, even in plays and works of fiction. There is a rare example of food talk in the form of (3) in the Oriya novel kanaa maamu (blind uncle). This occurs in a conversation between a Hindu young man and a Muslim elder who comes to visit this young man and his friends at their village gymnasium. The relation established between the young men and the visiting elder is like that between the grand children and the grand father from the mother's side. This is a relation where leg pulling and jokes are permitted, including the ones with mild sexual undertones. The visitor tells the young men about his passing through Lanka on his way to Mecca on pilgrimage. In order to impress them he tells them things that they know are clearly false, but he doesn't know that they know. This creates a perfect situation for some pleasant leg pulling. One young man asks him what he ate there (sethi kana khaaila?). The objective is obviously not to find out what he had eaten, since they know that there was no truth in what they were being told; it is to please the visitor, make him feel good and encourage him to talk.

The following occurs in informal interaction of both the rural and the urban population, especially the people who are not generally uncomfortable in life:

(4) kebe khaibaaku dauca?
when – eat-non-finite-post position – give-prog-2p
(When are you feeding us?)

This is a friendly way of telling the hearer that something good is coming his way (he has got a job, an increment or a promotion, or found a girl for himself, etc.), and of congratulating him for it. In some instances this is simultaneously a way of mildly complaining to the hearer that although he did not tell the speaker the good news about himself, the speaker knew of it. Thus in (4) eating is used not in its literal sense, but in the sense of celebration.

In the coastal town of Puri one occasionally comes across the use of (5) as part of informal and cordial interaction:

(5) chenaa chakataa te hau[4]
cheese - mash-nom – part – be-subjunctive[5]
(Arrange a cheese party.)[6]

Its conversational function is to bring some casualness into the interaction or relief in a rather not-so-pleasant conversation, as part of the effort to maintain cordial social relations. We are not sure whether such an expression is part of the local idiom of Puri and its neighbourhood alone.

Such food metaphors as the following could perhaps be considered as instances of food talk. Consider (6) and (7), containing lexical couplets tela luna ("ordinary, day-to-day"; literally "oil-salt") and saaga bhaata ("very ordinary food"; literally "green leaves-rice") respectively:

(6) taara tela lunara sansaara kaunasimate calijaauthilaa
he-poss–oil-salt–world–somehow–going on-prog-past
(He was somehow managing.)

(7) se saaga bhaata khaai calijaauthilaa
he–green leaves rice–eat-non finite–go on-prog-past
(He was managing with very ordinary stuff.)

Very ordinary existence is expressed in terms of food. In saying (6) or (7) one is not talking about or inviting attention to food, but to the difficult situation of the referent. Now if the lexical couplets in the above are metaphors of deprivation, khiri puri ("pudding – puri") or khiri khechadi ("pudding rice cooked with black gram") are metaphors of prosperity.

The following, which is a proverb, might be viewed as an implicit food expression:

(8) soilaa puara bhaaga naahin
sleep-rel.part – son-poss – share – neg-be-prs
(The sleeping child has no share.)

The basic sense of bhaaga here is share in food; but it is not so in every instance. Sometimes the predicate, as in (9) and sometimes the verb phrase, not the predicate alone, as in (10), determines the sense of this nominal, as in:

(9) hari taa bhaaga khaaidelaa
Hari – he-poss – share – eat up- pst
(Hari ate up his share.)

(10) hari bhaagare sahe aamba ghacha padilaa
Hari–share-in–hundred–mango–trees-fall-pst
(A hundred mango trees fell in Hari's share.)

Bhaaga remains ambiguous when the context does not contribute to the restriction of meaning. Consider (10):

(11) hari taa bhaaga raamaku delaa
Hari – he-poss – share – Ram-acc – give-pst
(Hari gave his share to Ram.)

Dissociated from the context, share in the above could refer to anything: from food to money or property.

There is a code of food talk; it is an expression of power relations, as are other codes such as the address code or the dress code. One important aspect of food talk is that it is horizontally or downward oriented; the norm is that it is used among equals, or by the speaker who has a higher social status vis-à-vis the hearer. Deviation is rather rare. When in an interaction the social superior uses any of (1) - (5), it is viewed as an expression of good will and even a degree of cordiality for the hearer, although in some context – say, when the hearer is fairly highly educated and has a decent job - some hearer might regard it as condescending behaviour on the speaker's part. But when the social superior is the recipient of such talk, it is viewed as unacceptable, something not done. A generous interpretation of it is that the speaker's behaviour is rather cheeky. On occasions, for example, when the addressee's status is very low with respect to the addressor's, it can even be construed as rather rude behaviour. Similarly, when someone whose social status is very high in relation to that of the addressee says (2), let alone (4), to the latter, it is very condescending, in fact, crudely so. As far as (6) and (7) are concerned, these describe the situation of a certain person who is the subject of the talk, and these can be uttered even in his presence, and then it expresses the speaker's sympathy for that person. When the speaker, who is well-to-do, utters versions of these with appropriate grammatical changes to talk about himself, these are regarded as politeness expressions, but when the speaker is poor, then these expressions sometimes tend to get interpreted as attempt by him to elicit the hearer's sympathy.

II

Food talk is not confined to Oriya. One finds instances of food talk in other Indian languages too, for example, Bengali, Hindi, Telugu, and Kannada.

Consider the following from standard Bengali:

(12) khaawaa daawaa hoiche (ki)
eating , etc.– has taken place – (Q word)
(Have you had your meal?)

(13) bhaat khiecho?
rice – have eaten
(Have you had your meal?)

(14) aajke ki raandhnaa holo?
today – what – cooking – happened
(What has been cooked today?)

(15) aaj ki khele?
today – what – ate
(What did you have today?)

A word about the gloss: khaawaa daawaa in (12) is a lexical couplet, in which the second word does not have the meaning of "give" that it has when it occurs independently. In (13) bhaat is the cover term for the major meal, as it is in Oriya. In (14) the implicit reference is not to rice or daal, the minimal items, but to the curry, as in (15). More used in rural Bengal than urban Bengal, these "good will" expressions are often used by elders and social superiors when they respond to the greeting of the youngsters and the ones lower on the status hierarchy. When used as such, they do not require literal interpretation by the addressee, who merely has to give some response, including a non-specific one.

In Telugu the following have the same function:

(16) annam tinnaawaa?
food - have eaten
(Have you had your meal?)[7]

(17) iroju mi inclo eem kura cesaaru?
today – you – home – what – curry – made
(What curry did you make at home today?)

Kannada the following expressions of greeting:

(18) utaa aaitaa?
food – have eaten
(Have you had your meal?)

(19) tindi / kaaphi aaitaa?
snacks / coffee – have eaten
(Have you had your snacks / coffee?)

Among the urban educated, who are no strangers to each other, these are not used unidirectionally; a younger person can greet and initiate talk with an elder using the above. Around breakfast or tea time one could use (19), and lunch / dinner time, (18).

As in Oriya, in Hindi, a comfortable life style is expressed in food terms. Consider the following which belongs to the Kanauji dialect of Hindi:

(20) we halwaa puri khaayaa rahe
he – halwa puri – eating
(He is having a great time.)

In the same dialect the following constitutes an interesting response to the news that someone is leading a prosperous life somewhere. The hearer does not believe it, and expresses his disbelief using (21):

(21) huaan badi heshmi dahri hai
there – a lot of - heshmi – kept – is
(There is abundance of heshmi in that place.)

Now heshmi appears to be some imaginary rich dish that is invoked by the elder generation to talk about something almost impossible.

III

Food talk is metaphorical, saying something in terms of something else, such as calling a crooked person jilebi (a syrupy sweet that has a crooked form), an easy task halwaa (a sweet dish), a boring person kadoo (pumpkin) in Hindi, or expressing good will by using language that relates to food in some way. As (1) and (2) and their cognates in other Indian languages would suggest, food talk is part of the repertoire of politeness expressions in these languages, which accounts for some of its crucial features such as its unidirectionality, and its sensitivity to power relations among the interactants We might speculate why good will is expressed in food terms in at least some of our languages. It is well known that in our tradition food enjoyed an eminent place since it was believed to be connected with not only the physical but also the physical and spiritual well being of a person, and the importance of food in the day-to-life of the poor villager especially in the feudal society and economy can hardly be over-stressed. It is presumably in this context that enquiring about the well being of a person came to be synonymous with asking whether he had eaten (1) or had eaten well (2) – eating a curry as part of the meal is more often than not a poor man's luxury. Now if (1) and (2) are implicitly good will expressions, then one would reasonably expect the language to have explicit good will expressions too. Oriya indeed has the following which often function as alternatives to (1) and (2):[8]

(22) sabu bhala (ta)? / bhala acha?
all – good – Q part / good – be-pr-2p
(Is everything all right? / Are you fine?)

To conclude, the paper draws attention to food talk in Oriya which has remained unnoticed so far by scholars working on this language. It deals, in some detail, with only those constructions that are greeting expressions. It maintains that food talk is by no means restricted to Oriya, and instances of it can be found as well in Bengali, Hindi, Telugu and Kannada, among other Indian languages, and speculates how some food talk expressions may have come to be used as expressions of greeting.

References

Dash, Kunja Bihari (1958). Odiaa loka gita o kaahani. Santiniketan: Vishwabharati.

Maharana, Surendra Kumar (1992). Saaralaa saahitya parikramaa. Cuttack: Orissa Book Store. (Revised and Enlarged Second Edition)

Malamoud, Charles (1995). Cooking the World (Ritual and Thought in Ancient India). Delhi: Oxford University Press. (Translated by David White) Mohapatra, Lakshmikanta (1964). Kaanta saahitya maalaa (Volume I). Cuttack: Orissa Book Emporium.

Patnaik, B.N.(1996). "A Study of Some Politeness Expressions in Oriya in Relation to Social Change", In Verma, S.K. and D.Singh (eds.) Perspectives on Language in Society. Delhi: Kalinga Publications.

Foucault, Michel (1991). The Foucault Reader. (ed. Rabinow Paul) London: Penguin Books.

Ramanujan, A.K. (1999). "Food for Thought: Towards an Anthology of Hindu food-Images", In Dharwadkar, Vinay (ed.) The Collected Essays of A.K. Ramanujan. Delhi: Oxford University Press.

Ray, Sudha (2005). "The Discourse of Food and Matrilineages in Contemporary Women's Writing". In Gupta, Santosh, P.C.Kar and P.D.Mukherji (eds.) Rethinking Modernity. Delhi: Pencraft International.

9

Language Contact Induced Changes in *Kurukh*

Awadesh K. Mishra

Kurukh [kurUx] belongs to the North Dravidian group of languages. The speakers of Kurukh (also known as Oraon) are found in the states of Assam, Jharkhand, Madhya Pradesh, Orissa and West Bengal. The maximum concentration of Kurukh population is to be found in the Chotanagpur plateau of Jharkhand. According to Census of India, 1991 there were 1,426,618 Kurukh speakers.

The present study is limited to the dialect of Kurukh spoken in the Ranchi district of Jharkhand. Sadri (an Indo-Aryan pidgin) is the lingua franca of Ranchi district. Through education, the Kurukhs have made great change in their economic conditions and have attained economic and social security. The spread of education also necessitated the use of Hindi, Sadri and even English by the Kurukhs.

The size of the Kurukh tribal population relative to that of the neighboring Aryans in Ranchi district is a significant factor. The Kurukh language has an ethnolinguistically minority status and it is in the rolc of a recipient language. The symbiosis between the Kurukh and the non-tribal (mainly Aryan) population which is numerically, economically and socially dominant is a multilingual milieu where Kurukh does not function as a dominant language. Urbanization and industrialization, in many areas, has exposed the tribal population to ethnically diverse non-regional people (speaking Indo-Aryan languages like Hindi, Sadri, Bengali, Assamese and Oriya), which subsequently brought linguistic, social and economic changes. The Kurukh tribal population has adopted the socially dominant languages in favor of Kurukh in all communicative networks, even in the home domain.

At all levels of linguistic structure, mainly in the lexicon, Kurukh has been highly influenced by the co-existing dominant languages, especially Sadri and Hindi. The degree of linguistic interference varies spatially, from the rural to urban, and temporally, from the older generation to the younger. The older generation retains archaic, conservative speech forms, while the younger generation's speech is highly Aryanized.

We now discuss the changes due to language contact/ Aryanization of the Kurukh lexicon, phonology, morphology and syntax one by one.

(1) Loanwords in Current Usage

The largest proportion of the loan vocabulary is from Indo-Aryan (I-A) consisting mainly of material artifacts introduced to the Kurukhs in their interaction with Aryan culture. E.g., *ja:it* 'caste', *sona:* 'gold', *ba:sa:* 'abode', *kar?ma:* 'blanket', *bhi:t* 'wall', *khuta:* 'pillar', etc.

Apart from material artifacts, much of the basic vocabulary from divergent semantic domains has also been incorporated, as kinship terms (*kaka:* 'uncle', *bhatija:* 'nephew', *sais* 'mother-in-law', etc.); animal names (*bandra:* 'monkey', *gadaha:* 'donkey', *hathi:* 'elephant', etc.); household terms (*puthi:* 'book', *chippa:* 'bowl', *d?ibya:* 'small wooden box', etc.); color terms (*li:l* 'blue', *hariyar* 'green', etc.), which have completely displaced their Kurukh counterparts, and religious terms (*dutas* 'angel', *dharmi:* 'religious', *dharmes* 'God', *girja:* 'church', etc.). The incidence of Indo-Aryan verbs is high (*ubasna:* 'to fast', *ghatrna:* 'to lessen', *latxrna:* 'to hang', *gan-na:* 'to count', etc.) defying the assumption of the resilience of the vocabulary to incorporate loan verbs.

(2) Indo-Aryan Loanwords in Kurukh 'basic' Vocabulary

In the analysis of the basic vocabulary (representing high-frequency-use words), an infiltration of loanwords is evident. The common I-A loans identified in the basic vocabulary are in the domains of:

(*i*) **Numerals**: The data on numerals in the basic vocabulary indicates that except for the numerals 'one', 'two' and 'three', which uniformally generated the Kurukh forms *o:nd* 'one', *e:kʔ* 'two', *mu:nd* 'three', the higher numerals have been displaced by their I-A counterparts.

(*ii*) **Kinship terms**: *babas* 'father', *bhaiyas* ', brother', and *bahin* 'sister' have been borrowed from I-A.

(*iii*) **Body part nomenclature**: This shows predominantly Kurukh forms with marginal lexical interference from I-A as in *buka:* 'heart', *cutʔtʔi: / ke:s* 'hair', *dʔena:* 'wing'.

(*iv*) **Natural objects** : Those natural objects geographically remote to the Kurukh habitat, as, *darya: / samundr*[a] 'sea', *baraph* 'ice'; some objects which are part of their natural habitat are also denoted by I-A terms as *ghãsi:* 'grass', *dhuli:* 'dust', *bada:li:* 'cloud', *kuhas / dhudh* 'fog', *cando:* 'moon', *xa:rʔ* 'river', *pakhna:* 'stone'.

(*v*) **Temporal organization**: The nouns used to denote discrete time consist dominantly of I-A forms, even in the basic vocabulary as *mahina:* 'month', *bachar* 'year', *pakkhe:* 'fortnight'.

(*vi*) **Adjectives**: Most of the basic adjectives are native. There are some loan adjectives such as *be:s* 'good', *digha:* 'long', *dʔhe:r* 'many', *cikan* 'smooth', *tani:* 'some/a little', *motʔ* 'thick', *cakarʔ* 'wide', *patla:* 'thin', etc.

(*v*) **Artifacts**: In the basic vocabulary there are only very few borrowed words for object of artifacts. *sotʔtʔa: / dʔanʔdʔa: / dʔa:ʔg* 'stick', *pagha:* 'rope', and *balam / barcha:* 'spear' are I-A loans.

(*vi*) **Verbs** : A number of I-A verbs have been identified in the basic vocabulary, as, *bhukna:* 'to bark', *habka'a;na:* 'to bite', *gan-na: / lekhna:* 'to count', *khanʔdʔna:/ bhangna:* ' to cut', *larʔna:* 'to fight', *katʔhua:rna:* 'to freeze', *dharna:* 'to hold', *gamka:rna: / mahka:rna:* ' to smell', *t?ut?ªrna:* 'to split/ break', *bhokna:* 'to stab', and *socna:* 'to think'.

(*vii*) Adverbs, form words, etc.: In the basic vocabulary, which includes very few 'form' words or grammatical markers, only *agar* 'if', *karne* 'because', and *aur* 'and' are I-A loans. However, an analysis of the extended vocabulary reveals that several indeclinable words (adverbs, etc.) and grammatical markers have been incorporated, co-existent with native Kurukh forms.

(3) Changes in Phonology

(*a*) Aspiration: Kurukh has all the aspirated consonants (voiceless as well as voiced) found in I-A languages, viz., / ph, bh, th, t?h, dh, d?h, ch, jh, kh, gh, r?h /. The aspirated phonemes are found in loanwords as well as native Kurukh words. Consider the following examples.

/ph/ *pho:phar* 'blowpipe/hollow', *rãph* 'ray', *napha:* 'gain'

/bh/ *ra:bh* 'alluvium', *morbha:* 'aloe', *bhokr?o:* 'hole/ cavity'

/th/ *ottha:* 'heavy', *kaltha:rka:* 'stout'

/t?h/ *sort?ha:* 'blunt (of speech)', *t?hekta'a:na:* 'to adjust'

/d?h/ *d?hapa?* 'ajar', *d?hod?hro:* 'hollow (of tree)

/dh/ *dhir?hi:* 'flower bud', *ma:dhri:* 'kite'

/ch/ *nichak* 'abject', *chalko:* 'vain', *geccha:* 'far'

/jh/ *jhongh* 'abyss', *me:jhªrna:* 'to adorn'

/kh/ *khota:* 'nest', *melkha:* 'throat', *nalakh* 'work'

/gh/ *dagha:* 'blot', *ghaska:rna:* 'to abscond'

/r?h/ *nõr?harna:* 'to take one's ablution', *p?:r?he:* 'flute'

(b) Nasalized vowels: Kurukh has nasalized vowels, common in I-A, Tibeto-Burman and other families but not found in Dravidian in general. For example, /i, ?, ã, u/ in *ci:xna:* 'to cry', *b?d?a:* 'wooden bolt for door', *kohã:* 'big', *kura:* 'large earthen pot'.

(c) Initial alveolar and retroflex consonants: Alveolar and retroflex consonants do not occur initially in Dravidian (Zvelebil, 1970). But in Kurukh alveolar consonants /r/ and /l/, and retroflex consonants /t?, t?h, d?, d?h/ occur initially. This is presumably a recent phenomenon.

r?o	'alluvial'
rakrak^{a}rka:	'parched'
lelles	'baby boy'
lun?d?a:	'brush'
t?at?xa:	'mango'
t?okke:	'ankle'
t?hekta'a:na:	'to adjust'
d?hod?hro:	'hollow (of tree)'

(4) Changes in Morphology

(a) Aryanization in word morphology: Kurukh has borrowed several I-A prefixes and suffixes for word formation. Consider the following examples.

an-t?heka:n	'untold'
be-lu:ras	'blockhead/stupid'
ni-saugya:	'delicate'
ku-ber?a:	'late'

ca:ir 'four' + *-o:* → *ca:iro:* 'all the four'

mo:t?h 'obstinate' + *-ai* → *mot?hai* 'obstinacy'

d?o?ga: 'boat' + *-ait* → *d?o?gait* 'boatman'

pi:t?- 'kill' + *-u:* → *pit?u:* 'fatal'

guda: 'pulp' + *-gar* → *gudgar* 'pulpy', etc.

(b) Classifiers: Languages of the Dravidian family do not have nominal classifiers in general. The use of nominal classifiers in Kurukh is an I-A phenomenon. The classifiers *jhan*, *tʔho: / tʔhu:*, *gotʔa:* and *gotʔaʔ* are directly borrowed from I-A languages (Bengali, Sadri, etc.).

jhan is used with 'human' referents; *tʔho: / tʔhu:* and *gotʔaʔ* are used with 'non-human' referents and *gotʔa:* is generally used with inanimate referents. Consider the following examples.

1. pance: ***jhan*** a:lar
   five CLASS man-PL
   'five men'
2. satte: ***gotʔaʔ*** iñjo:
   seven CLASS fish
   'seven fish'
3. ʔ:rʔ ***gotʔa:*** mann
   two CLASS tree
   'two trees'
4. paca:s ***tʔho:/ tʔhu:*** alla:
   fifty CLASS dog
   'fifty dogs'

(*c*) Echo-formation: The phenomenon of echo-word formation in Kurukh seems to be a recent phenomenon for the replacer sound ***–u*** is a loan from Sadri (I-A), whereas "In Dravidian, the echo-word...usually begins with the sequence **ki-* ...(Zvelebil, 1990).

na:d – u:d	'ghost, etc.'
nalna: - ulna:	'dancing, etc.'
bera:m – ura:m	'sick, etc.'

(*d*) Morphologically marked passive: According to Caldwell (1956), "..None of the Dravidian dialects possess any passive particle or suffix or any means of expressing passivity by direct inflexional changes...". But Kurukh forms passive verbs by adding the morpheme ***-r / -ta:r*** to the root. The tense and aspect markers are added after the passive marker.

co:x- 'pluck'	co:x-ta:r- / co:x^{a}-r- 'be plucked'
la:'o- 'beat someone up'	la'o:-r- / la'o-ta:r- 'be beaten up'

(*e*) **Numerical system:** The numerical system in Dravidian in general has the base in 'ten' "with traces of 'octogenal' (base 'eight')" system (Zvelebil, 1990). But Kurukh has the vigesimal number system; higher numbers are counted in twenties (with the base ***kur?i:*** 'twenty') as in Bengali, Sadri and other I-A languages of eastern India.

1. o:nd kur?i: dasse
   one twenty ten
   'thirty (lit., a twenty and a ten)'
2. kur?i: ?:r?
   twenty two
   'forty (lit., two twenties)'
3. ?:r? kur?i: das
   two twenty ten
   'fifty (lit., two twenties and a ten)'
4. ca:ir kur?i:
   four twenty
   'eighty (lit., four twenties)'

(5) Changes in Grammatical System (syntax)

(*a*) **Grammatical gender:** Kurukh has taken the feature of grammatical gender from I-A languages of the region. There are adjectives which agree with nouns for gender. In the case of irrational beings, special words borrowed from I-A languages indicating the sex are used. Consider the following examples.

cad?ra: me:t	'bald man'
cad?ri: mukka:	'bald woman'
cad?ra: xall	'bare field'
bañjha: mann	'barren/fruitless tree'
bañjhi: o:y	'barren cow'
an?d?ra: lakr?a:	'(male) tiger'
bur?hi: lakr?a:	'tigress'

(*b*) **Relative-correlative construction:** Absence of relative pronoun is one of the main characteristics of the

Dravidian family (Caldwell, 1956). Hahn (1900, p.119) had noted that "..Kurukh has no relative pronoun, and no third person personal pronoun – very characteristic Dravidian features."

It seems that under the areal pressure Kurukh has gained the feature of use of relative pronouns from the I-A languages. The interrogative pronouns ***ne:*** 'who (for animates)' and ***je:*** (< Sadri) / ***endra:*** 'who (for inanimates)' are used as the relative pronoun. In temporal constructions the Hindi relative pronoun (of time) ***jab*** 'when' is used. The correlative of ***ne:*** / ***je:*** is usually either ***se:*** 'that' (< Sadri) or the third person pronoun ***a:s*** 'he' / ***a:d*** 'she/it', etc. with different case and number markers. A nominal clause may also take the place of a correlative pronoun. Consider the following examples.

1. ***ne:*** / ***je:*** *ce:ro: barcka: ra'cas* ***se:*** / ***a:s*** *kirrim biccyas.*
   who yesterday came AUX he leave ECV
   'He, who came yesterday, has left'.

2. ***je:*** *purbe: turu: bar'a: helar* ***a:r*** *gahi: bansaj-dim*
   who east from came AUX they of ancestor-DAT
   dravir? ja:itar hindusta:n tara: bar?h-rar.
   Dravidian caste India towards proceed-AGR

   'Those who came from the east, their ancestors were Dravidians, and they moved/proceeded towards India'.

3. ***jab*** *cero: ja:itar,* ***ne:*** *ki: taman a:ryargane hedde: manar a:rya*

   when Chero caste-PL who CP themselves Aryan-PL consider AUX Aryan

   ujjna: tari:kan hocckar rahcar, rohta:sgar?he nu: akraman nañjar.

   living way-ACC learn-AGR AUX-AGR Rohtasgarh at/in attack do-AGR

'When the Cheros, who considered themselves to be like the Aryans, had learnt

the way of living of the Aryans, (then) they attacked the Rohtasgarh (fort)'.

4. *enne: hu: a:lar ra'nar, ne: tamhai adiba:si: bha:kha:n*

such too man-PL are who their tribal language

ambar, sa:dri:n adiba:si: aya? kattha: ba'nar.

abandon-AGR Sadri-ACC tribal mother language say-AGR

'There are such men, who, after having abandoned their tribal languages, call Sadri (their) mother tongue'.

Although Kurukh has retained many Dravidian features, e.g., presence of first person inclusive and exclusive plural (*na:m* and *e:m*), presence of human or epicene plural, etc., but, at the same time, Kurukh has gained many phonological, morphological and syntactic features from I-A languages of the region (Hindi, Sadri, etc.).

The long period of interaction between the Kurukh tribal population and the Sadri/Hindi speakers, and the urbanization and industrialization in Chotanagpur area has brought many linguistic and socio-economic changes in Kurukh. At all levels of linguistic structure, mainly in the lexicon, Kurukh has been highly influenced by the Indo-Aryan languages.

Kurukh has changed in such a way that it has become more homogenized with the surrounding languages. From a typological heterogeneity situation it has moved to a typological homogeneity situation. Kurukh has borrowed features from Indo-Aryan as well as Munda languages, and having done so it has incorporated features of both the language families and thus has become more consistent with the typology of this region rather than with the typology of the family. The changes are language contact induced changes. If these languages were not in contact, these changes would not have arisen. The language has developed differently: instead of loss, it has gained structures by way of both adoption and adaption. The language has changed in a drastic way in order to move towards typological homogeneity of the region.

References

Abbi, Anvita. 1991. "Language contraction, language shrink and language conflation: a case study of Kharia". Paper presented in a seminar organized by the Institute of Advanced Studies, Shimla.

Batsch, Rev.F. 1866. "Language of Dravidian aborigines: notes on the Oraon language". Journal of the Asiatic Society of Bengal, Vol. XXXV, Special no., App. E.

Beames, John. 1966. Comparative grammar of the modern Indo Aryan languages of India. Munshiram Manoharlal, New Delhi.

Bhat, D. N. S. 1965. Kudux pronouns. IL 26: 221-26.

Blain, E. 1975. English-Sadri dictionary. The Society of the Divine Word, Jharsuguda.

Bright, W. 1976. Variation and change in language. Stanford University Press.

Burrow, T. and M. B. Emeneau. 1961. A Dravidian Etymological Dictionary. Oxford University Press.

Caldwell, R. 1956. A comparative grammar of the Dravidian or South-Indian family of languages. Univ. of Madras (Reprint).

Ekka, Francis. 1967. "Language contact : Hindi and Kurux". Bulletin of the Cultural Research Institute, Vol. VI, Nos. 1 & 2.

Hahn, Rev. F. 1900. Grammar of the Kurukh Language. Mittal Publication, New Delhi. (Reprint : 1989).

Mishra, A. K. 1996. Word formation and language change in Kurux. Tara Book Agency, Varanasi.

Shanmugam, S.V. 1971. Dravidian nouns: a comparative study. Annamalai University Press, Annamalainagar.

Subrahmanyam, P. S. 1971. Dravidian verb morphology. Annamalai Univ. Press, Annamalainagar.

Zvelebil, Kamil. 1970. Comparative Dravidian Phonology. The Hague, Mouton.

__________. 1990. Dravidian linguistics: an introduction. Pondicherry Institute of Linguistics and Culture, Pondicherry.

10

Hindi Infinitives

Rajesh Kumar

Introduction

Categorical classification of some of the elements in natural languages is not so clear. Such elements are referred to as mixed category. There has been extensive discussion in the literature on so-called mixed categories represented by English gerund phrases and infinitive phrases in Spanish and Romance languages (Pullum 1991, Lapointe 1998, Malouf 2000 among others), as shown in (1).

(1) a. *John's singing an aria* surprised Mary. (English)

b. No acepto [el susurrar palabras obscenas constantemente] (Spanish)

Neg accept-1sg the whisper words obscene constantly

'I do not accept the constant whispering of obscene words'

As mentioned above there are several analyses of mixed categories, there are some consistent and theory-neutral facts about mixed categories that most of the analysis tries to account for. Mixed categories show verbal properties internally, while externally they have nominal distribution. That is, as we can see from both the example in (1), mixed categories take a verbal complement, that is, internal arguments subcategorized by a verbal head in that the relevant complements carry accusative or dative Case assigned by a verb. In this respect, mixed categories show verbal behavior internally. But at the same time mixed categories show nominal distribution externally in that it functions as a subject or an object of a sentence and complement of preposition or postposition. Even internally mixed categories show partial nominal properties as well since it allows possessive or genitive external argument, which is usually found in the specifier of a noun phrase (Spec, NP). Even though it may not be a universal property, so-called nominalizer uniformity is cross-linguistically observed for example in English, Spanish, and Quechua, etc. as shown in Yoon (1996b). In other words the same (de)verbal form is used in both lexical and phrasal nominalizations. Despite of the mixed properties of mixed categories, mixed categories are not exocentric like a headless construction. They have consistent endocentric phrasal properties which is hard to dispense with in any analysis. Hence most studies try to analyze the mixed categories in accordance with endocentricity. Phrasal coherence is cross-linguistically observed in mixed categories. In other words, there is some point in the structure of the mixed categories that demarcates nominal property from verbal property with no chaotic mixture of verbal and nominal properties.

In this chapter, we present a discussion of Hindi infinitival constructions and show that Hindi infinitives are consistent with regard to the all the properties of mixed categories discussed above. In particular, we argue for the lexical and phrasal nominalizations on the basis of verbal infinitive forms in Hindi. We discuss the internal verbal properties and the external nominal distribution of the infinitival phrases. Hence we claim that the Hindi infinitival phrase has the internal syntax of a VP while externally they behave like an NP. With regard to the analysis of mixed categories, there are two major approaches, lexicalist (e.g, Pullum 1991, Lapointe 1993, 1998, etc.) vs. non-lexicalist approach (Yoon 1996a, b, etc.). Since the focus of this paper is on characterizing Hindi infinitival constructions, we won't argue for either of these two approaches. For the purpose of illustration, we will take non-lexicalist approach for the analysis of Hindi infinitival phrases.

1. Phrasal vs. Lexical Nominalization

1.1 The morphology of the infinitive verb

In this we introduce the verbal morphology of infinitival forms in Hindi. Examples in (2) show the possible conjugations of the verb 'play'.

(2) a. khel-naa
play-Inf
'to play' (infinitive)

b. khel-taa
play-Pres
'plays' (present)

c. khel-aa
play-Perf
'played' (perfect)

d. khel rahaa hai
play
'is playing' (present progressive)

e. khel-te hue
play-Part
'while playing' (participle)

Verb stems ending in '*-naa*' has been analyzed as the infinitival form of the verb (cf. Butt 1994 among others). Hence the verb in (2a) corresponds to the infinitival form of the verb 'play', the one in (2b) third person singular present form, the one in (2c) perfect form, and the verbs in (2d) and (2e) periphrastic expressions of the present progressive and the participle, respectively.

There are certain auxiliary verbs that require infinitival verb forms. For example, the auxiliary verb *cahiye* in (3a), which corresponds to an English auxiliary verb 'should', can co-occur with the verb ending '-naa' only. Also, as shown in (3b), the auxiliary verb *hai* 'is' always takes an infinitive complement in dative subject constructions. Other auxiliaries such as *paRnaa* 'must' also take infinitival complements as shown in (3c). The auxiliary *paRnaa* 'must' inflects for different tenses aspects, numbers, and gender.

(3) a. aap-ko har din kriket khel-naa/*khel-taa/*khel-aa cahiye
you-DAT everyday cricket play-INF/plays/played should.
'You should play cricket everyday'

b. raakesh ko jaa-naa/*jaataa/*gayaa hai
Rakesh DAT go-INF/goes/went is
'Rakesh has to go'

c. mujhe har din skuul aa-naa/*aataa/*aayaa paR-taa hai
Me-DAT everyday school come-INF must (in HAB) is
'I have to come to School everyday'

Therefore following the traditional view, we suggest that the verb ending '*-naa*' are infinitival forms.

In the following section, we will discuss the phrasal nominalization on the basis of the verbal infinitive forms.

1.2 Phrasal nominalization on the basis of the infinitive

In this section we will look at the internal nominal property of the infinitive phrase.

1.2.1 Internal syntax of an NP

In (4) and (5), we show that the infinitive phrase has some internal property of noun phrases.

The subject argument also termed as subjectoid, by Pullum (1991) within the infinitive phrase is followed by a postposition which expresses genitive Case, while in case of pronouns, it is inflected for the genitive form, just like regular noun phrases. That is, the subjectoids of infinitive phrases are exactly like the possessive determiners of ordinary NPs as shown in (4) and (5).

(4) a. mukesh kaa ghar
Mukesh Poss house
'Mukesh's house'

b. mukesh kii kitaab[1]
Mukesh Poss book
'Mukesh's book'

c. tumhaarii kaar
your car
'your car'

(5) a. tumhaaraa novel likha-naa mere liye ek suprise thaa
your novel write-INF me for one surprise was
'Your writing a novel was a surprise for me'
(=/= 'Writing your novel was a surprise for me')

b. tumhaaraa gaanaa gaa-naa mujh-ko achaa nahiiN lagataa hai
your song sing-INF me-DAT good not seem-HAB is
'I don't like your singing a song'
(=/= 'I don't like singing your song')

c. mukesh kaa sigret pii-naa mujh ko achaa nahiiN lagtaa hai
Mukesh GEN cigarette drink-INF me to like not seem is
'I don't like Mukesh's smoking a cigarette'

d. raakesh ka biif khaa-naa uske dostoN ko pasand nahiiN thaa
rakesh GEN beef eat-ING he-DAT friend-OBL to like not was
'Rakesh's eating beef upset his friends'
(=/= 'Eating Rakesh's beef upset his friends')

As English parallel shows in (5), the subjectoids are not associated with the following noun but with the whole infinitive phrase and function as a subject of the phrase.

Hence the infinitive phrases in (5) suggest the tentative structure (6):

(6)

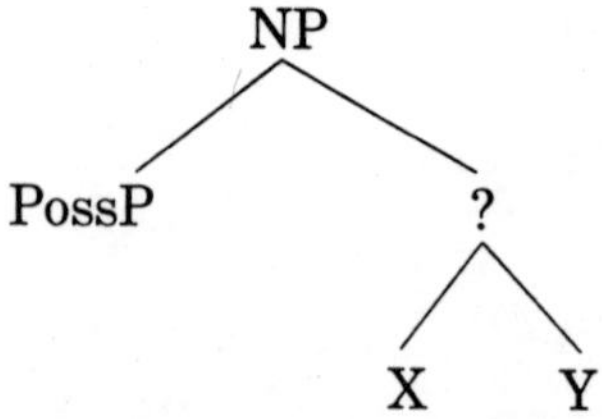

The exact picture of the internal structure will be drawn after discussing the internal properties of the infinitive phrase.

Next we discuss the external nominal properties of the infinitive phrase. That is, why should the infinitive phrase be a Noun Phrase externally as depicted in (6)?

1.2.2 External syntax of a NP

Let us look at the external syntax of infinitives as an NP. No extraction is allowed from the subjectoid in an infinitive phrase just like a possessive in a canonical NP cannot be extracted (Ross's left branch condition), similar to other languages such as English, Korean, etc. As shown in (7a), possessive noun phrases cannot be relativized. Similarly, possessive phrase within the infinitive phrase cannot be extracted as shown in (7b) where the possessive phrase is extraposed.

(7) a. *raakesh kaa jo mohan ko t ghar pasand nahiiN hai
rakesh GEN that Mohan to house like not is
'Rakesh's that Mohan hated t house
(Intended: 'Rakesh's house that Mohan hated')

b. *t sigret pii-naa mujh ko achaa nahiiN lagtaa hai mukesh kaa
cigarette drink-INF me to like not seem is Mukesh GEN
'Of Mukesh, I don't like (his) smoking a cigarette'
(Intended: 'I don't like Mukesh's smoking a cigarette.')

Infinitive phrases can be the complements of postpositions, which can take only noun phrases as their complement as shown in (8).

(8) a. kamrae meN koi nahiiN hai
room in anybody not is
'There is no one in the room.'

b. raakesh ke liye ek kursii laao
Rakesh for one chair bring-IMP
'Bring a chair for Rakesh.'

c. tebul par kyaa hai
table on what is
'What is on the table?'

Exactly the same postpositions used in (8) can appear after the infinitive phrases, as shown in (9). If postpositions follow the verb forms other than infinitive, such a construction is ungrammatical.

(9) a. [raakesh ke biif khaa-ne/*khaate] meN uske dostoN ko
rakesh GEN beef eat-INF/while eating in he-Gen friend-OBL to
koi aaptti nahiiN hai
any objection not is
'Rakesh's friends do not have any objection in his eating beef.'

b. [raakesh ke biif khaane/*khaata] par uske dostoN ko
rakesh GEN beef eat-INF/eats on he-DAT friend-OBL to
koi aaptti nahiiN hai
any objection not is
'Rakesh's friends do not have any objection on his eating beef.'

c. [raakesh ko biif khaane/*khayaa] ke liye uske
rakesh DAT beef eat-INF/ate for he-Gen
dostoN ne majboor kiyaa
friend-OBL ERG forced
'Rakesh's friends forced him to eat beef.'

Another piece of evidence in support of the nominal status of infinitival phrases comes from the variation on the ending *-naa* in infinitive verbs. In Hindi, nouns, ending with *-aa* show systematic variation with *-aa* changing to oblique form *-e* when followed by a postposition. For example, as shown in (10), regular noun phrases ending with *–aa* become ungrammatical without replacing the ending by the oblique form when they are followed by postpositions.

(10) a. *laRk*aa* ko
laRk*e* ko
boy to
'to a boy'

b. * tang*aa* par
tang*e* par
horse cart on
'on the horse cart'

Similarly we can find exactly the same variation in infinitives when they are followed by postpositions as shown in (11).

(11) a. [raakesh ke biif khaa-*ne*/**naa*] meN uske dostoN ko
Rakesh GEN beef eat-INF in he-DAT friend-OBL to
koi aaptti nahiiN hai
any objection not is
'Rakesh's friends do not have any objections in his eating beef.'

b. [raakesh ke biif khaa-*ne*/**naa*] par uske dostoN ko
Rakesh GEN beef eat-INF on he-DAT friend-OBL to
koi aaptti nahiiN hai
any objection not is
'Rakesh's friends do not have any objections on his eating beef.'

b. raakesh ne sariita se [paani laa-*ne*/**naa*] ko kahaa
Rakesh ERG Sarita to water bring-INF for say-PST-mas
'Rakesh told Sarita to bring water.'

In addition, in Hindi noun phrases, genitive markers usually appear between two nouns. Similarly as we can see from the data (12), a genitive marker should appear when the infinitive phrase is followed by a noun phrase, and the infinitive form changes to the oblique form due to the intervening genitive marker which can also be analyzed as a postposition.

(12) ramesh ki diimaagi haalat ko dekhte hue maine [[dost ko apmaanit
Ramesh GEN mental situation DAT see PRSP I-ERG friend DAT insult
karne] (**ki** baat) **ki** andekhi] kar di
do-INF GEN matter GEN disregard do give-PST
'When considering Ramesh's mental situation, I disregarded insulting his friend'

Finally, we can find another evidence for the external nominal status of the infinitival phrases on the basis of the coordination. Noun phrases are coordinated by the conjunct *aur* 'and' as shown in (13).

(13) a. [raam aur shyaam] skuul jaa rahe haiN
Raam and Shyamm school go PPRP are
'Ram and Shyam are going to School.'

b. maiN [seb aur kele] khaataa huuN
I apples and bananas eat-HAB am
'I eat apples and bananas.'

Note, however, that regular noun phrases can be coordinated with infinitive phrases as shown in (14).

(14) a. [[raakesh kaa kitaab paRnaa] aur [uskii imaandaari] ne]
rakesh GEN book read-INF and his honesty ERG
mujhe cakit kar diyaa
me-DAT surprise do give-PERF
'Rakesh's reading the book and his honesty surprised me.'

b. [[raakesh kaa aalas] aur [uskaa der se ghar aa-naa]]
rakesh GEN laziness and his late home come-INF
uski maaN ko acchaa nahiiN lagtaa hai
his mother to good not feel is
'Rakesh's laziness and his coming home late bother his mother.'

The possibility of coordinating NPs and Infinitive phrase again shows that the constituent [POSS X V-inf] as a whole is nominal.

Hence the discussion so far strongly suggests that the infinitive phrase has the external distribution of noun phrases. Before examining the internal properties of the infinitive phrase, let us point it out that with regard to the coordination fact, the sentence in (15) also suggests that the infinitive phrase has the internal structure of the VP. As far as the coordination is concerned, the bracketed phrase corresponds to the VP coordination.

(15) [raakesh kaa [ghar bec-naa aur kar khariid-naa]] uski patnii ko
rakesh GEN house sell-INF and car buy-INF his wife to
pasand nahiiN thaa

like not was

'Rakesh's selling the house and buying the car upset his wife'

The data examined so far lead us to the conclusion that the syntactic structure of the infinitive phrase requires both NP externally and VP internally. Before we draw any conclusion with regard to the syntactic structure of the infinitive phrase, however, we need to get more convincing evidence for the internal VP properties of the infinitival phrase.

1.2.3 Internal syntax of a VP

In this section we discuss that the infinitival phrase also has verbal properties internally.

In other words, the part of the infinitival phrase after the possessive/genitive phrase behaves just like a VP.

As we already saw in the preceding discussions, the infinitive form of the verb takes a bare NP as its complement as far as it can take one. As the contrast (16b) shows, the genitive marker cannot intervene between the infinitive verb and its object complement, suggesting the verbal status of the infinitive itself.

(16) a. raakesh kaa kitaab paR-naa
Rakesh Gen book read-INF
'Rakesh's reading the book'

b. *raakesh kaa kitaab kaa paR-naa
Rakesh Gen book Gen read-INF
'Rakesh's reading of the book'

Another piece of evidence in support of the internal VP status of infinitival phrases of Hindi comes from the fact that it can be modified by adverbs but not by adjectives. As the example in (17) show, adverbs do not modify nouns while the adjectives do. The reverse is true for verbs. That is, the adjectives do not modify verbs while adverbs do. Hence, if infinitival phrases have internal verbal properties, the same adverbs disallowed in (17) should be permitted while the adjectival modification allowed in (17) should not be permitted in the context of infinitival phrases. This prediction is borne out as shown in (18).

(17) a. *jor se aavaaz
loudly sound
*'loudly voice'

a'. tej aavaaz
loud sound
'loud voice'

b. *dhiire kar
slowly car
*'slowly car'

b'. dhiimii kar
slow car
'slow car'

(18) a. raakesh kaa *jor se* kitaab paR-naa
rakesh GEN loudly book read-INF
'Rakesh's reading the book loudly.'

a'. *raakesh kaa *tej* kitaab paR-naa
rakesh GEN loud book read-INF

b. suniitaa kaa *dhiire* kar calaa-naa
suniitaa GEN slowly car drive-INF
'Sunita's driving a car slowly.'

b'. *suniitaa kaa *dhimii* kar calaa-naa
Sunita GEN slow car drive-INF

Finally, infinitival phrases allow the VP-internal scrambling while the noun phrases do not allow such scrambling. As shown in (19), the direct object and the dative object of the verb can be switched.

(19) a. raakesh ka sariitaa ko ek kitaab de-naa
Rakesh GEN Sarita DAT one book give-INF
'Rakesh's giving a book to Sarita.'

b. Rakesh ka ek kiitaab sariitaa ko de-naa
Rakesh GEN one book Sarita DAT give-INF
On the contrary, the scrambling inside the regular noun phrase is not allowed as the contrast in (20) shows.

(20) a. raakesh kaa city kaa vidhvans
rakesh Gen city Gen destruction
'Rakesh's destruction of the city.'

b. *city kaa rakesh kaa vidhvans
city Gen rakesh Gen destruction

Therefore the data examined in this section clearly suggest that the infinitival phrase should have the structure of VP internally. Putting the discussion so far together, we can propose the following structure for the infinitive phrase, which is not final version and should be reconsidered with regard to endocentricity and phrasal coherence.

(21)

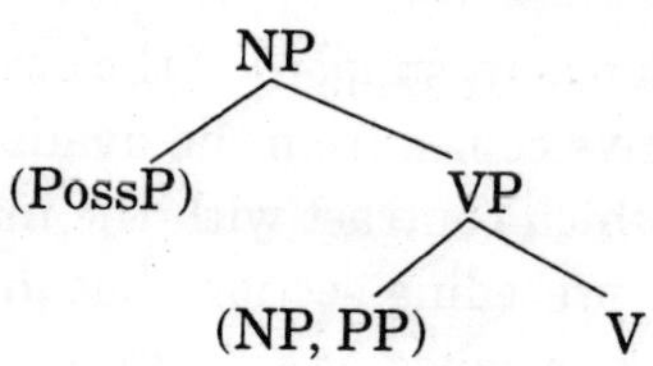

1.3 Lexical nominalizations

In this section, we show that de-verbal lexical noun is also derived on the basis of the infinitival form, which confirms so-called 'Nominalizer Uniformity' pointed out in Yoon (1996 a, b). That is, the same infinitival form of the verb, which functions as the verbal head of the phrasal nominalization, can also function as a lexical noun, i.e. de-verbal noun.

The infinitival form of the verb itself can appear where regular noun phrases can occur, i.e., subject, object position of transitive verb, and in particular can be followed by postpositions. That is, they show nominal distribution, as shown in (22).

(22) a. [likha-naa] meraa shOkh hai

Write-INF my hobby is
'Writing is my hobby.'

b. mujh-ko [likh-naa] pasand hai
me-DAT write-INF like is
'I like writing.'

c. mai [likh-naa] pasand kar-taa huN
I write-INF like do-Hab am
'I like writing.'

d. [gaa-ne] meN majaa aataa hai
Sing-INF in enjoyment come is
'Singing is fun.'

Hence, the infinitival verb in (22a) functions as a subject of the sentence, the ones in (22b-c) function as objects of conjunct verbs (light verbs) and the one in (22d) is a complement of the postposition.

Another piece of evidence in support of the status of a lexical noun of the infinitive comes from the availability of the adjective modifiers, which contrast with the infinitival phrases as we saw in the preceding section that infinitival phrases cannot be modified by adjectives. As in the English, once the infinitival form of the verb is modified by an adjective like in (23a) and (23c), it does not function as a verb which is related to the event or process but it functions as a regular noun which is related to the result. On the contrary if it is modified by an adverb like (23b) and (23d), it corresponds to the verb which is the head of the infinitive phrase as we saw in the preceding sections.

(23) a. raakesh kaa tej gaanaa
rakesh GEN loud sing-INF
'Rakesh's loud song.' (=/= 'Rakesh's singing loudly.')

b. raakesh kaa jor se gaa-naa
rakesh GEN loudly sing-INF
'Rakesh's singing loudly.' (=/= 'Rakesh's loud song.')

c. raakesh kaa mahNgaa khaanaa
rakesh GEN expensive eat-INF
'Rakesh's expensive food.'

d. raakesh kaa dhire khaa-naa
rakesh GEN slowly eat-INF
'Rakesh's eating slowly'

Another strong evidence for the claim that the infinitival form of the verb can be de-verbal lexical noun comes from the possibility of the attachment of the plural marker –*e* to de-verbal counterpart of infinitives, while the verbal head of infinitival phrases cannot take the plural marker as shown in (24).[2] As pointed out, adjectival modification of infinitives in (24a) and (24c) renders infinitives as de-verbal lexical noun and hence they can be pluralized. On the contrary, true infinitive verbs in (24b) and (24d) cannot be pluralized.

(24) a. raakesh ke tej gaane
rakesh GEN loud sing-INF-Pl
'Rakesh's loud songs'

b. *rakesh ke jor se gaane
rakesh GEN loudly sing-INF-Pl
'*Rakesh's singings loudly'

c. rakesh ke mahNge khaane
rakesh GEN expensive eat-INF-Pl
'Rakesh's expensive food'

d. *rakesh ke dhire khaane
rakesh GEN slowly eat-INF-Pl
'*Rakesh's eatings slowly'

Furthermore we can get the evidence for de-verbal lexical noun status of an infinitive the fact that the lexical noun counterpart of an infinitive can be modified by demonstratives, in contrast to infinitival phrases in which demonstrative modification is not allowed. Hence, as shown in (25), de-verbal lexical nouns modified by demonstratives in (25a) and (25c) are grammatical while the infinitival verb modified by demonstratives in (25b) and (25d) are ungrammatical.

(25) a. vah tej gaanaa
that loud sing-INF
'that loud song'

b. *vah jor se gaanaa
that loudly sing-INF
'that singing loudly'

c. vah mahNgaa khaanaa
that expensive eat-INF
'that expensive food'

d. *vah dhire khaanaa
that slowly eat-INF
'that eating slowly'

Final evidence for lexical noun status of infinitives can be found in the possibility of the modification by a restrictive relative clause. Infinitival phrases cannot be modified by the restrictive relative clause. However, de-verbal noun counterpart of infinitives can be modified by the restrictive relative clauses as shown in (26). De-verbal lexical noun modified by a relative clause in (26a) and (26c) are grammatical while infinitival phrases modified by relative clauses in (26b) and (26d) are degraded in grammaticality judgment.

(26) a. raakesh kaa tej gaanaa jo kisii ko pasand nahiiN hai
rakesh GEN loud sing-INF that anybody DAT like not is
'Rakesh's loud song that nobody likes'

b. *?raskesh kaa jor se gaa-naa jo kisii ko pasand nahiiN hai
rakesh GEN loudly sing-INF that anybody DAT like not is
'Rakesh's singing loudly that nobody likes'

c. raakesh kaa mahNgaa khaanaa jo kisii ko pasand nahiiN hai

rakesh GEN expensive eat-INF that anybody DAT like not is
'Rakesh's expensive food that nobody likes'

d. *?raakesh kaa dhiire khaa-naa jo kisii ko pasand nahiiN hai
rakesh GEN slowly eat-INF that anybody DAT like not is
'Rakesh's eating slowly that nobody liked'

Therefore, the discussion in this section strongly suggests that the same infinitival form of the verb that is used in infinitival phrase can undergo lexical nominalization and hence can function just like a regular noun. This conclusion also suggests that the nominalizer uniformity, which was pointed out in Yoon (1996a), holds in Hindi as well. That is, the infinitival form of the verb can be the anchor of both lexical and phrasal nominalizations.

1.4 The structure of infinitive phrases

The discussions in this chapter so far suggest that, we come to the conclusion that Hindi infinitive phrases have nominal properties externally as well as verbal properties internally. On the basis of this conclusion, we've come up with the plausible structure of Hindi infinitive phrase (27), repeated here.

(27)

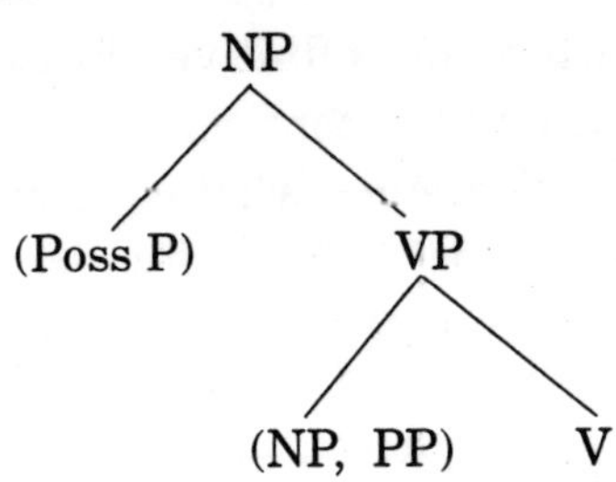

However, one obvious problem of this structure is that it fails to maintain endocentricity, which is central to all incarnations of phrase structures of x-bar. Hence the structure in (27) comes to regard infinitive phrase as headless construction. If endocentricity is the central to the theory with regard to phrase structure and Hindi infinitival phrases are far more like headed than headless construction, then the structure in (27) cannot be maintained any more. Then the next plausible structure would be to posit the (null) nominal head as shown in (28).

(28)

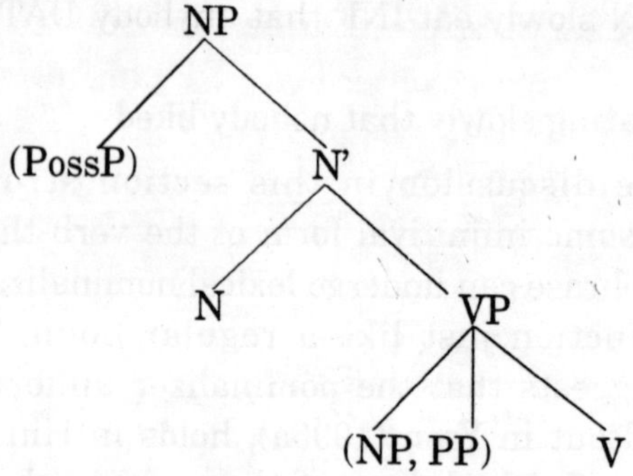

At the first sight, the structure (28) looks good since it maintains the central assumption of the x-bar theory namely, endocentricity, that is, it analyzes the infinitive phrase as headed construction. To the extent it maintains endocentricity, we can say it is desirable. However, it is not free from problems. The crucial problem of (28) is that it makes wrong predictions. Due to the fact that we posit N', it predicts that N'-adjuncts can occur within infinitival phrases. However, as we saw in the previous discussions, N' modifiers cannot occur within the infinitive phrase. Also coordination and relativization facts confirm the lack of N' within the infinitive phrase. Therefore, what we need is the structure that captures the external nominal distribution but has no nominal structure inside whatsoever. The most plausible one seems to be a DP. That is, we postulate the null head for DP, which is sister to VP as shown in (29). The Possessive NP is assumed to be assigned genitive Case under Spec-Head Agreement with the functional head D, which is the widely held assumption. Due to this outer layer of DP, infinitive phrases are predicted to show nominal distribution while allowing genitive subjectoid. Due to the lack of NP or

N' internally or the existence of VP only internally, however, it also predicts that no nominal modifiers are allowed inside the infinitive phrase and it shows verbal properties only. Hence the structure (29) not only maintains endocentricity of the x-bar theory, but it also makes correct predictions and captures empirical generalizations. Furthermore, due to this hierarchical structure, that is, outer layer DP plus internal VP, phrasal coherence naturally follows.

(29)

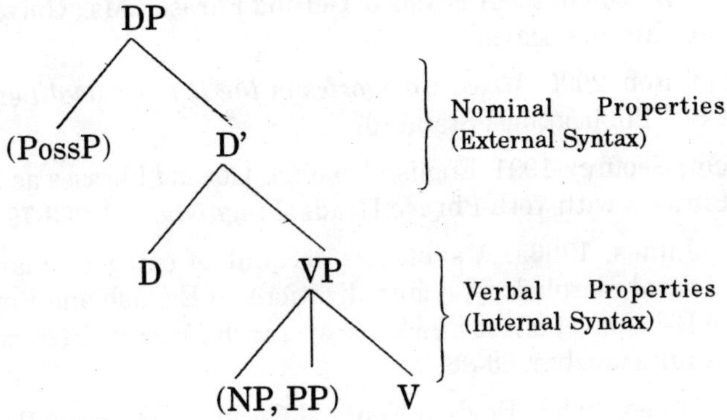

2. Conclusion

In this chapter we discussed Hindi infinitival constructions as an example of mixed categories. Throughout the chapter, we have shown that the Hindi infinitival phrases have internal syntax of a VP, the partial internal syntax of an NP and the external distribution of an NP. Then we concluded that we should recognize both VP and NP structure with regard to infinitival phrases. This conclusion, however, does not warrant exocentric structure of infinitival phrases. Infinitive phrases are too endocentric to analyze as the exocentric structure. Hence proposing plausible phrase structures of Hindi infinitival phrases while pointing out the problems of each proposal, we come to the phrase structure that consists of DP outer layer plus internal VP. The proposed phrase structure provides the principled account of the empirical generalizations found in Hindi infinitival phrases, at the same time they maintain theoretical assumptions of the phrase structure.

References

Butt, M. 1994. *The structure of complex predicates in Urdu*, Dissertations in Linguistics, CSLI Publications, Stanford, California. Doctoral thesis at Stanford University.

Lapointe, Steven. 1993. Dual Lexical Categories and the Syntax of Mixed Category Phrases. In A. Kathol & M. Bernstein (eds.), *Proceedings of ESCOL*, 199-210.

Lapointe, Steven. 1998. Dual Lexical Categories Vs. Phrasal Conversion in the Analysis of Gerund Phrases. Ms., University of California, Davis.

Malouf, Rob. 2000. *Mixed Categories in the Hierarchical Lexicon*. CSLI Publications: Stanford.

Pullum, Geoffrey. 1991. English Nominal Gerund Phrases as Noun Phrases with Verb-Phrase Heads. *Linguistics* 29: 763-799.

Yoon, James. 1996a. A syntactic account of category-changing phrasal morphology: nominalizations in English and Korean. In H-D Ahn et al. (eds.), *Morphosyntax in Generative Grammar*. Seoul: Hanshin, 63-86.

Yoon, James. 1996b. English Nominal Gerund Phrases as Phrasal Zero Derivations. *Linguistics* 34: 339-356.

There are three different morphological variants of the GEN/POSS marker *ka* in Hindi: *ka* (masculine singular), *ke* (masculine plural) and *ki* (feminine singular or plural).

Similarly to other languages, the pluralization of the deverbal noun is not a productive process. In particular, for the lack of the pluralization of the phrasal nominalzation, we can appeal to semantics. Given the observation Grimshaw (1990) with regard to the 'complex event nominals' that plural marking is disallowed even in purely nominal constructions, we could invoke semantics to rule out plurality on the infinitive phrases as well as English gerund heads.

11

'What is Under New Sun?' Nation and Narration

Shailendra Kumar Singh

Introduction

In the western countries minority ethnicity is something 'private' while majority ethnicity is a 'public' phenomenon. Looking at the texture of western pluralism, one is forced to conclude that it is a potential source of destabilization in the individual makeup. Wretchedness of hyphenation, which is part and parcel of western pluralism, needs to be examined more carefully. Perhaps, even more naively, such fundamental questions as 'Was it always so?' and 'Why, when or how did it become so?' need to be raised. At this juncture it is interesting to see how Smolicz (1979: 95-96) gave an account of this problem:

> "The terms American, Canadian, and Australian have come to refer to the person's current allegiance to a nation state with its political institutions and economic structures, while labels such as Irish, Ukrainian and Italian indicate ethnic ancestry and cultural traditions in other areas of life such as family, friendship, religion, language and manners. Viewed in this way, the two types of identities are not mutually exclusive' it is quite possible for a person to identify himself (SIC!) as both Irish and American, Ukrainian and Canadian, Italian and Australian"

Therefore any discussion concentrating identity and national fabrics of India must represent a break with traditional models. At the turn of new century time is probably ripe to attempt to bring these issues into a thorough inquiry. A thorough introspection will certainly help us, in a refreshingly new way, in dealing with the insularity between East and West and protecting the interest of each group and stopping one from running over other. Since heterogeneous and poly-glossic societies such as those that go into making India a polity distinct from the typically singular western societies in many fundamental ways (Singh and Singh: 1999), these two kinds of society deserve absolutely different kinds of theoretical modeling in discussing the notion of identity. This work does not take any either-or position in favor of plurality that exists either in the West or in the East. Aversion for ours reveals ones ignorance and arrogance. This world can not be found fault with solely on the basis of what has been said or what is available in that world. If the 'First World' is a purist's dream and viewed as integrative then the 'Third World' is meta-cognitive and a culturalist's ideology (Singh, 2001). One can conclude with firm conviction that a thesis that guided, consciously or unconsciously, so much past research on identity formation and national fabric, was, to a large extent, a result of faux pas generalization from the limited western experiences.

1. Begin with the West

Bromley (1984:9) says self-identification is usually denoted by the term 'ethononym' derived from the word 'ethnos'. Ethnonymic self-identification is what he calls is endoethnonyms and it may differ from excoetnonyms, that is, ethnonyms given by other people. He gives example of ethnos with the endoethnonym as "Deutsch" so named because of "nemtsy in Russian, "allemagne" in French, "tedesco" in Italian. Bromley further realizes that this condition of self-identification may prove insufficient for identifying ethnos. He opens two other possibilities: 1) Politonym denoting "all people (citizens) living within the boundaries of one or another social organism ... or political formation" (p:10), and, 2) Toponym denoting "the group's self identification originating from the name of the territory it inhabits" (ibid, 10). In that case Belgians and French provide us with examples of one's politonyms. His theory becomes more complex when he says: when a group of people move outside the original settlement, both politonyms and toponyms are often not retained by the second and further generations. He gives an example "when the children of Russian settlers in Siberia resettle in the European part of the USSR they will call themselves Russians, and not Siberians; that is, they will miss their toponyms (Siberians) and will retain their ethnonym Russian" (p:10). In certain conditions all three or two coincide. As he says: "When the politonym of a group of settlers is retained from several generations, this means that the given self-identification is also the ethnonyms. The coincidence of politonyms and ethnonyms is especially characteristics of relatively mono-ethnical states: for instance, the words "Frenchman" ("Francaise") or "Italian" ("Italiano") are both the politonym and ethnonym" (Ibid, 10).

Skutnabb-Kangas uses the term endoethnonmy for the Finns in Finland using for themselves Finnish ("Suomalaiset"). "The Finns" can thus denote all three: ethnonym, politonym and toponym. According to her ethnonym' indicates the ethnic group of Finnish-speaking Finns in Finland in opposition to "Finland-Swedes", "suomenruotsalaiset" in Sweden and "finlandssvenskar" in Swedish. It declares all citizens of the state of Finland as politonym' regardless of their language or ethnic group whereas as `toponyms' includes all those who live in Finland. What emerges from the above description is that convergence of toponym, politonym and ethnonym is a major problem to find out the implication of self-identification in many cases (especially, for the Finnish-speaking Finns in Sweden). It is a futile exercise to try to do it linguistically. Therefore, it is reasonable to leave the politonym part by asking people themselves about their group affiliation or citizenship. But one can find another problem if someone changes nationality, whereas many remain Finnish citizens. Then, how can we differentiate between the politonym and ethnonym? What will happen in this situation: A Finnish - speaking Finn in Sweden describes himself a "completely Swedish" person. This could be interpreted as his ethnonym, politonym and toponym. But, problems do not end here: such a contrast does not help in clarifying the meaning for those who have not changed their nationality. The main difficulty then remains as to how to differentiate politonym from ethnonym, particularly for those who have not changed their nationality. As a sample it is interesting to mention at Skutnabb-Kangas (1987) empirical investigation about self-identification of Finns in Sweden, for whom complete switch over to Swedish would signal assimilation and would be mainly interpreted as an ethnonym whereas complete retention of only Finnish would signal segregation. In comparison, the other combinations such as Swedish and also Finnish, Finnish and also Swedish or both Finnish and Swedish signal tendencies towards integration. In this connection, the basic difference between Swedish-Finn and Indians living with labels such as Bengali, Bihari, Tamilian, Marathi, etc situations is that signaling of these processes in the first one raises certain inter-national issues whereas in the latter one it is restricted to the state level and the issue is intra-national. Assimilation and segregation tendencies of Swedish- Finns provoke a trivial question of hyphenation in-betweens, that is, whether they belong to this country or that country. The reverse is true in Indian case. For any Indian within India, assimilation, at the surface level, might provoke a sense of uproot-ness but super ordinate marker, say, 'Indian', is always intact and undisturbed.

According to Skutnabb-Kangas (1987) variable identification is the best solution. That would vary depending on to whom or where the identity is presented.

That is, for a person A or in country 1 one could define himself/herself as X, or X than Y; or Y but also X. If this problem of identification is viewed from the country of origin then only ethnonym remains but not toponym and politonym. But if it is viewed from the point of new country then it may be toponym, politonym, or ethnonym or combination of all three. Whatever it may be, self-identification in hyphenated form cannot be avoided here. For her, this hyphenation denotes some sort of a hierarchy as indicated in the following figure of Greek-American :

1.

E	P	T	Greek (ethnonym only if seen from Greece point of view) -
E	P	T	American (ethnonym, politonym and toponym, seen from USAs point of view)

2.

E	P	T	Irish (ethnonym)
E	P	T	American (politonym and toponym)

She recalls various lacunas in this pluralistic model. Any permanent solution for 'hyphenation' seems to be remote. It is almost impossible to conclude whether hyphenation will precede identity or whether it will follow. She strongly says that this framework operates also on monistic contexts and is not typical of only western societies. She suggests two changes are needed to prevail: firstly, majority ethnicity has to become conscious and; secondly, a purely monistic view has to be altered. If these two changes are made, it is possible to conceive of a space where one could belong to two (or more) ethnoses without any of these ethnoses accusing them of lacking in loyalty because of their other allegiances. However, she accepts that this ideal condition prevails as a rule in many Asian and African countries but it seems to be not there in the European or Europeanized contexts.

Therefore, her suggestion to bring changes to prevail real pluralism in western countries seems to be a conditional solution. In fact, she fails to understand as to why they can't be described in UN-hyphenated ways. In India, on the contrary, when a group of people move outside the original settlement within the country all upper levels, viz. ethnonym, politonym and typonym, are preserved. This may be presented diagrammatically as follows:

A.

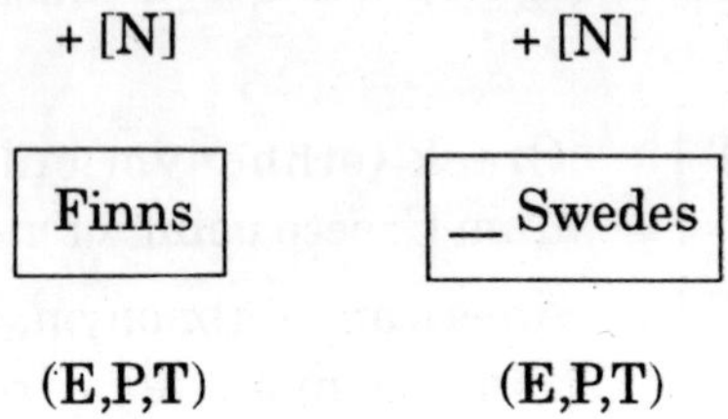

B.

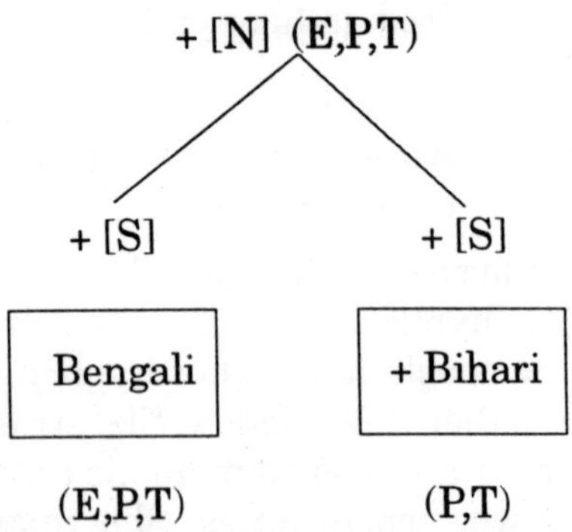

+[N] = nation

+[S] = State

Finns, Swedes and the two Concerned Minorities

Immigration (change of permanent residence to another country) and migration (temporary residence away from country and place) are the two phenomena that have created multilingualism in many western countries. As a result, many second-generation migrants experience marginality and a feeling of have-nots becomes a permanent features of their private and common 'selves'. It remains crucial to see how and to what extent, they eventually establish their own identity in generating hyphenated existence. A few multilingual countries can be cited as an example here:

Nation Linguistic groups-

Nation	Linguistic groups
Switzerland:	German, French, Italian, Romansch
Finland:	Swedish, Finnish
Belgium:	Flemish, French, German
Canada	English, French

In each of the resolution reviewed above, we have encountered identity- in terms of current political affiliation, returning to root, ethic memories and loyalty – as a potential source of destabilization in the individual make up.

2. Other side of the Globe: Remodeling Typological Schemata

Differences can be exhibited systematically by formulating typological **schemata of** ecological variables. In so doing, I think we would produce, in effect, a framework of variables, which would serve to illuminate marking features of self-identification at different levels. One could imagine, as well, that such scaffolding could be used to inform and guide relevant theoretical assumptions for demarcation. The following assumptions could be proposed:

1. A comprehensive and multidisciplinary analysis of ethnonym, toponym and politonym will be intrinsically useful.
2. Emerging generalities may be found which would permit comparision and classification of different contexts under certain rubrics.

It is now possible to move a bit further onward. In what follows, let us make the best use of variables as category labels, which are also available as a general framework of ecological factors and realized, in a hierarchical order.

A. Demographic variables:	home, community, region, state, any other subordinate boundaries and nation.
B. Linguistic variables: ↓	mother language home language, community language, state language, national language, traditional language, institutional language, colonial language, caste language, class language
C. Social political variables: ↓	panchayat, tha:na:, ta:luka, jila: state, nation.
D. Socio-cultural variables: ↓	Ancestry, clan, caste, religion, nation.
E. Social-Psychological :	commitments for preserving own traits, tolerance, strong integrative tendency, national feeling

One can point out that there are many other perhaps more subtle, but still important variables which operate in this context. Returning, then to our objective, it can be predicted that without describing the linguistic ecology as a whole, it would be almost impossible to draw the boundary of differences. Typological schemata has a number of distinct analytical advantages from Indian point of view: a) it provides a dynamic bridges between objective and subjective approaches to the definition of INDIAN identity and (b) accounts for similarity in the construction of collective identity. Such a model is helpful not only in exhibiting dynamic role of these variables in identity formation but also help in understanding political, demographic, linguistic and socio-cultural fabrics of India as a whole. Admittedly, through this project objective as well as subjective meanings in identity creation, projection and identification can well be explored. As a general guide to the analysis of ecological variables relating to construction of identity at the national level, the following agenda can be proposed which account for:

1. Preconditions of national identity, namely those factors which account for collective identity.
2. Bases of internal distinctiveness and uniqueness.
3. Conditions which block conflict, hyphenation, and anomie of identity.
4. Likelihood of success

Typological schemata of ecological variables are needed because there are wide varieties of factor and ways in which Indians identify variably and distinctively among themselves being sufficiently Indian and insider. Metamorphosing and reduplicating of identity features do not disbar either from the apexial marking or from any other available in the hierarchical ordering. At each level a new sense of positivism prevails without denying one another. Similarly, marked features for one do not necessarily act the same for others either at the corresponding level or even at the uneven level.

3. Paradox of Construction

Let us be sure that it is still in beginning phase and should be seen as preliminary sketches. This, then, is the state of affairs at the moment. Clearly, much more work needs to be done before a useful typology results. I believe that a comprehensive typology would be an useful tool for description and comparison, leading to more complete conceptualization of identity. These questions will necessarily help in process building upon previous insights and will also involve a considerable search of relevant literature:

1. How highly regarded are the levels such as Kashmiri, Tamilian, Gujrati, etc?
2. To what extent do the following groups [as above] correlate themselves with the super-ordinate marker [Indian] ?
3. How highly regarded are the levels such as Bihar, UP, Himachal Pradesh, Utteranchal, Jharkhand, etc ?
4. How highly regarded and differentiated are the levels such as Kanauji, Kumauni, Garhwali, Bhojpuri, Braj, Awadhi, Bhojpuri, Maithili, Magahi, Sadan, Kortha, Madaya Pradesh, Chattisgarhi, Bagheli, Rajstani, marwari, Dhundari, Mewari, Malvi, Rahari, Mandeali, Sirmauri, Kului, Chameali, etc ?
5. How highly Sanskrit, Urdu and English are regarded as markers of self-identification, self- categorization and self-projection at ethnonymical, toponymical and politonymical levels?
7. How Konkani, Santhali and Sindhi are identified at intermediate or subordinate levels?
8. How and in which conditions linguistic pockets such as Saurastri in TamilNadu and Bengali in Benaras are surviving?

In an attempt to answer these questions, one also has to have a clear cut answer for the following also:

A. How do Indian evaluate the importance of language as compared to religion, race, territory as a marker of collective as well as individual identity?

B. Under what conditions India as a whole assumes greater importance to ethno-national communities?

C. What are the causative variables that combine the nation into ethnonymical, politonymical and toponymical units?

D. What are the instruments of nation building?

E. How and under conditions maintenance of linguistic pluralism are carried at trans-ethnic political unit?

3.1. Possible Typology

To substantiate a better analytical perspective, let us begin with the formulation of these three categories, which may well be labeled as indigenous: 1) Super-ordinate: national (culminated) 2) Indoor: state (equidistant) and 3) Base: pedestal (core or grass root)

These orders presumably explain why Indian-ness supersedes various indigenous idioms either at the subordinate levels or at the grassroots levels. This is why any expressions of political ideology derived or based upon western observations like non-functional models in the process of nation building. Here point to be noted is that the trans-generational consciousness of togatherness was derived from trans-historicity stretching back to immemorial times, which has transcended in the fuzzy order of nation building. The heart of the matter is this: for Indians the conditions are reasonably favorable to attach at a time with apex, indoors and base levels without accusing each other. This can be shown diagrammatic:

Indian

Bounded	territory
	Extension
Apexial	Integration Output
Indoor	Expansion
	Demographic
	Freedom of choice
	Socio-cultural
Surfacial	

The ramifications of ecological variables make the substance of identity an enigmatic subject. Most importantly, therefore, issues which are to be investigated: 1) as to what are the factors and preconditions which are likely to be operational in ensuing a 'collective identity' in such a diversity, 2) what motivates Indians to identify themselves differently at different levels keeping preceding and following identities intact. Variables are toponymically, politonymically and ethnonymically mutually enforcing and re-enforcing because of trans-generationality.

At the heart of each Indian, there is a real self in which resides the essence of authentic self as an Indian. As a marker, it is neither patchable nor exchangeable. Culminating into wholeness, a maker such as this behaves as an open and reserved choice within which every individual is forced to define himself/herself differently. At all the ethnonymical, politonymical and toponymical levels in the hierarchy, it has a demonstrative capability to cheek all other causal differences that might sound even very sharp at lower levels. At the apex level privilege of altering, categorizing, maintaining and adopting personal identities is uniquely preserved without destroying and disturbing national identity. As a matter of fact, it does not matter how sharply local and regional identities vary with political, linguistic, socio-cultural boundaries.

At the apex level, the reverse is true in the multilingual countries of the west as selfhood is toponymically and politonymically legitimized but suffers from some sense of ethnonymical hyphenation. For instance, at the apex level, French speaking Canadians and English speaking Canadians posses dual identity within the same politonymical, toponymical and ethnonymical boundary. In such a situation, the issue of hyphenation consistently remains suspicious. For French and English speaking Canadians, the justification for [trans-generationality] does not hold true. It may also hold true that in many western and multicultural nations, identity features at apex level may be toponymically, politonymically and ethnonymical unified, but indoors form is not historically derived as people of different ethnicities who join from different countries have well defined national identity attached to their host country. Australia, with several long settled ethnic groups such as Jews and Chinese, is composed with a number of smaller aboriginal inhabitants and majority, staasvolk, is English speaking of Anglo-Celtic origin.

A French in America, with French or without French may remain ethnically French until and unless he/ she surrenders himself/herself. His French-American symbol remains unchallenged as the first part is related with ancestry, legend and history and the second part symbolizes adopted toponymical and politonymical identities. In this case it is hard to decide which is more dominating, open and powerful and which part is less dominating, open and powerful. Migrants from the western multilingual countries face the crisis of hyphenation. Multilingual countries of the west in majority have similar kinds of structure.

At the immediate subordinate level, Ethnolinguistic units are always breakable into politonym (political boundary), toponym (geographic region) and ethnonym (ethnic group). Nation, as a whole, is an amalgam of these units and at this level all traits get integrated into such a way that even theoretically no more upward fragmentation sounds logical. At subordinate levels, as many boundaries are possible but, taken together, justifies the off-quoted idiomatic expression of 'unity in diversity'. Various names like Bengali, Tamilian, Telugu, Marathi, etc. are various ethnolinguistic units within the nation, whereas terms like Bihar, Uttar Pradesh, Madhya Pradesh, etc, do not evoke the sense of ethnolinguistc units but signify only political and geographical significant boundaries.

In the hierarchy, below superordinate ethnonymical, politonymical and toponymical layering, there lies a complex network of 'indoor identity' which can, in the real sense, be called branching of apexial identity into subordinate identities. By its virtue it may also be called 'medial. Politonymically and toponymically, it is post independent political restructuring. At this level ethnonymical definition of self does not always stand in one to one correspondence with politonym and toponym. In many cases, indoor identity also bears ethnonymical significance along with toponymical and politonymical. But this does not happen like a rule; in fact, restricted to as an exception. However, Pan-India-ness lies very much with it.

Its features are more cosmetic in nature. It allows expansion and distribution of subordinate markers with internal boundaries for maintaining group differentiation. It is to be mentioned here that indoor identity is neither aberration of super-ordinate identity nor devaluation. In the topological schemeta duality represents tolerance. In a situation where state demarcation is done linguistically, ethncnymical makeup guarantees the position. Indoor features are very handy for differentiation and may also be treated as a binding force with a democratic sense of liberation for self-perception, categorization and identification. Therefore, its legitimacy in socio-political divisions is sanctioned and guaranteed.

States are not created on linguistic divisions and objectives: they are demarcated largely to strengthen federal system and smoothen administrative functioning. The issue of state formation on the linguistic basis was something of an ideological pacemaker for administrative advocacy. As a whole, within this category, if language is taken as a base, six types of zone are identifiable:

(*a*) **Stable linguistic zone** (with well defined demographic and political boundary):

Ethnonym	toponym & Politonym
Bengali	Bengal
Tamil	Taminadu
Marathi	Maharastra
Gujrati	Gujrat
Oriya	Orissa
Punjabi	Punjab
Kanada	Karnataka
Telugu	Andhara Pradesh
Malyalam	Kerla
Kashmiri	Kashmir
Assamese	Assam

(*b*) **Comprised linguistic zone** (with different political boundary):

Politonym & toponym	Ethnonym & Toponym
Uttar Pradesh	Kanauji, Kumauni, Garhwali, Bhojpuri, Braj, Awadhi, etc
Bihar	Bhojpuri, Maithili, Magahi, Sadan, Kortha, etc.
Madaya Pradesh	Chattisgarhi, Bagheli, etc.
Rajsthan	Rajstani, Marwari, Dhundari, Mewari, Malvi, etc.
Himachal Pradesh	All Pahari Languages: Rahari, Mandeali, Sirmauri, Kului, Chameali, etc

(*c*) Linguistic zone without definite politonymical and toponymical boundary:

Konkani, Santhali , Sindhi

(*d*) Language without indoor boundary:

Superordinate level :	Sanskrit -	Traditional/ religious/ritual
	Urdu -	Religious/political
	English -	Colonial/Official

(*e*) Greater linguistic region: Use of Hindi in Punjab, Gujrat and Maharastra: Punjabi in Delhi, Himachal and Jammu

(*f*) Survived linguistic pocket: Saurastri in TamilNadu Bengali in Benaras

4. Surgical Diagnosis and Political Dilemma

Political restructuring in India never justifies the dream of linguistic homogeneity. It seems impossible also. Even on the issue of creating provinces the congress had neither adopted hard plan for reorganizing the provinces on linguistic basis nor violently demanded a full-fledged reorganization. In 1937, at the Calcutta session - Andhra and Karnataka - were demanded on the linguistic basis. Almost after a month demand of creating Kerala on the same ground was raised. Two years before the independence, when the congress was preparing for election, declared in manifesto that administrative units would have to be constituted as far as possible on linguistic and cultural basis. For the first time in 27 November 1947, Nehru, under severe socio-political constraints, announced his Government's commitment to accept the principle of linguistic provinces. Though the Government had shown her commitment to satisfy the demand, but had no plan as to how it could be completed. Formally, for the first time, a four men commission was set up to examine the criteria and impact of reorganizing provinces on the linguistic ground.

Bihar and Orissa had been separated from the Presidency of Bengal at the time of repeal of the partition. Both were created separate states only after the enforcement of the Government of India Act, 1935. According to the Act 1935, the government was given the following authoritarian powers: a) to create a new province; (b) increase the area of any province; c) diminish the area of any province; d) alter the boundaries of any province without mentioning of any hard and fast rule of linguistic principle. It is evident from the Act that linguistic issue was not a sole criterion in the creation of new states.

The Committee had argued strongly that linguistic based provinces should not be created for the sake of boundary reorganization, but favoured for linguistic based provinces only in the situation if it would provide administrative convenience. The committee recommendation was that the emphasis should be primarily on administrative convenience and homogeneity of language will enter into consideration only as a matter of administrative convenience and not by its own independent force. However, many argued in favour of linguistic criterion as the fittest choice for fulfilling administrative convenience. The commission agreed that linguistic homogeneity in the formation of new provinces is certainly attainable within certain limits but only at the cost of creating a fresh minority problems. Gandhi was also not against the linguistic provinces if it meant to serve the linguistic demand of local people and in case language has to grow. As it is clear from his this message during prayer's meeting: The redistribution of provinces on a linguistic basis was necessary if provincial languages were to grow to their full height. Hindustani should be a lingua franca and Rashtra Bhasa of India. Nehru's comment was almost similar as he said that state education should be given in the language of each linguistic area. This language should be the dominant language in that area.

The Congress Election Manifesto of 1951 advocated for creation of provinces depending upon people choice and preference. The congress policy in the revised version supported the separation of Telugu-speaking Andhra from Madras presidency. After the death of Potti Sriramulu demand became more violent. Touched with this tragedy, the then Prime Minister felt seriously about the concern and as a result the Government announced decision to establish the state of Andhra consisting of the Telugu-speaking areas of the Madras state. On 1 October 1953, Andhra was born. In 29 December 1953, the government announced to set up a State Reorganization Commission to consider the matter in a refreshingly new way. The Commission presented rigorous study on as to how political rearrangement of India on the basis language can be done. The basic problem of State Reorganization Commission was with border people who are unlikely confined to particular uni-lingual identity. In the process of the creation of Andhra, real problem was with two organic bilingual districts: Ganjam and Vizag-patnam. The problem was whether to place them in Orissa or in Andhra. On the finding and recommendation of the Commission, Ganjam and koraput districts were finally given to Orissa. However, local people were not happy over the decision as they wanted Koraput to be retained with Andhra. Andhra people also claimed that half of the Bustar district, which is in MP, to be included in Andhra on the basis of the majority of Telugu speakers. But demand was rejected. This makes the fact obvious that instance of multilingual in India not only exists at the national and state levels but also at the district level. In the Ganjam about 20% belongs to Telugu community and in the rest Oriya and others. Ganjam is not a single district; in fact, there are many districts in India whose linguistic composition is multilingual. Kolar district is a case to be presented with much interest as it presents an unique example of organic pluralism: District as whole comprised of Telugu majority and city comprised of Tamil majority but it has Kannada politonymical definition. During the inquiries of 1953, kolar district was comprised of 54% Telugu population and only 21% Kannada. The commission said since Kolar had long standing and intimate tie with Mysore it cannot be separated. In the first phase of linguistic reorganization, all the four Southern states had been in grim confusion over the accumulation of border districts who had become true multilingual and multicultural through the process of acculturation. In the process of bifurcation of states, linguistic criteria were unworkable to the satisfactory level. Bellary was an another problematic Zone. A majority of the population was Kannada, but demanded by the Andhra Government. But due to economic and political reasons it was allocated with Andhra Pradesh as Bellary town continues to be connected with all the district headquarters of the Rayalseema area by rail and road and it is nearer to Kunnool than Bangalore. To reach Bangalore by rail from Bellary, the shortest route lies only through Andhra territory. At the border area it was always impossible to create a line of control. Similarly, Madhya Pradesh had divisional problem with Andhra and Maharastra. Demand was also made for the inclusion of some of the areas of Bihar, i.e. Purnea, Santhal Pargenas and Manbhum by West Bengal. Hence is the case with Tripura, where almost 59% people are Bengali speaking. The Commission had also doubted the linguistic composition of Assam on the following ground:

(1) not all the language groups are so placed that they can be grouped into separate states;

(2) there are a large number of bilingual belts between different zones; and

(3) there exists areas with a mixed population each within unilingual areas.

More than that at the border areas Assam include many tribal groups with their own languages, and there were even known as autonomous districts.

5. Justifiable Dilemma

A state may exhibit both configurations: 1) [+ethnonym, +toponym, +politonym]; 2) [-ethnonym, +toponym, +politonym]. In the second case, the first rule is largely violated because the states in the Hindi regions had been reorganized only on toponymical and politonymical grounds. But, this gives a clear-cut picture that because of this variation the super ordinate level is unaffected. Reorganization of states based upon the consideration of majority ethno linguistic group has injected misunderstanding on many counts. However, at all points there are evidences of tolerance. For example, Dogri and Kangari in 1961 census were regarded as varieties of Punjabi. But since 1971, under the reclassification scheme, Dogri has been recorded an independent language status and Kangari is reclassified under the Hindi amalgam. See the profile of Hindi as a mothertongue as a result of return from first mothertongue.

State	*1962*	*1971*	*variation*
U.P	85.4	88.5	+ 3.1
Bihar	44.5	79.8	+ 35.3
M.P	78.1	88.3	+ 10.2
Rajsthan	33.3	91.1	+ 57.8
H.P	10.1	86.9	+ 76.8

The highest variation with 76.8% is noticeable in Himachal Pradesh between 8 Pahari languages and Hindi. Apart from comprised linguistic groups elasticity or fluidity in the assertion of Hindi as mother tongue is noticeable in the greater Hindi regions as the trend of gain between 5.4 to 6.1 was reported in the same census report. Let us come to the conclusion that Indoor compartmentalization on the linguistic ground is largely based on majority configuration of language use within politonymical and toponymical boundaries which also has ethnonymical significance. Naming of politonym and toponym units based upon linguistic criteria falls on the principle of predominance of language within the unit. Here are examples:

Language	Unit	Percentage of Population
Bengali	Bengal	84.3
Gujrati	Gujrat	90.5
Tamil	Tamilnadu	83.2
Oriya	Orissa	82.3
Punjabi	Punjab	55.6
Manipur	Manipuri	64.5
Marathi	Maharastra	76.5
Assamese	Assam	57.1
Kanada	Karnataka	65.2
Kashmir	Kashmiri	54.4
Malyalam	Kerla	95.0
Telugu	Andhra Pradesh	86.0
Rajsthani	Rajsthan	56.5
Tripura	Tripuri	24.9
Nicobar Island	Nicobarese	21.9

However, for two states - Andhra Pradesh and Kerla- linguistic criteria of politonymical and toponymical divisions seem to be justifiable, but the name of these two states do not follow linguistic criteria as the terms like Telugu and Malayaliesse do locate person's politonymical and toponymical boundaries along with ethnonymical emblem. Rajstahni language rightly stands as a justifiable criterion for characterizing Rajsthan as a politonym and toponym unit. Ethnonymycally, it is a part of large Hindi populus. Similar may be the case with Tripura. Tripuri language, with about 25% of population, may be one of the factors in the development of Tripura as a separate politonym and toponym unit but the majority language of state is Bengali with almost 65.2% population. Comprised linguistic group is largely Hindi speaking which is distributed into seven politonymical units with wide regional varieties. Indoor politonym with toponymical organization is made on the basis conceivable demands. Creation of new boundaries into Jharkhand, Uttranchal and Chattisgrah is perhaps the best example of politonymical restructuring for administrative purposes. In the third category, there are some traditional linguistic groups, which carry same politonymical and toponymical identities with that of majority group. This could be an answer to a question why these languages are surviving over years.

Linguistic Group	*State*
Bodo	Assam
Dogri	J & K
Konkani	Maharastra
Saurastri	Tamil NaduSanthali
BiharKui	Orissa
Kurkh	Madhya Pradesh
Coorgi	Karnataka

6. Exception

Urdu, with religious affinity and without any toponymical definition, is a case to be treated with care. Politonymically Urdu receives respectable positions in many states as second/third or minority language. Hindi and Urdu present a live picture of unmarked interchangeability and intelligibility as distinction between Standard Hindi and Urdu is even not as compartmentalized as two distinctly prescribed literary standards of Yugoslav language, Serbo-Croatian (Serbian in the Cyrillic and Croatian in the Latin Script). Since Muslim population is scattered through out the country, so as Urdu, it can not have indoor politonyical and toponymical definition except ethnonymical within the super-ordinate politonyical and toponymical and ethnonymical boundaries. A large proportion of Muslims in many regions tend to have native like control over the languages of region along with Urdu. It enjoys the status of minority language with an additional privilege of being a second and third language in many states and has privilege to attach lingo-religious marker for self identification at any level irrespective of majority's politonymical and toponymical definitions at the indoor levels. In many cases, toponymical and politonymical and linguistic identities precede the religious and cultural features as the name such as Tamil-Muslim, Kerla Muslim often recalled with respect. However, in the Hindi belt linguistic identity other than Urdu does not precede in the same fashion, but again hard to differentiate on linguistic basis.

7. Paradox of Construction and Countable Differences

Nation, in its totality, must be treated as evolutionary, formational, behavioural and cognitive entities. In the process, therefore, many factors are equally functional. The basic problem in theory building is identification of significant components, which correspond and integrate with the creation of national image. The most important characteristics of significant component is to act as distinct feature which help in distinguishing one nation from another in terms of evolution and construction. It is to be remembered that significant component should be considered in terms of signifying factor. Every nation creates its own national image in terms of significant component. Some of significant components are identifiable:

Significant component:

Language		**Nation**
	Korean	South and North Korea
	Italian	Italy
	French	France
	Germany	Germany
	Spanish	Spain

	Portugese	Prutugal
	Nepali	Nepal
	Russia	Russian
Religion		
Muslim	Pakistan	
	Bangla Desh	
Geography:	Complusory to all	
Political Unit	Complusory to all	

In the first category, slogan like one language one nation resonates well. The linguistic ecology of these countries is plain. Even the names of these counties correspond with language. In the countries like India, Indonesia, Nigeria and many other others diversity stays at the level of language, religion, ethnicity, therefore theory of monism doesn't apply. Roughly estimated even not more than 10 percent nations come under mono-category in their linguistic, religious and ethnic composition. Therefore, 10% can be turned as an exception, rather than a rule. Nations like Greece, Portugal, Iceland, Japan, Korea, and Norway fall under this category. Within this category, again there are obligatory and optional features. Geography, political unit, population and resources are obligatory features whereas language and religion are optional features. Significant components become significant only when they are also understood subjectively. Significant components are not absolute and often reveal quite relative phenomena. Once the co-ordination between objective and subjective factors are established, the expressive value of significant component becomes functional. Also, at one point, every nation is known and identified through objective factors. In Canada, features such as toponym and politonym do not correlate with ethnonymical significant components as it is composed of two linguistic ethnonymes. Somalia, on the other hand, as a single dominant ethnic group uses two imported tongues for official purposes. A logistic like this gives solid evidences to prove as to how and why the homogeneity is labeled as a narrow conception.

Towards Concluding

Linguistic fabrics of India demand many more optional significant components other than what we commonly presume language, geography and politics as only determinant factors to play the role of signifiers. Such a marker forms core territory from toponymical point of view, core political autonomy from politonymical point of view and core ethnic determination from ethnonymical point of view in which every individual- irrespective of one's belongings to various **'isms'**, remains sufficiently a part of national homeland. It creates a widespread collectivism while transforming regional, linguistic and parochial loyalties. At this level, collectively all symbols are equally mobilized. How does it function? One may prefer to call India as a trans-generational unit as it is socio-culturally and historically reconstructed. Super-ordinate is an integrated reproduction of ethnic properties and represents historical meta - ethnographic region. Trans-generational reproduction of aesthetic character has historical-ethnographic structure. Important thing to be noticed here is that India as a transgenerational ethnographic entity never seem to be in the process of fading. Multiplicity of identity, at any category level, is visible. Characteristics such as stratified roles, cross-cultural overlapping, regional variations, cross-linguistic geographic boundaries, ethno-behaviorism, stratified social structures and hierarchical polities are either anaphoric or patchable. Pluralistic ethos is, therefore, neither on compromise nor on suppressed visibility. Hierarchical ties are indicatively justifiable. Singularity is seldom allowed to act as a definable parameter either in identity creation or in identity projection. The principle of projection is hardly always governed by a single local governing; rather all categorical constituents are multiplied in such a way that each conducts itself in a very smooth and negotiated manner.

The assumption that one can only understand the nature and possibilities of a new community in the third world by referring only to new political structures and mechanisms, which are distinctively and readably available, is justified. Without explaining the distinctive degrees of divisions and multiple interactive networks, today it would be a mistake to conclude about the fate and borders of the third or the postcolonial world based on the throughout nineteenth and twentieth centuries debates which were very close to the heart of western model. Thus questions may be raised: 1. about the fate of the western theories; and 2) about the appropriate locus for articulation of the **New World order**. To avoid misunderstanding, these arguments need further unpacking in relation to the idea and prospects of linguistic visibility in the New World order. Therefore, there is a fundamental question about whether features embodied in this part of the world any longer be sustained simply within the framework of western model. Postcolonial ecology has created the possibility of extending and expanding the new interconnectedness in which a sharp division between the East and the West is no longer based upon the dichotomy of have and haven't but mostly upon how the gap between two has wrongly been read. No doubt, the tests of extensiveness and intensity of the new order are yet to be done objectively as well as subjectively. However, this could be proposed as a filter and a guide model to the different levels of existing differences.

References

Bromley, Yu. V. 1984. theoretical Ethnography, Mascor: Nauka Publisher.

Singh, U.N. & Singh, S.K. (1999) Issues of Language choice in India : Returning to WH–Questions. South Asian Language Review, Vol. IX. No.1.

Singh, S.K. (2001). Multilingualism. New Delhi, Bahari Publication.

Skutnabb-Kangas, T. 1990. Legitimating or delegitimating New forms of Racism—the role of Researchers. Journal of Multilingual and multicultural Development. Vol. 11. Nos. 1 & 2. 77-100.

Smolicz, J.J. 1979. Culture and Education in a Plural society. Canberra : Curriculum Development Centre.

Index